# WHEN DOCTORS GET IT WRONG

Dr Nicholas Rae

Copyright © 2019 Dr Nicholas Rae

The moral right of the author has been asserted.

Apart from any fair dealing for the purposes of research or private study, or criticism or review, as permitted under the Copyright, Designs and Patents Act 1988, this publication may only be reproduced, stored or transmitted, in any form or by any means, with the prior permission in writing of the publishers, or in the case of reprographic reproduction in accordance with the terms of licences issued by the Copyright Licensing Agency. Enquiries concerning reproduction outside those terms should be sent to the publishers.

Matador
9 Priory Business Park,
Wistow Road, Kibworth Beauchamp,
Leicestershire. LE8 0RX
Tel: 0116 279 2299
Email: books@troubador.co.uk
Web: www.troubador.co.uk/matador
Twitter: @matadorbooks

ISBN 978 183859 161 8

British Library Cataloguing in Publication Data.
A catalogue record for this book is available from the British Library.

Printed and bound in Great Britain by 4edge Limited
Typeset in 11pt Adobe Garamond Pro by Troubador Publishing Ltd, Leicester, UK

Matador is an imprint of Troubador Publishing Ltd

To the memory of my kinsman Dr John Rae, Hudson's Bay Company Chief Factor, explorer and general practitioner. He set out to discover the fate of the Franklin expedition and to discover the North West Passage. He got it right.

# CONTENTS

| | | |
|---|---|---|
| 1 | Introduction | 1 |
| 2 | Pathology | 18 |
| 3 | Doctors & NHS Management | 34 |
| 4 | Skeletal Problems – Joint Pathology and Fractures | 57 |
| 5 | Back Conditions | 81 |
| 6 | The Breast | 99 |
| 7 | Gastrointestinal Problems | 112 |
| 8 | The Genitourinary System | 133 |
| 9 | Nerves | 153 |
| 10 | Cardiovascular System – The Heart | 182 |
| 11 | Cardiovascular System – Circulation | 201 |
| 12 | Gynaecological Problems | 221 |
| 13 | The Skin | 237 |
| 14 | When Things Go Wrong | 256 |
| 15 | Putting Things Right | 267 |

Chapter 1

# INTRODUCTION

This book is to help people who have no medical training but who want to know if their doctor should have done better. It removes some of the mystery surrounding medical practice and also explains how accidents can occur. It is based on a training manual written when I was Chief Medical Officer for an insurance company.[1] Their clerical workers needed to know enough about medical practice to handle disability claims. That manual – and now this book – was written so that the average person may understand the basic principles of medicine.

The things that can go wrong in medical practice are illustrated by real-life medical accidents. These are mainly UK general practitioner cases, collected over a period of ten years, where lawyers requested me to provide a medical opinion in cases of alleged negligence. The principles of medicine are, of course, universal but the cases themselves mostly centre on care delivered under the UK National Health Service. The examples give a guide to patients who are considering a complaint about a general medical practitioner. They may also provide an explanation for patients and relatives to show that even if things have turned out badly the doctor may still have done all that was possible.

## DOCTORS – WHO ARE THEY?

Because we are looking at doctors' mistakes, it is worth considering the sort of person who gets to be a doctor. A professor at University College London Medical School once described his policy when interviewing applicants – predominantly sixth-form schoolchildren – who wanted to be doctors. This was his interview technique:

"So why do you want to be a doctor?"

"To work with people."

"So why not work at Harrods, Waitrose or even Tesco? Perhaps what you really want to do is not to work *with* people, but *on* people!"

To his credit, this line would only be taken with a promising candidate by way of testing reactions, but in fact his retort held a lot of truth. Being a doctor confers a huge amount of power, to an extent not usually enjoyed even by senior statesmen or royalty. One obvious example is that if most people take a sharp instrument and cut someone open they can expect a lengthy jail sentence. The surgeon, performing a similar manoeuvre will (usually) receive the accolade of a grateful patient and be (reasonably) well paid. Doctors often request their patients to undress or to submit themselves to other indignities, and then provide them with the dangerous compounds known as medicines. In some circumstances, doctors can deprive patients of their liberty simply on a signature and with no trial. There is no doubt that this amount of power can appeal to the wrong sort of person. Fortunately, it is only rarely that the desire for control is overextended. The most prolific serial murderer of modern times was an apparently respected general practitioner Dr Harold Shipman who administered lethal doses of narcotics to unsuspecting patients. The rest of his practice was

## Introduction

considered perfectly acceptable. The problem was, of course, not that Shipman was a bad doctor – if anything, rather the reverse. He just happened to be a psychopathic murderer who made full use of the enormous privileges attached to his medical qualification. He went undetected for years. So what other attractions are there to a medical career? Money is always a consideration, but although some doctors in private surgical practice may expect to make a great deal of money, this career path is too uncertain for the aspiring medical student. Anyone able to get into medical school and pass the examinations for specialist qualifications would almost certainly make more money as a senior business executive. Most careers in medicine are stable, so in that sense there is financial security, but people looking for big bucks do not go into medicine. What other attraction is there? Up until relatively recently, doctors were regarded as pillars of society. This situation applies less and less, partly because of the publicity given to the type of incidents mentioned in this book, and partly because of the public perception that doctors are overpaid and inefficient – myths which some politicians often find convenient.

Against this background selection panels for medical schools will try and find candidates whom they consider to 'have a vocation' or to be 'caring'. This is not easy and there are a few people who are complacent, self-satisfied and arrogant but still get into the profession. These doctors are particularly dangerous because they cut corners in the belief that they cannot be wrong. Even if they go undiscovered they may do an awful lot of damage to their patients. Their activities feature in this book.

### MEDICAL TRAINING AND REGISTRATION

All doctors have similar undergraduate medical education, usually through a five year university course at medical school. After this they are required to work in a range of approved junior hospital doctor posts under close supervision. These are the foundation posts after which they are entitled to be entered onto the Medical Register. At this point a doctor will decide whether to become a general practitioner or a specialist. To become an independent general practitioner in the UK, the doctor must then undertake three years of GP Specialty Training (GPST), normally including 18 months in an approved training practice and 18 months in approved hospital posts. The hospital posts may be in General Medicine, Elderly Care Medicine, Paediatrics, Community Paediatrics, Obstetrics and Gynaecology, Psychiatry and old age Psychiatry, ENT, Accident and Emergency, Dermatology, Ophthalmology or Palliative Care. Obviously, not all trainee general practitioners, in their 18 months of hospital posts, will work in all these specialties. For this reason the degree of expertise may vary from general practitioner to general practitioner in terms of knowledge of any single specialty. Even so, every general practitioner should have a core of basic knowledge which he must bring to bear in diagnosis and management of his patient.

For specialists, the period of further training can be up to seven years, again rotating through a series of hospital posts prior to receiving a certificate of completion of training as a specialist and entry to the General Medical Council (GMC) Specialist Register.

A "Registered Doctor" is one who has got his name on the Medical Register. At the time of writing, EU rules apply. Under these rules, a doctor from any country of the European Union, if he is registered in his own country, is entitled automatically to have his name put on the Register. Registration does not equate to a License to Practice and so does guarantee him or her a job. Even so, where there is a shortage of doctors candidates may be accepted simply on the basis of their competence in English rather than their competence in medicine. This led to the widely-reported case of a German doctor who killed a patient in 2008 while undertaking a GP locum shift on his first day in the UK.[2]

# Introduction

THE SCIENTIFIC BASIS OF MEDICINE

To get into medical school as a young undergraduate in the UK and Europe a student will usually require the equivalent of A levels in scientific subjects, with chemistry often being compulsory. This is because medicine is a science-based subject in which knowledge and experience is placed on a rational basis to apply guiding principles. This knowledge is shared and may then be used to build further experience, so that a practicing doctor will build on his knowledge of former cases and also acquire knowledge through textbooks and journals as reported by colleagues. This process is referred to as practising evidence-based medicine.

Having said that, most experienced doctors would say that application of scientific principles will only carry them part of the way. After this there is a question of experience, even if this is not applied scientifically, and sometimes just general flair. Medicine is therefore to some extent an art as well as a science. Criticism of a doctor's management cannot always push scientific principles to the limit – even when things have gone wrong.

Although doctors have to spend a long time in training, the basic principles of medicine are actually fairly simple. A lot of the time spent in training is necessary so that the doctor can gain experience in simply talking to the patients and acquiring the habit of marshalling his or her thoughts effectively.

Teaching for doctors follows a tried and trusted system and this book follows the same traditional pattern. The chapters dealing with medical accidents correspond to the major clinical specialities of cardiology, orthopaedics, gynaecology, gastroenterology and so on. All these specialties have the same underlying scientific principles and so each chapter will deal with the subject by covering the *basic medical sciences* of anatomy, physiology and pathology as follows:–

- **Anatomy** – this is, put quite simply, a study of the way the body is put together physically. If we think of a body as being

a machine, all the parts of which must work together to keep the machine running efficiently, then anatomy is the parts list. Anatomy can be studied from dead bodies, or even picture books.
- **Physiology** – this looks at the way that the life process actually happens – how the body works. It represents vast numbers of chemical processes behind everyday activities like walking, eating, breathing and even thinking.
- **Pathology** – another 'ology'. This is the scientific study of things going wrong with the anatomy or physiology to cause disease. Perhaps surprisingly, these causes can be grouped under relatively few headings. They are looked at in detail in a separate chapter.

CLINICAL ASSESSMENT AND DIAGNOSIS

The word 'diagnosis' comes from a couple of Greek words meaning 'through knowledge'. Most people would agree that this is a fair description, because a doctor's diagnosis is, after all, intended to be more than an educated hunch. This knowledge is gained through *history* taking, *examination* and *investigations* (tests). Diagnosis is the first stage of the doctor's management, and provides a label to the patient's complaint based on the doctor's knowledge of anatomy, physiology and pathology. Once the diagnosis has been made the next logical step, based on experience and research, will be to provide the patient with treatment to try and get him better. So medical management becomes a two-step process, diagnosis and treatment. Diagnosis alone is no use. While it may provide the practitioner with some intellectual satisfaction the simple application of a label does not help his patient. A patient with a sore tongue may be told he has glossitis, but do not expect him to feel any better as a result!

# Introduction

MEDICAL NOTES

The process of diagnosis and treatment will (or should) be recorded in the patient's notes. It has to be said that the quality of medical note-keeping varies enormously. Medical students are taught to write comprehensive and thorough hospital notes. This is important to establish a standard pattern of history taking and examination – essentially, training in the diagnostic process. At the other end of the scale general practice notes will usually concentrate only on the essentials – if only for lack of time. One way or another, however, it is important to record the necessary information concerning a patient's illness. The following system shows the basic information which would be written in a new hospital case, sometimes known as "clerking". The details will vary from doctor to doctor, depending on which medical school they went to, but the essential information should be the same.

Patients have a right to see their own notes but even when they get them they can be highly confusing because they will contain a lot of abbreviations. The examples below may help to explain the abbreviations. Later chapters explain what the notes actually mean.

HX (HISTORY)

| | |
|---|---|
| CO | (complains of) a brief description of the patient's presenting problem |
| HPC | (history present complaint) duration, severity, previous occurrences, exacerbating/relieving factors |
| PMH | (past medical history) previous serious illnesses, operations, medication, allergies, vaccinations |
| ODQ | (on direct questioning) systems review: |
|   GIT | (gastrointestinal tract) abdominal pain, bleeding, diet, weight change |
|   RS | (respiratory system) cough, sputum, shortness of breath |
|   CVS | (cardiovascular system) palpitations, shortness of |

| | | |
|---|---|---|
| | | breath, chest pain, ankle swelling, exercise tolerance |
| | CNS | (central nervous system) headaches, fainting, fits, numbness, weakness |
| | GUS | (genitourinary system) bleeding, pain, discharge, urinary difficulty, childbirth & periods |
| | MSK | (musculoskeletal system) joint pain, stiffness, weakness, |
| SH | | (Social history) occupation, smoking, alcohol*, recreational drugs*, sexual orientation*<br>*(Some questions are, of course, best omitted or at least deferred until they become necessary in the light of investigations!) |

EXAMINATION

| | |
|---|---|
| OE | (on examination) Whether anaemic (pale), jaundiced (yellow), cyanosed (blue), or clubbed (deformed finger-ends).<br>The system indicated by the patient's complaint will usually be described first, and in greater detail. Some but not all of these examination features (and abbreviations!) may be found in a reasonably comprehensive clinical assessment: |
| GIT | (gastrointestinal tract). The notes may show a small hexagonal diagram with labels indicating the site of any abnormality. The following abbreviations may occur: L K2 S: (liver, two kidneys, spleen), =N (normal) |
| BS | (bowel sounds) |
| PR | (rectal examination). |
| RS | (respiratory system) L=R (left equals right chest movements), |

# Introduction

| | |
|---|---|
| ↓ | (trachea central) |
| Sats n% | (oxygen saturation n percent), |
| res | (resonant on percussion) |
| BS vesic. | (Breath sounds vesicular, i.e. a normal rustling sound) |
| | |
| CVS | (cardiovascular system) n/n (BP in mmHg e.g. 120/80), |
| R n | (respiratory rate n/breaths per minute) |
| HS=N+nil | (heart sounds normal with no added sounds) |
| SOA | (swelling of ankles) |
| | |
| CNS | (central nervous system) |
| CN I – XII | (cranial nerves 1 to 12), |
| PERLA | (pupils equally reacting to light and accommodation) |
| Reflexes. | The examining doctor may record a table with the first letter of the standard reflexes on each side: **b**iceps **t**riceps **s**upinator **k**nees **a**nkles **p**lantar with a √ or x, and ↓or ↑or for the plantars. (The supinator is a forearm muscle. The plantar reflex depends on whether the toes go up or down when the sole of the foot is scratched–supposedly with the key of the neurologist's Bentley!) |
| T,P,C | (tone, power and coordination of the limbs) |
| Sens. | (sensation – testing for touch and pain on each peripheral nerve – rarely done completely) |
| | |
| GUS | (genitourinary system) |
| PV/VE | (vaginal examination). |

Abnormalities of the male genitourinary system may be indicated by a diagram.

# When Doctors Get It Wrong

MEDICAL TERMINOLOGY

As in any complex subject, medicine has its own specialised words which are understood by those whose everyday work involves medical matters. To the outsider, they may seem to be a bewildering vocabulary, but accurate description is essential in any scientific discipline. Having said that, good medical notes should avoid a great deal of jargon. Some terms do remain and are likely to be used regularly because of their convenience and because they are understood between professionals. It is unfortunate – or at least problematical – that medical vocabulary has evolved from the classical languages of Greek and Latin. Happily, knowledge of a very few words (or even part of words) will give the meaning of most medical terms. This list does not cover everything but gives commonly used words or prefixes and suffixes used in medical notes:

| TERM | DEFINITION |
|:---:|:---:|
| Adeno– | Gland |
| –aemia | Blood |
| –algia | Pain |
| Angio– | Vessel |
| Arterio– | Artery |
| Carcin– | Cancer |
| Cardi– | Heart |
| Cephal– | Head |
| Crani– | Skull |
| Cysto– | Bladder |
| Derm– | Skin |
| –ectomy | Excision |
| Hepat– | Liver |

# Introduction

| | |
|---|---|
| Hyper– | Excessive/Above |
| Hypo– | Deficient/Below |
| –itis | Inflammation |
| My– Myo– | Muscle |
| Myel– | Marrow/Spinal cord |
| Nephr– | Kidney |
| Neur– | Nerve |
| Os– Osteo– | Bone |
| Spondyl– | Vertebra |
| –stomy | Opening/hole |
| Trans– | Across/Through/Over |

DIFFERENTIAL DIAGNOSIS

So far the notes will have described the history and examination – hopefully using only standard abbreviations – and the clinical assessment is complete. Once this is done the doctor must next consider a differential diagnosis. It has to be said that this part of the diagnostic process is the most demanding – it is certainly the part that causes most trouble in terms of medical accidents. What does it mean? From the history and examination the doctor will have arrived at a number of symptoms (from the history) and signs (from the examination). The differential diagnosis is a list of the conditions which *could* be responsible for these signs and symptoms. This list of diagnoses may actually be written down or remain in the clinician's head but it must be there.

So by now the doctor will have this list of potential conditions, most of which must be eliminated or *ruled out* so as to arrive at, ideally, one condition which the doctor can get on and treat. It is this rule out process which so often causes trouble. There is a strong temptation to place the most likely diagnosis at the top of the list, having ruled out other less likely conditions on probability alone.

"Well, why not?" says Dr Botchup. "The health service is underfunded, I am short of time and it is a waste of resources to go looking for unusual conditions when the most likely diagnosis is staring me in the face".

This attitude, still quoted by some senior doctors who should know better, is summarised by the adage: "common things are common". Unfortunately, it works in many cases, which is why it persists. It is in the remaining few cases that problems occur. Ruling out conditions by simply opting for the one most likely is fraught with hazard. In this situation it is essential to apply a "restricted rule out". To put it simply, a doctor must not consider only those diagnoses which are the most likely. He must also think of possible diagnoses which are so urgent and/or dangerous that he cannot afford to miss them.

This difficulty is illustrated in many cases appearing later in this book. By way of immediate example consider a patient who has consulted his doctor with a complaint of chest pain. The patient is not sure what brings the pain on, but thinks it might have got a bit better when he took an indigestion tablet. There is little to find on examination, and the pulse and blood pressure are normal. The differential diagnosis includes simple indigestion (most likely) or several serious chest conditions (much less likely, but may need immediate treatment). Should the doctor get hospital tests for a heart problem or should he simply proceed to treat (presumed) indigestion? Statistically, for every hundred patients in this situation well over ninety will indeed have some sort of mild indigestion. One or two of the others, however, could have critical coronary artery disease, an aortic aneurysm or a pulmonary embolus. These conditions require immediate treatment. They cannot be ruled out on history and examination alone and the doctor must organise his investigations accordingly.

At this stage, therefore, assuming a proper differential diagnosis has been considered, the doctor will have arrived at a shortlist of possible conditions to include the most likely, together with those dangerous conditions which cannot be ruled out. At this stage the notes may say:

IMP (impression). There then follows a list of conditions which may now need investigation. Alternatively (and sometimes mistakenly) history and examination alone may have suggested only one condition which he will proceed to treat.

**Investigations.** In some cases the diagnosis will now be clear if a careful history and examination have been undertaken. In other cases it may be necessary to do some investigations. Put simply, these are special tests to look for pathology – physical or chemical abnormalities. Blood samples may be taken by the nurse in general practice but the actual investigations involve the hospital laboratory. The blood may be processed to look at the red or white cells in the blood (haematology). Other blood tests will involve biochemistry and may be used to detect abnormalities in the liver, kidneys and glands. The rate at which red cells settle in blood, the erythrocyte sedimentation rate (ESR) is a long-established test for inflammation. Other tests may include biopsy, where small anatomical sections are taken for microscopic examination (histology). Depending on the differential diagnosis, imaging may be required to look for abnormalities of the anatomy. These may range from broken bones to brain tumours and imaging may be by ultrasound, X-ray, computerised tomography (CT) Scan, or Magnetic Resonance Imaging (MRI) – the latter especially useful for the brain and nervous system.

**Treatment.** Once a doctor has made a diagnosis he will decide on a treatment plan. Depending on the illness, the patient may be referred to the care of an appropriate specialist (if not already under specialist care for investigation) or may be treated in general practice. Specialists may treat the patient at the hospital, or may provide treatment suggestions back to the GP. At this stage a doctor will also be able to give some idea of the *prognosis*. This is from another couple of Greek words – meaning 'forward knowledge' – and is really an educated guess at what is going to happen to the patient, and how long the illness – or the patient – is likely to last.

MEDICAL SPECIALISTS

Specialists fall into two broad groups, physicians and surgeons. Physicians (as in Shakespeare's 'physic') will primarily rely on medicine to treat the patient. Surgeons resort to operation, traditionally described as 'performing' in a 'theatre'.

**Surgeons.** A member of a surgical specialty is known as Mr, Mrs or Miss once he or she obtains the postgraduate qualification MRCS (Membership of the Royal College of Surgeons). They may later advance to Fellowship – FRCS. Surgeons may sub-specialise into the following categories:

- Upper gastrointestinal – stomach, oesophagus (gullet) and upper bowel
- Lower gastrointestinal – colon rectum and anus
- Thoracic –surgery of the heart and lungs
- Vascular –surgery to the major blood vessels (aorta, femoral arteries etc.)
- Orthopaedic –surgery to the limbs and bones
- Neurosurgery – surgery of the brain and spinal cord
- Urology –surgery of the kidneys, bladder prostate and urinary tract
- Gynaecology – surgery of the female pelvic organs. (Qualification FRCOG)
- Plastic– Reconstruction after burns & trauma. Also cosmetic.

To this list may be added anaesthetists, without whom most surgery

Introduction

would not be possible. The anaesthetist is an essential member of the surgical team, and the responsibility of anaesthesia is often greater than that of the surgery. They have the qualification MRCA – Member Royal College of Anaesthetists

**Physicians** are known as 'Doctor' (not Mister, etc.) even when specialists. They have the post-graduate qualification FRCP or MRCP (Fellowship or Membership of the Royal College of Physicians. In District General Hospitals many physicians will act as general physicians, being responsible for all acute general medical care, but may also have special interests:

- Cardiology. –Medical care for the heart.
- Endocrinology – Glandular problems (notably Diabetes).
- Rheumatology – Joint problems.
- Respiratory –Lung problems, e.g. asthma.
- Gastroenterology – Stomach & intestines.
- Dermatology – Skin
- Ophthalmology – Eyes
- Psychiatry – Mental illness. (Qualification MRCPsych)

TOPICS BY DISEASE OR BODY SYSTEM

Because specialists concentrate on a particular area of the body or a particular type of disease it is traditional to look at medical topics along the same lines. This is what I have done here, so the following chapters of this book describe ways in which medical accidents can occur in different areas of medicine. There is also a chapter on the general principles of pathology – the causes of illness – since these are common to all body systems. I have also included a chapter on NHS management because a poor outcome may sometimes be the result of systemic failure rather than individual clinical error. The sections start with a brief explanation of the anatomy, physiology and pathology of the system concerned. Diagnosis and treatment are discussed in terms of the ways in which they may have caused problems, with examples drawn from actual cases.

Although I have been involved with medical negligence for about twenty-five years I have drawn the cases from the last ten years (which I have called the period in question) so as to be reasonably up-to-date. This explanation of the medical background, illustrated by examples, should enable patients or relatives to approach a situation with a poor medical outcome from a proper basis of knowledge rather than relying on anecdote. It is intended to provide fair and rational way of moving forward, whether the decision is to accept that the doctors acted reasonably or alternatively to take matters further.

Although these are real cases and the circumstances of the medical accidents have been retained, the patients' details have been changed so as to prevent recognition. Not all medical conditions are included in this book. Experience shows that the majority of complaints and clinical negligence claims arise from a relatively small number of areas. These are as follows:–

| | |
|---|---|
| Skeleton & Joints | Chapter 4 |
| Back | Chapter 5 |
| Breast | Chapter 6 |
| Gastro-intestinal | Chapter 7 |
| Genitourinary | Chapter 8 |
| Nerves | Chapter 9 |
| Heart | Chapter 10 |
| Circulation | Chapter 11 |
| Gynaecology | Chapter 12 |
| Skin | Chapter 13 |

REFERENCES

1. Medicine for Disability Insurers. Aviva Insurance in-house publication.
2. *Independent.* 4th February 2010. https://www.independent.co.uk/life-style/health-and-families/health-news/locum-overdose-patient-unlawfully-killed-says-coroner-1889368.html

Chapter 2

# PATHOLOGY

INTRODUCTION

The word pathology comes from the Greek word "pathos" (παθος) meaning suffering (as in pathetic). It is the scientific study of things that can go wrong with the body, or as Shakespeare put it: "...*the thousand natural shocks that flesh is heir to*..."

In its strict sense, pathology is concerned with the abnormalities of the body at tissue level. Diagnosis in medicine and surgery is concerned with the effects of that pathology on the patient. For this reason we should not confuse the study of pathology with the process of diagnosis of disease processes. While the difference may seem academic (and is often a source of confusion to medical students) it is still a distinction worth making. This chapter on pathology is included here because working out the underlying pathology in an illness usually makes it easier to understand what is going on – and what the doctor should have done about it. Several patients may consult with the same complaint but the underlying pathology may be different. By way of example, consider the case of a patient with abdominal pain. The doctor thinks this is probably coming from the stomach. So far so good, but is this a side effect of medication (iatrogenic), food poisoning (infective) or undiagnosed cancer (neoplastic)? It is only by considering a range of possibilities that the doctor can reach the right diagnosis and be able to investigate and then to treat the patient properly.

Fortunately, the list of pathological possibilities is quite short. The usual classification is as follows:

CLASSIFICATION OF PATHOLOGY ('PATHOLOGICAL SIEVE')

A. **Congenital (i.e. born with)**
B. **Acquired**
   Degenerative
   Neoplastic
   Immune
   Metabolic
   Infective
   Toxic
   Iatrogenic
   Traumatic

So what do these terms all mean? Here is a brief explanation:

A. CONGENITAL CONDITIONS

These refer to pathology that is present when a baby is born. They may be *teratogenic* (acquired in the uterus through outside damage) or *genetic* (from the genes).

**Teratogenic** hazards that may damage the growing baby during pregnancy include smoking and drug or alcohol abuse by the mother, infection, radiation, toxins and prescribed medicines. German measles, Hiroshima, Marlboro' and thalidomide provide examples.

**Genetic** (*i.e.* inherited) conditions come from the genes rather than an event happening in pregnancy or during the rest of life, although many conditions may depend on adverse events plus a genetic background – an 'inherited tendency'. Family medical conditions should come to light during history taking (questioning) if the doctor asks the right questions. A family history is important, particularly in suspected coronary artery disease, cancer or some mental illnesses. Familial characteristics are inherited from both parents in the genes. Many genes simply define characteristics such as blue eyes, tallness or red hair. Other genes, however, may cause disease or abnormalities. Some of these are lethal and the foetus does not survive the first few weeks – the commonest reason for early miscarriage. Other disease-carrying genes may not be lethal, but may still represent serious pathology in the patient. In practice many disease-carrying genes are present but are not always expressed in the individual. For example, there may be a history of cleft palate in the family. This represents an increased risk but does not mean all individuals in the family are bound to be affected.

One unfortunate example of inherited pathology is the rare group of disorders causing abnormal muscle function. Muscular dystrophy has a strong family tendency, but does not cause problems until early middle age – by which time the patient may already have had children and passed the gene on. Natural selection has failed.

The possibility of familial (inherited) illness is important for diagnosis. This is why the doctor should take an accurate family history in arriving at his differential diagnosis. An early heart attack in his patient's parents may give additional weight to the possibility that this chest pain may be a lot more than indigestion. Genetic information may also be useful for the next generation, but can give rise to the controversial issue of foetal screening where early termination may be considered if a familial condition is detected in the foetus. For the grown individual, however, the family history is obviously of little use in treatment – one cannot choose one's parents!

B. ACQUIRED CONDITIONS

**Degeneration** is apparently straightforward. It is simply the process of wearing out. In reality matters are not as simple as this. We know that a car engine will probably last for about 100,000 miles if it is regularly serviced. Once it has done its mileage it will become unreliable, whether that mileage is done over two years by a busy rep. or over ten years by a housewife who drives the second car. In the human body things are quite different. Additional activity in early and middle age is positively beneficial, causing strengthening of the bones and muscles. As old age approaches, however, degenerative change is inevitable and may bear no relation to previous activity. It has to be said that we do not understand the full mechanisms for control of the growth process, but it is likely that a given line of cells has a definite life span, after which further growth and repair will not occur, or occur only slowly and inefficiently. One possibility is that there is a limit to the number of cell divisions that an individual stem cell line may undertake. After that the DNA controlling growth puts a stop on the process.

Interestingly, not all creatures are subject to degeneration. Even quite advanced animals high up in the animal kingdom do not all experience degenerative change. Some fish, for example, are potentially immortal – although of course in practice their long-term survival is limited by the presence of other predators, bigger fish, or the supply of food. In humans, however, degenerative change is inevitable if the individual lives long enough. Nearly all parts of the body are affected, an obvious example being the greying and thinning of the hair. *Elastin* is the protein that gives the skin its suppleness. As the years go by it is produced less and less, allowing the skin to require its familiar wrinkles. The hyaline cartilage lining the joints is also subject to the pathology of degeneration, and osteoarthritis is the inevitable fate awaiting those who survive into old age.

**Neoplastic** is Greek for 'new growth'. Growth is one of the few characteristics, which distinguish living creatures from machines. We tend to take this for granted, but growth is the complex process turning what we eat and drink into replacement parts for the body. Failure of growth and repair has already been discussed as degeneration. At the other end of the scale, however, the process may go wrong to the extent that growth is allowed to occur without proper controls. For the patient, this means the development of tumours. Tumour comes from the Latin for a "lump", although some tumours may be very small. The process of growth and repair is never perfect and nearly everyone has, for example, a few additional skin pigment cells clustered together as freckles. This is the most benign form of tumour. Most people have a few innocent lumps and bumps of the skin or underlying fatty tissue. It is probably not surprising, when we think about it, that those parts of the body which have the rapid cell turnover are also liable to the pathology of growth abnormalities – glands and the skin are obvious examples and discussed in later chapters. Fortunately, most of these abnormalities are benign and are at most a minor nuisance or blemish. Having said that, the process of growth can in some circumstances continue unabated. This is malignant growth – cancer. It is the opposite extreme to degenerative pathology. Cancer is the biological equivalent of leaning on the 'start' button of a photocopier – the machine will keep on churning out copies until it runs out of paper – in this analogy represented by the death of the patient.

Cancer cells are abnormal not only in their uncontrolled growth but also because they are different from the tissues from which they are derived. The appearance of the cells is important for the pathologist in the laboratory when he is studying a tumour from a patient's biopsy. The more a cancer cell differs from the original tissue, the more aggressive that cancer is likely to be. The amount of nuclear material (DNA) in the cells gives an important clue to the likelihood of rapid growth. This rapid growth brings the potential for invasion of adjacent structures. Bits of the tumour may break away and *metastasise* (spread) to distant parts of the body. ('Metastasis' comes from two Greek words meaning 'multiple sites' – an unfortunate characteristic of uncontrolled advanced cancer). As these tumour cells continue to grow they may erode or obstruct vital organs. This is how cancer kills the patient.

**Immunity** is the term describing the body processes that recognise and remove abnormal biological material. Abnormal material has chemical markers called antigens. These may be found on bacteria and viruses and some cancers. Unfortunately, they may also be found on a variety of other things including otherwise healthy foodstuffs. Study of the immune system is an important branch of medical research. Anatomically the immune system consists of the lymph glands and the spleen together with the circulating white blood cells. Physiologically the system may be compared to a military defence system with patrolling sentries and armed hit squads. The sentries (the white blood cells) constantly sample all the biological material with which they come into contact. If the white cells do not recognise these material they sound an alarm – the immune response – and a hit squad of antibodies and lymph cells is called up to attack the 'foreign' invader. Unfortunately, as in a real war, the parallel of 'friendly fire' may occur. This is the basis of the so–called **auto–immune** group of conditions.

The development of the immune system occurs in late pregnancy and early infancy. During this stage of development the white cells become programmed to recognise the body's own constituents. Once the system is mature then anything else is liable to be attacked. The circulating cells of the immune system stay in the blood and will not, in the normal way, come into contact with some specialised structures within the body. These may include the inside of the eye, the fluid within the joints and the cells within the thyroid gland and the pancreas. If, therefore, damage occurs or through some chance the structures of these tissues leak out into the circulation the inflammatory process will be activated because the body's own tissue is treated as 'foreign'. This is the basis of the autoimmune response. From the examples given above, *sympathetic ophthalmitis* may cause loss of an eye in the presence of damage to the other eye. *Rheumatoid arthritis* is considered in the section on joint disorders. The thyroid gland may be destroyed by the autoimmune process, and cause the clinical condition of *myxoedema; Type I diabetes* occurs if specialised insulin cells within the pancreas are destroyed.

The sensitivity of the immune system is an inherited characteristic. In particular, some patients appear to have very sensitive lymphocytes and it is not uncommon to find that a patient with, say, asthma will also develop an allergic reaction of the skin (eczema) and may also be susceptible to drug allergies or external allergens such as pollens.

**Metabolism** is the term applied to the vast range of chemical reactions which keep the body going – its biochemistry. Every cell in the body has its own isolating cell membrane and is separate from every other cell and, just as importantly, distinct from the fluid which surrounds it. (As a side observation, it is interesting to note that this surrounding tissue fluid closely resembles sea water in its chemical content, while the contents of the cells tend to resemble the chemistry found in primitive one-celled creatures found in their millions in the sea as plankton. Evolution has only taken us so far!) In the human, and indeed in all multi-cellular creatures, the individual cells become specialised for different purposes, but because of the difference between the inside and the outside of the cell a constant supply of energy is required to pump the salts to the outside of the cell membrane. If this energy supply fails then the cell – and potentially the whole body – will die. With the increasing sophistication found through the animal kingdom comes greater independence. Plankton is limited to floating round in the sea, waiting for food in the form of chemicals to be absorbed directly. Higher creatures are able to move in search of food. With further evolutionary sophistication creatures like ourselves have abandoned the sea. We are able to survive in a wide range of temperatures and able to absorb a wide variety of foodstuffs to acquire essential nutrition.

Problems with the metabolic process may seem rather remote, so consider, by way of example, another but very familiar biochemical process – cooking. The cooking process essentially consists of mixing the right amount of ingredients to produce the right amount of sweetness, acidity and other flavours. A chemical reaction is then promoted by the application of heat which may allow release of carbon dioxide as in bread making and also changes the characteristics of the proteins within the ingredients, producing the difference between raw meat and cooked meat and elastic dough to crumbly bread. Compare this relatively simple process of cooking (in which many things can still go wrong!) to the enormously complicated chemistry within the body. Glucose is present in the blood as the essential fuel, but this has to be produced from food in the gut, either by breaking down carbohydrate or by removing nitrogen from amino acids, which in turn are produced from protein. Exactly the right amount of sugar has to get to every cell in the body. (See the section on diabetes.) The fuel must be accompanied by oxygen, again in the right concentration. The complex chemical processes of combination of glucose and oxygen are sometimes referred to as "burning" but obviously the body does not normally produce smoke and flames. What actually happens is that there is a whole chain of reactions which produce energy-rich compounds for the cell membranes and for muscle activity. Each of these chemical processes occurs due to the presence of enzymes – biological catalysts. These can only operate within a very narrow range of acidity and temperature. Compared with our kitchen recipes it is perhaps surprising that the body manages to work at all.

Metabolic abnormalities – the pathology – can be caused by problems within the control systems. These are usually hormones produced by the glands and circulating in the blood. Thyroxine is produced by the thyroid gland and promotes many of the processes of energy production. Steroids are produced in the liver and in the adrenal glands and also affect the growth process. The pituitary gland sits in the middle of the brain and produces a range of hormones including growth hormone and the anti-diuretic hormone which controls the way in which the kidneys concentrate the blood. Some pituitary hormones are responsible for the function of other hormone-producing glands, notably the thyroid, adrenal cortex and the testes or ovaries. Insulin – controlling glucose – will be considered separately in the section on diabetes.

In the clinical situation known as respiratory failure, where there is an inadequate supply of oxygen to the blood, pathology at cell level may affect the muscles, where lactic acid is produced. This causes the familiar feeling of stiffness after unaccustomed exercise. While the muscles can survive without oxygen for about an hour, the brain and kidneys cannot. Anoxia (no oxygen) or hypoxia (low oxygen) cause irreversible tissue damage to these organs within minutes. This results in cardiac arrest, respiratory failure or sudden renal failure.

The body temperature is also crucial and bears out the comparison of metabolism with our kitchen recipe. It is a matter of common experience that a rise in temperature of even one or two degrees causes us to feel remarkably ill. The reason for this is that the metabolism is affected because the enzymes are temperature sensitive. It is likely that the rise in temperature is an adaptive change to infection. This has produced an evolutionary advantage because infecting organisms may be even more susceptible to temperature change than the human body and are rendered vulnerable by a rise in temperature.

**Infections** are probably the commonest type of pathology. By infection, we mean a pathological reaction caused by microscopic living organisms in or on the body. When looking at this it is worthwhile remembering that every inch of the outside of the body is colonised by viruses or bacteria – and so is a great deal of the inside. Every individual is outnumbered by billions to one by the microorganisms they carry around, but even so most of us remain fairly healthy most of the time. When these microorganisms gain the upper hand, however, we suffer from infection. This may show itself in various ways.

*Viruses* are small particles of nucleic acid (DNA or RNA). The name virus has been hijacked by the computer industry but the term is actually accurate in either situation. The biological virus represents a small section of a program which gets itself into a cell. The equivalent of the computer program in this case is the normal cell, but its program, which is written in the DNA, becomes corrupted by the virus and cell function is affected. In the commonest type of virus infection, in the upper respiratory tract, the cells then become abnormal. This is recognised by the immune system, which produces an inflammatory response, causing the familiar sore throat. A virus may spread throughout the body and the inflammation in the gut, muscles, head and stomach produces all the clinical symptoms familiar as influenza. More dangerously, some viruses can provide a false instruction pattern for growth.

In, for example, the skin, the clinical effect can range from a mild rash to smallpox. The association of human papilloma virus (HPV) with cervical cancer has been known about for years and has finally become the subject of an immunisation programme. In this situation, the virus infection is a lot more than a mere nuisance.

*Bacteria*, unlike viruses, have a cell wall and are capable of independent existence. They cause trouble either by production of toxins or by triggering an immune response. Toxin-producing bacteria include those of the *botulinus* group, which produce muscle paralysis – an effect used therapeutically in the form of Botox. *Staphylococci*, commonly found in the nose, can infect food and the toxin produced causes profuse diarrhoea. Staphylococci can also produce a wound infection. They are quite sophisticated bacteria and can develop enzyme systems allowing them to resist the effect of antibiotics. The phenomenon of methycillin resistant staphylococcus aureus (MRSA) is becoming a significant problem in UK hospitals. *Streptococci* produce enzymes to dissolve the tissues and allow spread of the bacteria. A useful derivative of this enzyme is the so-called 'clot busting' drug – *strepto*kinase. Unfortunately streptococci also produce other enzymes and toxins, which will cause inflammatory change and extensive tissue damage. When tissue damage occurs white cells are brought into play by the immune response. A lot of the white cells are killed in the process, and these together with dead bacteria form the battlefield corpses collectively known as pus.

When bacteria cause an extensive immune response, this may unfortunately cause an 'own goal'. A good example of this is tuberculosis which can cause extensive tissue damage within the lung because of the inflammation it produces. TB can be present for months or even years, walled off by this immune response.

**Toxic** changes represent another form of tissue damage. Toxins have been mentioned as products of bacteria. Many other chemicals may, however, obstruct the sensitive chemical processes of the body.

In practical terms 'poisoning' in its usual sense is rare outside of criminal activity. Alcohol and drugs, however, cause significant pathology because of their accepted 'social' use in some sections of society. Alcohol is a simple chemical product produced by bacterial breakdown of sugar. It is naturally present in the body in very low concentration, probably as a result of fermentation within the gut. It is, however, a tissue poison. Its effects on the brain are discussed in the section on psychiatry. In general terms, the body is able to tolerate a small amount of alcohol and the effect on the brain is to produce a sense of well-being. Alcohol is broken down in the liver. For this reason the liver cells bear the brunt of excessive alcohol concentration and may be overwhelmed. The first reaction is death of the liver cells to be replaced by scar tissue (cirrhosis). If the process continues the liver cells may attempt to repair, but the repair process becomes abnormal and primary liver cancer ensues. Probably the simplest toxin chemically is cyanide. It has the formula CN. It blocks the process which produces the energy rich compounds keeping every cell in the body going. An attack at this level produces death within minutes.

**Iatrogenic disease** should always be considered by a doctor when going through the list of potential pathological causes of his patient's illness. It comes from the Greek word "iatros" (ιατρος) – meaning doctor. This means that a doctor is directly responsible for the pathology, usually because he has issued a prescription or undertaken a surgical procedure. It is worth remembering that prescription drugs were first controlled by a piece of legislation called The Pharmacy and Poisons Act – the Act made no generic distinction between the therapeutic effect of pharmaceuticals and the toxic effect of poisons! This is because all drugs are intended to interfere with cellular processes within the body, the intention being that these will produce a desired effect. It is a matter of common experience, however, that the therapeutic effects are by no means the only ones to be found. Side effects can occur with almost any drug and in issuing a prescription a competent doctor is expected to consider the likely side effects on the principle of "risk versus benefit".

Considering surgical procedures, the potential risk of any procedure should be explained to a patient prior to obtaining his or her consent. Again, the risk versus benefit of a procedure should be carefully considered by the surgeon before the operation is suggested, not least because the consent has the legal effect of changing an assault under the Offences Against the Person Act into a health-giving therapeutic procedure!

**Trauma** is usually self–explanatory. The human body is soft and relatively vulnerable. For legal purposes trauma may be defined as pathology directly resulting from the application of violent external force. The word "violent" may in turn be defined as sufficient force to produce the injury. This produces something of a circular argument, but in practical terms the circumstances surrounding trauma should be fairly obvious. Implied in the definition is, however, a requirement that the anatomy may be changed, even though this change may be at microscopic level. Specifically excluded by this definition are pathological fractures where the bone is weakened by tumour. The natural history for physical trauma is that it will heal, firstly by the formation of a blood clot. The blood clot is replaced by fibrous tissue (scar), which in turn is replaced by the normal tissue relevant to that part of the body, such as skin, bone or tendon. In many tissues this process is not perfect and some scar tissue remains. The general tendency is, however, towards resolution of the scar and the development of normal tissue. This process should take a matter of weeks.

Iatrogenic trauma is one way of describing the effects of any operation. This is because the process of healing is rarely perfect and scar tissue is never as good as the original. The site of an operation may be vulnerable to infection as an early complication of surgery, or the wound may break down weeks or even months after healing has apparently completed.

So much for the classification of pathology. This classification is often referred to as the 'pathological sieve' because a doctor looking for the underlying cause of his patient's illness should go through these underlying possibilities systematically. Some of the ways in which the different varieties of pathology may produce abnormalities within the body have been discussed, often mentioning inflammation.

**Inflammation** is the final common pathway of many pathological processes. It is a standard response to what may conveniently be called any insult, whether this is a cut on the hand or a dose of 'flu. Classically, inflammation is described as a process whereby the part of the body becomes painful, hot, red and swollen. In addition to this there is usually some loss of function.

For descriptive terms the process of inflammation is usually given the suffix *–itis*, to indicate that the inflammatory process has occurred, as in appendicitis. Other terms with the same suffix are sufficiently familiar to be obvious. (Less familiar is the suffix *–osis*, which is used to indicate a pathological process – often degenerative – but without inflammation.)

It is sometimes helpful to think of the mechanism of the inflammatory response as a mobilisation of the body's defences – described above as a 'hit squad'. These are the white cells which are freely circulating in the blood but which are attracted to the 'trouble spots'. When they get there they release substances to cause an increase in blood supply – allowing further reinforcements by white cells. This also causes a concentration of proteins, together called complement, which circulate in the blood. These proteins stimulate the different type of white cells to produce the response necessary to kill invading bacteria or to surround them to minimise their damage. As the response to the infection progresses, pus may accumulate. It is a mixture of dead bacteria and dead white cells.

The inflammatory process should normally lead to repair – with the important proviso that any pus needs to be out of the way first. The next step is fibrous repair as scar tissue and finally re-growth of normal structure. If the insult continues, however, the process of *chronic* inflammation may occur, when the insult is just balanced by the repair process. This produces granulation tissue, a mix of new blood vessels and fibrous tissue. To correct a common misunderstanding, the word chronic comes from the Greek word for time (κρονος) and has nothing to do with the severity of the condition. It simply means that the inflammation has been going on for a good while.

PATHOLOGY AS A CAUSE OF DISEASE.

Having looked at different types of pathology it should by now be clear that the patient's complaint may arise from one of several pathological processes, all of which are different. This is the reason for considering pathology as a separate science.

By way of example, consider a cancer that has spread to the bone and eroded it. The bone may break with the minimum of effort. This is clearly a fracture but it is not really due to trauma. If the fracture causes the skin to be broken it is likely that infection will occur. There *could* therefore be three different types of pathology going on in the same site (neoplastic, traumatic and infective), but it is only by careful consideration of the *underlying* pathology (here, the cancer) that the true diagnosis may be reached and the best management provided for the patient.

The same considerations may apply in medico-legal situations.

## Pathology

The cancer is the underlying pathology, and the fracture and the infection have arisen as a consequence – a doctor who has negligently failed to diagnose cancer cannot say that the pathological fracture was simply a result of trauma and use this as a defence. Unfortunately, failure to consider the pathology is not the only mistake open to Dr Botchup – as we shall see in the following chapters.

Chapter 3

## DOCTORS & NHS MANAGEMENT

It may seem odd for a book on doctors' mistakes to include a chapter about politicians and civil servants. It is necessary because in the United Kingdom most medical treatment, and nearly every example mentioned in this book, is carried out under the National Health Service. Because the NHS is publicly funded it means that everything within it can, in theory and sometimes in practice, be questioned by Parliament and be regulated by civil servants. This must inevitably have an effect on doctors and the way they practice.

Historically the NHS was founded in 1948 to replace what was then a haphazard system for the provision of healthcare in the United Kingdom. Before this some individuals had access to healthcare because of a plan through their workplace; others had to rely on charity or pay the full cost of health care. The creation of the NHS was at the time held to be a model for the world. Some doctors welcomed it, particularly general practitioners in poor districts who had to earn a living by charging fees to impoverished patients. Other doctors, particularly specialists in fashionable London practices, felt threatened by a serious decrease in their income. This was to some extent foreseen by the Government, and Aneurin Bevan, the founder of the National Health Service, later explained (at a private dinner) how he had secured these doctors' consent for the 1948 settlement: – "I stuffed their mouths with gold."

There was also some opposition from the public because the health service was seen as a drain on the taxpayer – an argument repeated in the United States 65 years later by the opponents of 'Obama care'. In 1948 this argument was countered by what was probably one of the most inaccurate statements of the 20th century, even for a politician. The Minister responsible claimed that within a short time the system would effectively be self-funding. This was, he said, because the increase in the health of the nation provided by the NHS would allow greater productivity and wealth for all. Using dentistry as an example, the argument ran like this: A combination of poor diet and poor education meant that in some districts the number of people with dental disease was approaching 100%. In the absence of affordable dental care, the best patients could hope for was periodontal disease affecting the gums and causing loose teeth. This would mean that patients could extract the teeth themselves once the amount of infection round the teeth had made this possible. In other cases, dental decay would proceed relentlessly, involving the pulp (nerve) and proceeding to painful abscesses. These had to be endured, and the pain and associated ill-health continued unless the patient could afford an extraction. The argument provided by the government was that provision of NHS dental care would allow free extractions, free dentures, and the health and prosperity of the nation would improve.

Interestingly, insofar as it went, this was true. My grandfather provided a typical example. He had trained as a pharmacist but with the advent of the NHS saw more prospects in dentistry. This was prior to the registration of dentists – all he had to do was buy a set of extraction forceps. Working in a North Lancashire cotton town in the 1950s he had an anaesthetist come in to his surgery once a week. After these sessions there would be a large bin that contained nothing but extracted teeth. The rest of the week he spent constructing dentures. The patients were cheerfully pain-free and in better health, with no time lost from work. It was quite normal to have no teeth by your mid-20s. This level of care was taken as a model for the future of NHS dentistry. What was not taken into account, of course, was the more sophisticated application of dentistry. Instead of extractions and full dentures, patients began to demand fillings, metal partial dentures, crowns and bridges, and even orthodontics – all on the Health Service. With the mantra of "free health for all" no politician dared oppose this and costs escalated. This example applied to dentistry but the same principle applied across the board to include general practice and all hospital specialties. As the years went by it became apparent that the NHS was at risk of becoming an all-consuming monster.

The newly founded Ministry of Health inherited the system in 1948. Prior to the NHS medical care was to say the least patchy. Most general practitioners were single-handed. Because they relied on a panel system and a few private patients to provide their income they jealously guarded their practices, with GPs accepting responsibility for 24 hours a day, 7 days a week – whether sober or not. Perhaps fortunately, patient expectations were considerably lower and workload was reduced by the disincentive of patients having to pay a fee. This made general practice at least tolerable from the GP's point of view and the local doctor was usually seen as a pillar of the community.

The hospital system prior to the inception of the health service was also highly variable. The long established London teaching hospitals, followed by those in other major cities, had traditionally attracted the brightest and the best to be their specialists. The arrangement was that a consultant ran a 'firm' within the hospital, and delegated many of his routine tasks to his junior doctors. These 'junior' doctors could often be highly trained and knowledgeable, well on their way to getting a foot on the consultant ladder. The consultant himself would juggle his time between doing ward rounds at the hospital and his private practice. Surgeons undertook only the more advanced NHS operations, and even these were delegated once the juniors were considered reasonably proficient. While there were many conscientious hospital consultants there was clearly a conflict of interest, even in what were then centres of excellence. Outside the big cities, the hospital service consisted of what are now described as district general hospitals. These had frequently been founded by some charitable institution and were variously described as infirmaries or in some cases named after either a benefactor or perhaps a saint. Overall, the same medical system applied, with consultants nominally attached to the hospital but often gaining the majority of their incomes from their private practice.

After 1948, despite Aneurin Bevan having stuffed the doctors' mouths with gold, it could hardly be expected that the system would change overnight. General practitioners had a more assured income in that they no longer had to charge their patients, but they still depended for that income on the number of patients on the 'panel', or list. General practice was run very much at the whim of the individual doctor, and the management structure, in the form of so-called "Executive Councils" was mainly restricted to administering the GPs' payment system. It was not until a more complex system of fees and allowances was introduced that the concept of partnerships became more popular – the introduction of a partnership allowance overcame the concerns about individual list size. In hospitals things ran very much as before.

The consultants ran their firms with little reference to any hospital management system or, often, without reference to colleagues in the same specialty on a different firm. The matron and the hospital secretary headed the hospital management. The matron ran the wards very much on a hierarchal military system supervising the ward sisters – Florence Nightingale had, after all, been a nurse with the Army. Each ward sister had 'her' ward with no deputy. She was not expected to marry. The hospital secretary had a small support staff and was concerned largely with running the infrastructure of the hospital and ensuring that people got paid. There was no management input into any clinical decision-making and the doctors were responsible only to the General Medical Council. The hospital management was however responsible for the budget for each department and indeed each medical firm. This was the system that the health service had inherited, and which in practice continued for many years afterwards. The so-called "clinical freedom" of both consultants and general practitioners was held to be sacrosanct. Managers were not paid to interfere, and politicians did not dare.

The principle of "free health for all" was finally broken in an acknowledgement that the NHS could not fund everything. The first crack in the wall, interestingly, began in NHS dentistry – the craft that had been cited as promoting efficiency through health for all. Before the introduction of the present scaled charges dentists were paid on a 'fee per item of service' scale. This meant that the more work they did the more they got paid. There is no doubt that the system was abused. In particular, Commonwealth dentists, often newly qualified, would enter an NHS practice and pursue a relentless policy of 'drill and fill'. They would do this until the first income tax demand arrived, when they would go back to their own country with the capital to start their own (probably more conservative) practices. This perceived abuse made it politically possible to introduce a charge for NHS dental services – although this was initially limited to ten shillings irrespective of the treatment undertaken. At about the same time a prescription charge was introduced, in the form of one shilling per item. (The shilling is now 5p.)

This was the system that pertained in the late 1960s, the time when I entered a London teaching hospital as a student. Although a consultant had unlimited clinical freedom there was still discontent with the management. My first inkling of this was at a lecture from an ENT consultant. He had condescended to appear at the medical school lecture theatre – teaching was considered to be a prestigious activity. To be fair, the first half-hour of the lecture was indeed devoted to matters pertaining to ear nose and throat surgery. The second half of the lecture consisted of the consultant railing against the hospital management. He required an operating microscope for the hospital theatre. The best one (which he considered to be the only option) cost £6000. His departmental budget was £5000 per year. He had approached the hospital management, asking either for an additional sum or alternatively offering to reduce expenditure that year so that the budget could be carried over. The burden of his complaint was that the management had adamantly refused. The financial year ran from 1st April one year until 31st of March the next year. The budget could not be exceeded. Any funds not used within the year would be forfeited. The accounts must be kept in order. The hospital manager had his job to think of and that was that. One can see the consultant's point of view.

Financial constraints aside, however, both general practitioners and consultants could still run their firms or practices as they pleased. GPs were at liberty to run open surgeries without any appointments, and it was not uncommon to enter a doctor's waiting room to find 20 people waiting. This was held to be efficient and convenient for the doctor, irrespective of the time wasted by his patients. The GP contract at the time specified only that a doctor was obliged to provide "the services normally provided by a general practitioner". This was of course an absurd circular argument, and failed to pay any heed to the concept of introduction of preventive medicine. You went to the GP if you were ill. You could expect a consultation of six minutes or less. You probably got a prescription whether you needed it or not, largely as a way of terminating the interview. On the hospital side, waiting lists became standard. When working at a hospital in France some years later a French colleague asked me with total wonderment why patients tolerated the "listes d'attente". The answer of course is that the patient was not paying anything, and was therefore seen as having no right to complain. If a patient wanted urgent treatment, or sometimes any treatment at all, he always had the option of going – often to the same consultant – and paying privately. From the consultant's point of view there was obviously no incentive to make efficient use of hospital time. Rather the contrary – the longer the waiting list, the more chance of the patient opting for private treatment. In the 1970s as a registrar in a district general hospital it was my responsibility to organise the theatre operating lists. It became apparent that when patients were eventually called for surgery and attended the hospital for their preoperative assessment some of them no longer needed the operation. Others were found to be unfit, or unsuitable for anaesthetic. Would it not, I asked, be possible to have a secondary list of patients, perhaps those with less work or home commitments, who could come into hospital to fill these places at short notice? This would help reduce waiting lists and ensure that the theatre time was used efficiently. The firm response from the consultant in charge was that I should mind my own business and stick to the way things were done. The reason was, of course, that the quicker he finished his (now abbreviated) NHS list the quicker he could get off to the private hospital.

Eventually public discontent forced the politicians to act.

The problem of money still remained. The first attack (as it was perceived) on clinical freedom of general practitioners was in the form of a 'black list' of drugs that could not be prescribed on the NHS. Predictably, there was some opposition from the general practitioners and from the British Medical Association but this was overcome, not least on the rational grounds that many of the black listed items could be prescribed in other forms and others were generally considered to be useless. Although most of the items on the GP blacklist were hardly ever prescribed in any event, the fact remains that the mould had been broken. A few years later the general practice contract was changed to oblige GPs to provide preventive care for the first time. Advocates of 'clinical freedom' in general practice were heavily critical, suggesting that GPs would have to spend their time chasing perfectly fit septuagenarians round the golf course in order to check their blood pressure and get a urine sample. Most good general practitioners found that the contract simply paid them a little more for what they were doing already. At about the same time it became politically acceptable to question the freedom of consultants to run the hospitals in their own way. The government of the day introduced targets for waiting lists. These were still set at the limit – incredible to foreign eyes – of 18 weeks between the first GP referral and the time to be seen in a consultant-led clinic. This was probably the point where hospital management took on a new role, effectively extending management into territories that had previously been jealously guarded by the doctors. The hospital management put pressure on the consultants to reduce their waiting lists. The hospital management were, themselves, coming under pressure from the Department of Health. Incredibly, as explained by one head of Department, this was done by a system of fines! If, for example, a hospital had breached its waiting list target to any significant extent the reasons for this were not questioned. This was held to be too simplistic. The likely reason was of course that the hospital was underfunded and hence understaffed so the work could not be done. The Department, in their wisdom, therefore applied a fine, effectively reducing the available budget still further. This may beggar belief, but was nonetheless the system applied at the time. Coming under management criticism, the consultants, who still ordered the day-to-day management of their firms, felt that they had to act. The National Audit Office found a majority of consultants – who had themselves complained of heavy pressure from hospital managers – admitted distorting clinical priorities. 'Bean counting' became the order of the day. Operations to reverse vasectomies were performed at the expense of patients waiting for bladder surgery. Patients with minor ear, nose and throat disorders were given outpatient appointments before those with serious breathing troubles. Patients needing quick operations for what were termed "lumps and bumps" were treated before those needing surgery for hip and knee replacement. Numbers were up, but the concept of healthcare was down.

In an effort to improve the overall efficiency of the service, business management principles previously reserved for industry and commerce were applied. The principal of 'money follows the patient' was introduced. This was done in conjunction with the introduction of general practitioner budget holding. The idea was that a GP would have a notional budget, to be spent as considered clinically necessary. If there were any savings the GP would be able to spend the money on enhancements to his own practice. Not surprisingly, the incentive at the start of the programme provided generous funds. A few more business-like – or cynical, depending on your point of view – GPs profited enormously, ploughing the funds back into their own premises or paying relatives generous salaries to undertake health promotion clinics. Many GPs declined to enter the commercial rat race and after a few years the system was abandoned.

From the hospital point of view, this newly introduced commercial aspect of the NHS had unfortunate and unforeseen consequences. Here is just one example. In the early 1990s it had become customary for a group of my colleagues who had been students together to meet for an annual cricket match. The doctors and dentists attending for the day had graduated more than ten years previously, had completed their postgraduate training and were holding appointments as hospital consultants or in their early years of general practice in medicine or dentistry. Although there was no formal 'man of the match' it would have been generally agreed that Dr Steve Bolsin, who opened both the batting and the bowling, would undoubtedly have fitted the bill. The cricket was not the only feature of the day, which was very much a social occasion. It was also an opportunity for old friends, who by now were scattered throughout the country or even abroad, to exchange views and ideas with colleagues who were not involved at their own place of work. It was at one of these cricket matches that Dr Bolsin, with some reservations, sought the views of his peers. He explained his problem. In 1989, as a newly appointed consultant paediatric anaesthetist at the Bristol Royal Infirmary, Dr Bolsin had identified that babies were dying after routine heart surgery. His attempts to improve matters led to confrontation with paediatric cardiac surgeons whom the hospital refused to investigate. The hospital clinical director at the time was a physician. The senior paediatric cardiac surgeon had trained at a London hospital. Nursing colleagues who had worked with this surgeon later described him as one of the most conscientious and capable thoracic surgeons they had ever worked with – but in adult cardiac surgery. The unit was performing relatively few adult cardiac operations, with the consequent reduction in hospital income under the funding system. Babies requiring heart surgery were sent elsewhere. Under pressure from the management, via the clinical director, the unit started to perform paediatric cardiac operations – even though the surgeon had no training in this highly specialised area. Dr Bolsin had carefully confirmed the high mortality rates and attempted to improve the service. Initial attempts to keep the matter in-house had failed. The question he now put to his friends from student days was, what should he do? The advice was unequivocal. The situation had to be addressed, and having exhausted what were then seen to be the only official channels Dr Bolsin had no alternative but to seek extensive publicity over his concerns. Once the matter had become public, of course, the political incentives changed and action had to be taken. There was an enquiry, and recommendations as to personnel. This led to a fall in mortality rates for children's heart surgery in Bristol from 30% to less than 5% but this was all too late. The cardiac surgeon and the clinical director were struck off the medical register after a General Medical Council enquiry. Steve Bolsin had knowingly sacrificed his job, professional popularity and ultimately his young family's life in Britain in defence of his professional conscience for what he knew was right. Unable to obtain work in the UK after what is now known as the Bristol Heart Hospital Scandal, he took up a senior appointment at a hospital in Australia. His achievements in establishing Clinical Governance across the NHS and indeed globally have never been formally acknowledged in the UK.

So who are the people that allowed this to happen? It is impossible, and indeed unfair, to attempt to lay the blame at the door of any medical individual. At the enquiry surgeon Mr Dhasmana said: "My career is over. I have no reputation, I have no standing, I have no job, I have no possibility of a job, my family are distraught and destroyed, I am distraught and destroyed. I have tried to get a job elsewhere; I can't get a job." He then looked at a lady who was chairman of the group of parents whose children had died, and whose own child had died. He looked her straight in the eye and said: "But my loss is as nothing compared with the loss of a child." These were not the words of a man who regularly got up in the morning determined to protect his career no matter what the cost to his patients. The clinical director was a physician. While arguably the clinical statistics of mortality should gradually have become obvious, a physician could not be expected to be aware of the finer points of cardiac surgery. It is therefore arguable that this doctor, coming under pressure to increase the output of the cardiothoracic surgery unit, himself persuaded the surgeons to undertake procedures for which they had no training. Again, however, this was not a cynical man who strove for results no matter what the cost. Surely, ran the argument, an expert cardiac surgeon should be able to adapt his technique to young babies. If we have a higher mortality rate it is simply because the surgeons are undertaking more difficult cases.

So if the doctors had got things wrong was this due to management pressure? And was the pressure based on ignorance? During the enquiry the chair of the Regional Health Authority, the senior management board overlooking the Bristol hospital, was asked whether she had a track of the fact that there were some deaths taking place in the hospital. Her response said it all: "I did not know whether they came out dead or alive, it wasn't relevant to our task. Our task was to measure throughput, in terms of financial flows." Could the pernicious results of management disengagement be demonstrated more forcibly!

Unfortunately, it is this separation of clinical management from what happens in the hospital ward or the GP's surgery that makes things go wrong. The other permanent difficulty is a limitation of resources, but this cannot be the only answer because financial stringency applies across the whole of the NHS. Most of the time it is possible to muddle through but in some instances the management get it catastrophically wrong. One example of this was in the Staffordshire Hospital, again described in the popular press as a scandal. In February 2013 a report was published by Robert Francis QC. The report was the result of a public inquiry into the role of managers of Mid Staffordshire Foundation NHS

Trust between January 2005 and March 2009. Two previous inquiries into events at the Trust had uncovered a lack of basic care in many of its wards and departments. These earlier reports had described many distressing episodes of appalling care. Patients were left in excrement-soiled beds for lengthy periods. Assistance was not provided with feeding for patients who could not eat without help. Staff were described as treating patients and their families with indifference and a lack of basic kindness. The Francis report considered why these serious problems at the Trust were not identified and acted on sooner, and what should be done to prevent it happening again in future. The findings were highly critical of the management, describing "an insidious negative culture involving a tolerance of poor standards and a disengagement from managerial and leadership responsibilities".

Interestingly, the Francis report, which was after all commissioned by the Department of Health, makes no observations as to funding. The report was based largely on evidence from patients and their relatives, all of whom were understandably critical of the care provided by the Trust. Relatively few witnesses appeared from the staff, a fact that was commented upon favourably by Mr Francis who argued against compulsory attendance at an enquiry. The nursing witnesses who did give evidence described a scene of chaos, with the medical assessment unit being known as "Beirut". A salient feature was the lack of senior management on the wards. It was stated that managers would rarely be seen unless they happened to be accompanying a visitor. This disengagement from leadership responsibility, as described in the report, was arguably a method adopted by these managers in the face of what should have been recognised as chaos, and had indeed been the subject of two previous unfavourable reports. The response of the management in this situation was to suggest that the criticisms in these reports had been exaggerated. Again, who are the people that allowed this to happen? No one is suggesting that any individual manager had set out deliberately to allow vulnerable patients to suffer unnecessarily. There is however a very natural human tendency, in the face of unpleasantness, to adopt the self-comforting approach of retreat from those facts.

One patient's sad story illustrates this. In April 2006 a man in his early 20s, John Moore-Robinson, bled to death at home when casualty staff at Stafford Hospital failed to diagnose a ruptured spleen. The death was due to an accident and a coroner's report was therefore necessary. The coroner requested an expert report into the death. The report was not however commissioned from an outside expert; the coroner simply asked the Trust to provide a report. One of their own casualty consultants, Dr Ivan Phair, was asked to write it. Dr Phair's *initial* report said: "I would therefore raise the possibility that his unfortunate, untimely death may have been avoided had he been more properly assessed on his initial attendance to the A&E department at the Mid Staffordshire General Hospitals NHS Trust." Prior to being sent to the coroner the report was submitted to the hospital's legal department. The head of hospital legal services was a senior solicitor, Kate Levy. She noted that the report was highly critical of the hospital and suggested that it should be withheld, or substantially changed, on the grounds that it would cause distress to the family. She was sacked by the hospital over the matter. Mr Stuart Knowles, who worked as a solicitor for Stafford Hospital, was later investigated by the police on the grounds that he had withheld the doctor's expert report from the inquest in 2007. As part of this inquiry the police also interviewed Kate Levy. The police case was not pursued, although the Coroner for South Staffordshire, Andrew Haigh, confirmed he never received a copy of the report. As a final twist Ms Levy brought a case for unfair dismissal against the hospital, saying that she had been performing her duty as a solicitor to her client. There was minimal resistance from the management who accepted her contention with the obvious implication that they, too, agreed that protection of the reputation of the Trust came before patient care. Ms Levy was awarded £100,000.

On a lesser scale, but just as significant and tragic for those involved, HM coroner for North Devon held an inquest into the death of a patient who had suffered a diabetic crisis (ketoacidosis). The diabetes had not previously been diagnosed – the patient had telephoned for advice to NHS direct, saying that he had an unquenchable thirst. This is one of the symptoms of an acute diabetic crisis, but is difficult to establish, particularly over the telephone. The nurse who dealt with the call followed a protocol which led her to believe that the problem was dehydration. She urged the patient to drink and unfortunately he attempted to quench his thirst by consuming a large volume of commercial lemonade, rich in sugar. This hastened the crisis and, sadly, the patient died. I was engaged by HM coroner to provide a report as to the expected duties of the primary care team. While waiting to give evidence I entered into conversation with a man in a suit. He turned out to be the manager of the local NHS Direct. As we talked, it rapidly became clear that he was there to give evidence. His evidence was not, however, to the effect that the nurse had misunderstood the situation, still less that she was inexperienced or poorly trained. It was clear that he saw his sole function as distancing himself and his organisation as far as possible from the unfortunate front line practitioner. "She mucked it up and it's not the fault of the management," was the message he was there to deliver to the coroner. This was 15 years ago, but the long history of "disengagement from managerial and leadership responsibilities" as later described in the Francis report could not have been clearer.

One example of NHS management's distance from the realities of day-to-day patient experience has, interestingly, been the development of a special language. This may come as a surprise, but NHS management has nonetheless managed to achieve the status of its own entry in the classic reference work, Fowlers English Usage. Looking up the word "jargon" as long ago as the Third Edition published in 1996, one finds what the editors considered to be an emphatic representative example. A lengthy extract from an NHS management report is quoted. While the extract is superficially detailed and authoritative, it is worth reading through critically. Using three words where one will do, the report gives a spurious impression of professionalism but, on closer analysis, manages to say very little. If you can find a copy of the book it makes for interesting reading; alternatively, almost any other NHS management produced diktat at will probably demonstrate the same point. Try it![1]

Again at a local level, the effect of management pressure on professionals may be shown by the following example. Being obliged to reduce costs, a primary care trust in the South East arranged for one of their senior managers to undertake an analysis of surgical and other procedures, which, it was considered, may have been unnecessary. These were deemed to be low priority procedures, or LPPs in the jargon. The list included the ENT procedure known as myringotomy. Myringotomy is a procedure to incise the eardrum and place a grommet, allowing ventilation of the middle ear. It is a short operation, taking about 10 minutes, but is important for children who have blocked Eustachian tubes. These children can get 'glue ear', a cause of deafness at a significant time of a child's schooling and development. The list of LPPs was presented to the professional executive committee (PEC). This was an extended committee representing health professionals in the area of the Primary Care Trust. The list of procedures, which it was proposed to limit, included myringotomy. The enthusiastic manager duly presented the list to the committee. To my surprise, there was a general nodding of heads, and the proposal was about to be accepted by the committee – myringotomy would be done only after a complex consultative process. At this stage I raised a point of order. "Chairman, could anybody round this table please explain exactly what a myringotomy is, and what are its indications?" There was a vague muttering from another GP at the end of the table to the effect that this was something to do with ENT. The rest was silence. It was obvious that no one else had the slightest clue what a myringotomy was, or what it was intended to achieve, although all the members were prepared to defer to the manager and see a treatment for childhood deafness removed from the list of available surgical procedures. On my insistence, this part of the proceedings of the committee was minuted in detail. This was yet another example of professionals being pressured by management attempting to adopt a position which was clinically and ethically untenable – in this case by withdrawing the availability of what was clearly a useful and sometimes essential operation.

Worryingly, the Francis Report on the Mid Staffordshire Trust ultimately concludes that responsibility is not confined to the Board of that Trust alone, but runs right through the National Health Service. Francis stated that events at the Trust are *"not… of such rarity or improbability that it would be safe to assume that it has not been and will not be repeated"*. The report calls for a "fundamental change" in culture whereby patients are put first and makes 290 recommendations covering a broad range of issues relating to patient care and safety in the NHS.

Happily there is the occasional heartening story that bureaucracy and political pressure can still be overcome if doctors are properly motivated. In 2005 the system of training for hospital doctors and general practitioners was about to be modernised in a Government initiative known as modernising medical careers (MMC). An offshoot of this organisation was the medical training application service (MTAS). This appears to have been modelled on the University Central Application Service without considering any local requirements, or indeed consulting the people concerned.

The result was an application form, which went to such politically correct extremes as to be unusable. The name of the applicant was withheld (this could allow nepotism to occur), photographs were banned (skin colour might allow racism) and references were sanitised so as to be unrecognisable. The situation was summed up by one junior hospital doctor saying: "There's no point in working hard and trying to do a good job and get on; your next job is now completely random anyway." Fortunately, an all-too-rare situation arose, where doctors stood up to the managers and politicians. A group of surgeons at a Birmingham hospital pointed out that they knew most of the doctors who were likely to be applying for their junior posts, either from medical school or from previous jobs. Under the system now proposed they were faced with an allocation of doctors about whom they knew nothing, although they were expected to work with them and delegate responsible tasks for the next six months. They simply refused. It was finally recognised that the system was unfit for purpose and abandoned. In an almost unheard-of gesture, the Minister of Health Patricia Hewitt actually offered an apology. Sadly, such instances of doctors standing up to managers and politicians are all too rare. Until more people are prepared to stand up and say "the Emperor's got no clothes" the present situation is likely to continue.

In 2017 surgeon Mr Ian Paterson was convicted of unlawful wounding and sentenced to 20 years in prison. He had been working at a hospital in the Midlands. Concerns about his practice had been expressed many years before but he continued to operate. His practice is described in this book in the section on breast disease. Eventually Sir Ian Kennedy was commissioned to produce a report. His conclusions make chilling reading: "This is a tragic story. It is not a story about the whole of the NHS. It is about something that happened in one corner of one hospital Trust in one part of the NHS. But, it has lessons for the whole of the NHS. It is a story of women faced with a life threatening disease who have been harmed.

It is a story of clinicians at their wits' ends trying for years to get the Trust to address what was going on. It is a story of clinicians going along with what they knew to be poor performance. It is a story of weak and indecisive leadership from senior managers. It is a story of secrecy and containment. It is a story of a Board which did not carry out its responsibilities."

With each new scandal comes a government response. One response at around the time of the Staffordshire hospital scandal was to introduce the Care Quality Commission – CQC. This organisation has sweeping powers to inspect and even close down hospitals, general practices and dental surgeries. Although it was later recognised that many of the inspectors were inadequately trained, and really had no idea what they were looking for or which evils they were supposed to prevent, the programme continued uninterrupted. It had to. It was rapidly obvious that the Commission was unfit for purpose and really only provided unnecessary administrative burdens to an already overworked service. Even so, any politician who suggested that the Care Quality Commission should be scrapped or even watered down would immediately be laying himself open to the accusation that he was trying to remove 'Care' and 'Quality' from the National Health Service. The CQC lumbers on, at best an irritant and at worse a positive disincentive for the brighter students to think of a career in the health service – whether as managers or doctors.

By way of example, when my practice premises were inspected by the CQC no comment was made about the quality of care. Patients could get an appointment at their convenience, and were invariably able to see a doctor that day should they so wish. There had been no complaints. A few 'critical incidents' had been analysed as learning points rather than as errors. Nonetheless, the inspector came up with two requirements. Firstly, the plumbing in the hot water tank had to be rearranged to reduce the likelihood of Legionnaire's disease. When it was pointed out that Legionnaire's disease had never occurred in our surgery in the last 25 years or, as far as we know, in any other surgery in the county this was held to be a fatuous argument. Secondly, the comfortable cloth covered chairs in the waiting room were deemed unhygienic and should be replaced with plastic covered substitutes on the basis that these could be wiped down with disinfectant. It was pointed out that these were simply chairs for patients to sit while waiting; the waiting room was not intended to provide a sterile area. Our nurse's treatment room and operating area were well up to antiseptic standards but this, too, was held to be irrelevant.

In general practice, the pressure from government, via its civil service managers, continues apparently unopposed. The British Medical Association is supposed to represent doctors, but very little opposition has been shown to the imposition of measures which a generation ago would have been considered unthinkable. The concept of professional freedom, or even professional discretion, has been almost entirely swept away. In 2004 general practitioners had a contract imposed upon them. One of the central features of the contract was the quality of outcomes framework, 'QOF'. This replaced a scheme which paid doctors via a capitation system. The theory then was that the more patients you had the more you had to work so the more you should be paid. The concept of preventative care was then gradually introduced. The perfectly reasonable idea of checking patients' blood pressure and doing annual checks against diabetes and kidney failure was something which many practices had been doing already. The QOF system, however, replaced this with a series of targets. The idea that individual health can be streamlined into a general 'one size fits all' series of targets has so far met with little opposition from doctors. This is probably because, whether they like it or not, it is the only way that general practitioners can keep their businesses afloat. In theory the principle is sound, but in practice it becomes unworkable to the point of absurdity. Obviously, people suffering from mental health are more vulnerable but this vulnerability is not reduced by a regulation requiring their doctor to call them in every year to complete an elaborate form with questions which the patient probably cannot answer. It is also a good idea to stop people getting too high a blood pressure, because this can lead to strokes and heart attacks. What is "too high" a BP will however depend on the individual. Not with QOF. A Doctor must get 90% of his patients to a blood pressure of 150/90 or less or he does not get paid. As far as I am aware, neither Nazi Germany, African dictators, nor even Soviet Russia have ever gone as far as to decree the blood pressures of the population.

The obvious point arising from all this is, what effect does the imposition of management strictures have on doctors' treatment of their patients? The proper answer should be that doctors are generally brighter and better educated than the management, should have their patients' interests at heart, and act accordingly. This does not always appear to be the case however. During a recent influenza outbreak a senior manager sent an email to all general practitioners in his area asking them to be aware of the hospital situation and to make an urgent referral of patients to hospital only where necessary. At first sight this may seem sensible enough, but the implication was that the urgency of a given clinical situation should be considered, not against the background of the patient's needs but against the background of the hospital's convenience. A few of the more senior, or more realistic, general practitioners emailed back to the manager telling him that they would continue to do as they had always done, and that an urgent case was an urgent case. The rest were silent. This insidious downward pressure or temptation to compromise coming down from above undoubtedly influences some doctors' thinking. The extent to which it may have caused some of the tragedies mentioned in this book may never be known.

NICE. Although free at the point of delivery, healthcare in

the United Kingdom still has to be paid for. Because it is paid for by 'The Government', the politicians have seized the opportunity to control spending and, by implication, to provide input (some would say to meddle) into every aspect of the National Health Service. Curiously, although the NHS started in 1948, governments have been reluctant to provide significant input into actual medical management until the last 30 years or so. The controls, which started in the late 1980s when prescribing restrictions were imposed on general practitioners, were mostly sensible and applied only to drugs which no one prescribed anyway. This was probably an initial step simply to test the water but since then there has been a gradual increase in the amount of government input. The agency responsible for this is the National Institute for Health and Clinical Excellence. This provides the snappy acronym NICE – the name by which the agency has come to be known. (Ironically, this works provided you leave out the 'Health'.)

From their humble beginnings of controlling GP prescribing, NICE have gradually ventured into previously uncharted territory and now regularly publish documents on Clinical Guidance. The Guidance papers are compiled by a panel of advisers, who in turn rely on peer-reviewed evidence or where this is not available expert opinion. As a general rule, NICE Guidance will provide an up-to-date and effective summary of current clinical practice. It has to be said, however, that the purity of scientific reasoning may occasionally be influenced by government pressure. Whether this causes these eminent academics to look over their shoulders at a possible honours list may never be known; it is possible to be cynical but in a cash-limited environment pragmatism may sometimes take precedence!

So what influence should NICE Guidance have on medical management? Can it automatically be said that if a doctor does not follow the guidance, then he has got things wrong? Although there is a tendency for some negligence lawyers to regard NICE

Clinical Guidance with the same rigid approach they would give to, say, the Road Traffic Act, the fact remains that every patient is different and a doctor's management must be influenced by circumstances. Having said that, if there is an obvious departure from the Guidance then a practising doctor may well find himself in a position of having to explain and justify this departure. In the final analysis, should a complaint proceed to the extent of litigation for breach of duty, the issue will have to be decided by a judge who will himself have been trained to follow rigid rules. A doctor departing from these rules may well have done so for a good reason, but will have to be persuasive in explaining why he has done so. Where relevant the clinical chapters of this book quote appropriate NICE Guidance with its application to the cases under discussion. To this extent, at least, management interference in the NHS may be said to have produced some positive results.

Finally, for those who remember the late Peter Cook and Dudley Moore, I quote an extract from 'Frog and Peach', featuring the absurd character Sir Arthur Greeb-Streebling:

Dudley:"Do you think you've learned from your mistakes?"

Peter: "Oh yes. I've learned from my mistakes and I'm sure I could repeat them exactly."

REFERENCE

1. *Fowler's Modern English Usage.* Third edition (1996) p426.

Chapter 4

# SKELETAL PROBLEMS – JOINT PATHOLOGY & FRACTURES

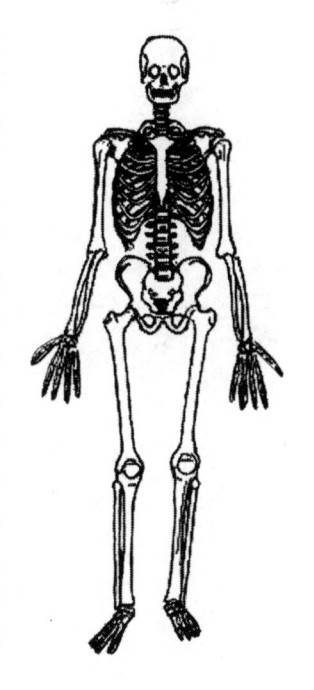

The skeleton is made of bones together with the joints that hold them together. Medical problems of the skeleton are dealt with by the disciplines of orthopaedic surgery and rheumatology. Rheumatology is the medical care of inflammatory conditions including the joints. Apart from problems with the spine, which are dealt with in a later chapter, over a period of ten years I was asked to assess four cases of bone cancer and three cases of bone-marrow cancer (myeloma). Mismanaged childhood orthopaedic problems occurred often, with nine cases of missed congenital dislocation of the hip (congenital dysplastic hip) and three cases of slipped epiphysis. There were fourteen cases of missed fractures. Tendon injuries included seven cases of missed Achilles tendon rupture and two of cruciate ligaments (in the knee). Nearly all these cases represented medical errors, although only about half were directly attributable to fault on the part of the general practitioners. This was usually because in the cases involved the general practitioner had followed incorrect advice provided from a hospital casualty department.

ANATOMY AND PHYSIOLOGY

Most people will be aware of the approximate shape of the skeleton – if only from cartoons or the occasional horror film. It is worth thinking about what the skeleton actually does. Simple creatures do not need a skeleton and are able to move by changes in the shape of their soft tissue. Amoebae, primitive one-celled creatures, are able to move through their environment in this way. Other creatures have specialised parts of the cell membranes (cilia) that produce a brush like movement and propel the cell along. More complicated creatures still, a good example being the earthworm, are able to move because a series of circular muscles will elongate the body and longitudinal muscles will contract it. They make forward progression by alternatively changing shape. Once past a certain size in the animal kingdom, however, the sheer bulk of the muscles means that they have to be attached to some sort of scaffolding – hence the skeleton.

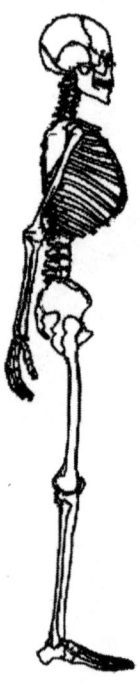

**Muscles** produce movement. In butcher's shop terms these are the red meat. Their only function is to produce movement. Even this can only occur in one direction – by contracting. Muscles have a special type of protein, which has an electrical charge in the resting state. When this charge is triggered off by the motor nerve to the muscle the protein shape changes and the muscle contracts. Since contraction (and not expansion) is the only type of active movement available to the muscles they are usually found in pairs in the body, so that one set of muscles of a pair will contract while the other relaxes. For movement in the other direction the opposite applies.

**Bones** consist of special tissue rich in calcium. Calcium as its carbonate salt is familiar as chalk, either in the schoolroom or in parts of the country such as the South Downs. The calcium salt in bone is called hydroxyapatite. This is less soluble than carbonate, although still susceptible to removal by specialised cells called osteoclasts. Hydroxyapatite in teeth can be dissolved by acid in the mouth, the start of dental decay. Sweet eaters beware! When a skeleton is examined it is only the harder calcified mineral elements that are obvious although bone also has an important protein component. Another feature of some bones, particularly the long bones of the limbs, is that they are actually hollow tubular structures. The space in the centre of these bones is full of marrow. The marrow is not a part of the skeleton dealing with movement, but is still an important structure. It is richly supplied with blood, and consists of a jelly-like substance producing stem cells. These are immature cells with the capacity to go on and form either red or white blood cells and connective tissue – in fact nearly everything else the body.

The bones grow, not as may be supposed at the very ends, but at growth plates, called *physes*, a little way from the ends. This arrangement means that the part of the bone within the joint can keep working even while alterations are occurring. This growth plate represents a potential structural weakness, particularly in weight bearing areas and specially the femur. This femoral epiphysis is particularly vulnerable in overweight adolescents.

Look at the diagrams of the skeleton. At first it may seem overwhelmingly complex. In fact it is fairly simple if we consider the skeleton in sections. The limbs (both upper and lower) originally evolved for movement. Under the skin they consist of bone and muscle, together with the blood vessels and nerves to supply them. The limbs are attached to supporting bones, the pelvis below and the shoulder blades and collarbones above. The whole structure is then linked by the bones of the spine, which also extend upwards to the skull. (The spine is considered in more detail in the chapter on back problems.) We are one of the few four-limbed creatures to use mainly the back legs for movement – the arms have evolved to supply a platform for the hand. It is worth remembering that it is in the fine development of the hands, and particularly the opposable thumb that allows us to grip tools accurately, that has enabled our species *(homo sapiens)* to become dominant on earth.

**Joints** are the parts of the skeletal system between lengths of solid bone. They allow movement. The type of joint influences the extent of movement that is possible. The shoulder and hip

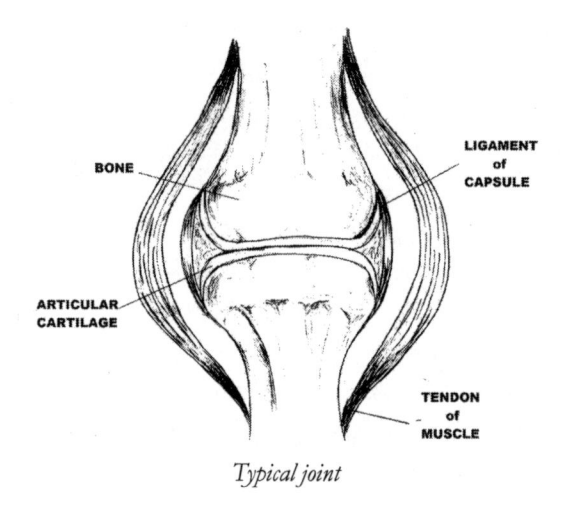

*Typical joint*

joint are ball and sockets, allowing movement over a wide range, particularly in the shoulder. The ankle and wrist joint have movement to a lesser extent, being hinge movements, although some movement is possible in two directions. Other joints such as those between the fingers, and the elbow and knee joints, allow only hinge movement.

Tough soft tissue is found adjacent to the joints. Ligaments attach one bone to another, and surround a joint. Tendons are attached to bone at one end with the other end of the tendon fusing gradually with the outer surface of the muscle. This how muscles act on the bones.

Most joints in the body are lined with a synovial membrane that secretes a lubricant within the joint, the synovial fluid. The common features of these synovial joints appear in the diagram below. Note that bone does not articulate (touch) directly with bone on the other side of the joint. There is (or should be) a fine layer of cartilage covering the ends. Cartilage is the white gristle-like material seen in the butcher's shop on, for example, the ball and socket joint on a shoulder of lamb. It is smooth and shiny and allows easy movement between the articulating surfaces. The capsule is a tough elastic structure of ligaments holding the bones together.

**Movement Control.** This is also considered in the section on back pain, but remember that joints have at least two sets of muscles acting on them, working in opposite directions. The ideal situation for movement would be that one set of muscles is completely relaxed while the other contracts. In practice, all muscles keep a certain degree of tension. The degree of muscle tension may depend on our degree of alertness, which in turn may increase in times of stress and anxiety. This is actually a protective mechanism, as the muscles are already partly tensed and so able to 'spring into instant action'. This increased muscle tone can, however, be a disadvantage because if the muscles are constantly

*A joint in action*

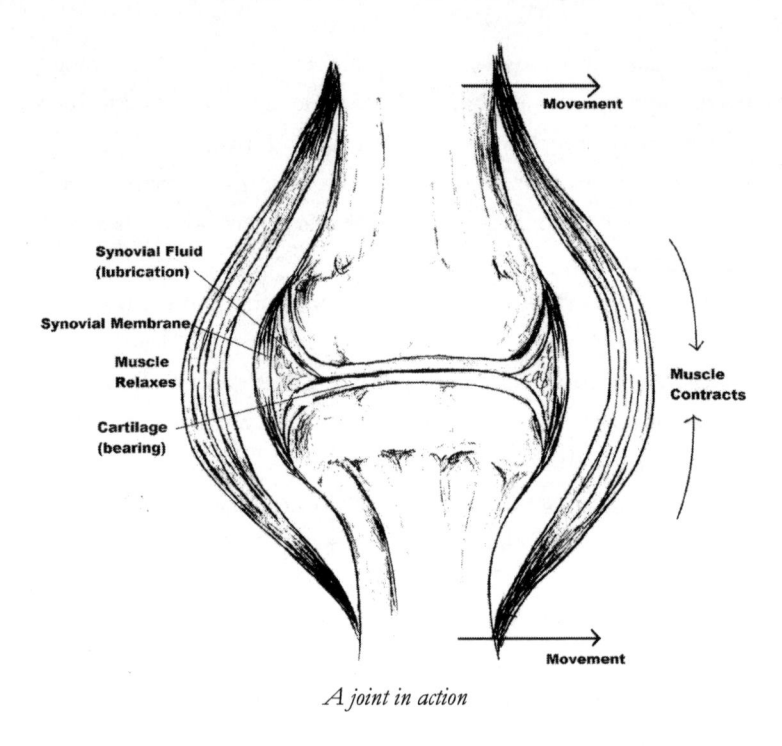

under tension then additional forces are transmitted back through the joints and indeed the muscles themselves can start to become fatigued and ache.

## CLINICAL ASSESSMENT OF MUSCULOSKELETAL PROBLEMS – THE DOCTOR'S JOB

**History.** The patient will usually complain of pain, irrespective of the underlying pathology. One trap for the unwary doctor – such as our old adversary Dr Botchup – is that pain from a joint is often referred to muscles acting on that joint. The site of the abnormality may therefore be difficult to detect and the doctor should be aware of this. For example, a patient with arthritis in the knee may actually feel the pain in the thigh and attribute the problem to pathology in the hip. In addition to pain, the patient may also complain of stiffness. This may be painful but with a normal range of movement, or there may be a limitation of movement to below the usual range. The doctor should note any variation in the timing of joint stiffness. Pain from osteoarthritic joints is frequently worse in the morning and improves as the joints are used more throughout the day.

**Examination** The joints can only be inspected directly by the orthopaedic surgeon using an arthroscope, but in the GP surgery the doctor should palpate (feel) over an area where the patient complains of pain. This is to detect any abnormal swelling or tenderness of the bones, joints or muscles. An inflamed area may be warm to touch. The range of movement should be assessed, both with the patient relaxed and the examiner performing the movement (passive) and then by asking the patient to move the joint himself (active). The passive range of movement is often greater, particularly where there is reduced muscular activity.

**Investigations.** History and examination may provide only limited information for orthopaedic and rheumatological patients' problems and the clinician will often need to resort to imaging or biochemical tests.

Plain x-rays are the simplest form of imaging but ultrasound, CT and MRI may have a place once a patient has been referred to hospital. Ultrasound avoids high doses of radiation. CT and MRI usually provide detailed information, but these resources are limited. Injecting a short half-life radioactive isotope and

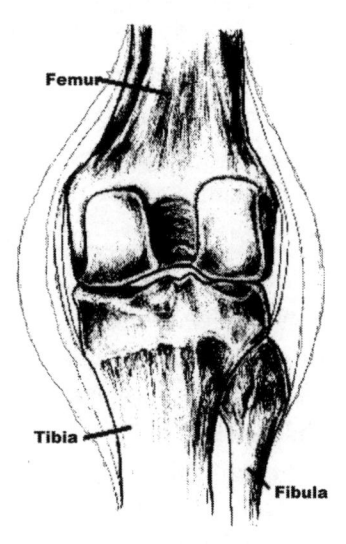

*Knee joint from behind*

scanning the patient for "hotspots" of increased skeletal activity gives even more sophisticated imaging.

Blood tests in the GP surgery are important for diagnosing rheumatological conditions. A high erythrocyte sedimentation rate (ESR) may point to a problem that is otherwise unsuspected. It is a non-specific test, and the ESR may be raised in a wide variety of conditions. A normal ESR is reassuring, while a high ESR justifies further investigation. Bone turnover is measured indirectly by the enzyme alkaline phosphatase, which is part of the routine battery of tests done when the liver function tests are requested (alkaline phosphatase is produced in the bones as well as the liver).

PATHOLOGY AFFECTING THE BONES AND JOINTS

When considering the problems that can occur in the skeleton it may be helpful to look through the chapter on pathology. This is because nearly any type of pathology can occur within the joints or bones. Indeed, applying the pathological sieve to the skeleton provides good examples of the "thousand shocks the flesh is heir to". Unfortunately, this wide variety of problems also provides an opportunity for Dr Botchup to jump to unjustified conclusions.

The chapter on pathology also defines inflammation, noting that when an area becomes inflamed it is usually described by a word ending in *–itis*. *Arthr*itis comes from the Greek for inflammation of the joint. The hot, red, swollen, painful and dysfunctional joint is a clear example of inflammation.

**Congenital** joint problems may cause a problem in diagnosis, particularly if there is no previous family history. Congenital hip disease (congenital dysplastic hip, CDH) occurs because prior to childbirth the baby is curled up in the uterus. The ball and socket hip joint is bent so tightly that it is dislocated. This is normal, but after birth the ball should slip back into the socket in the new-born infant. If this does not happen then the pelvis and the

## Skeletal Problems – Joint Pathology & Fractures

femur grow without proper establishment of the joint. If this is not picked up within the first few months of life the joint will never develop properly, giving rise to problems throughout adult life. Screening is done at birth, six weeks and three months but of course the infant is not walking at this stage and the clinical test is somewhat crude. Ortolani's manoeuvre consists of flexing (bending the hips forwards) and pushing down in an attempt to feel any instability, manifested as a "clunk". It is recognised that clinical examination alone may miss some cases of congenital hip dislocation. Once the child starts to walk any suggestion of limping should be viewed with suspicion. Examination may reveal some leg shortening, and an increased skin crease between the hip and the buttock when compared with the other side. If in doubt a referral should be made to a specialised orthopaedic surgeon. The orthopaedic surgeons recognise that there will be a significant percentage of so-called 'negative' referrals and accept this. Failure to make the referral, however, is negligent once suspicion has been aroused. If congenital hip dislocation is neglected the condition may not become apparent until the teens or even later. At this stage the joint may be severely deformed and hip replacement is usually necessary. If a negligence case is brought then damages may be substantial, but only if it is possible to find the doctor or doctors responsible who failed to make the referral – the screening examinations may have been done many years previously.

**Case report**
A new-born infant underwent a check by the health visitor, who found a clicking hip. The child was referred to the orthopaedic surgeon for further investigation. Before this consultation took place the general practitioner visited at home. The mother was a consultant on the staff of the local hospital. The GP re-examined the child and failed to detect any abnormality, overruled the health visitor and cancelled

the orthopaedic consultation. Seventeen years later the boy was noted to have a painful hip after a football game. This persisted, and an x-ray was taken. This showed that there had been a congenital dislocation of the hip, which was now significantly deformed, requiring extensive surgery. At trial the judge accepted my evidence to the effect that clinical assessment was prone to error and that *any* positive finding on screening, by *any* health professional, should be followed up by further investigations. The teenager was awarded a substantial sum.

*Comment*: In this case, although the GP had failed to find a clicking hip this had been detected by another competent professional. Since the test is variable and can have full false negatives the child should have been submitted to x-ray or ultrasound for definitive diagnosis. The judge accepted the principal that a positive clinical screening result by any healthcare professional should be followed up by definitive tests. The case has passed into English law.

**Cancer** in bone is unfortunately common but primary cancer is rare. Primary cancers (those arising from the bony tissues themselves) occur as osteosarcoma (bone) or chondrosarcoma (cartilage). *Secondary* cancer in bone occurs when cancers elsewhere have got to the point where they break off into the bloodstream and form metastases. A case of missed cancer is described in the section on back problems. These secondary bone cancers may be from breast, thyroid, prostate, lung or kidney. A patient who is known to have one of these types of cancer, even if it is apparently in remission, should be investigated or referred if there is any unexplained bone pain.

NICE provides guidance on *primary* bone cancer. For bone sarcoma in adults the advice is to consider a referral for an appointment within two weeks for adults if an X-ray suggests the possibility of bone sarcoma. In children and young people with unexplained bone swelling or pain the advice is to consider a very

## Skeletal Problems – Joint Pathology & Fractures

urgent direct access X-ray, to be performed within forty-eight hours. In the case of suspected bone sarcoma in children and young people the advice is to consider a very urgent referral for an appointment (within forty-eight hours) for specialist assessment if an X-ray suggests the possibility of bone sarcoma.

Cancer of the bone marrow is called myeloma. The bone marrow lies within the long bones but is functionally separate from the musculoskeletal system. Abnormalities within the bone marrow do not usually present as musculoskeletal pain. The bone marrow may be replaced by fibrous tissue and this can be a cause of anaemia. Diagnosis requires specialist referral to a haematologist and is made by marrow biopsy. (This is not as bad as it sounds – a small sample can easily be taken from the front of the pelvis just below the waist!)

**Case report**
A 62-year-old lady presented with severe headache. The general practitioners did routine blood tests, revealing a high ESR suggesting temporal arteritis. She was referred to the local hospital and successfully treated with steroids. A year later however, she re-attended with persistent general illness and feeling tired all the time. The GP undertook screening blood tests and once again found a high ESR. On this occasion there was also significantly raised protein on the liver function tests. She was referred to the local hospital and the on-take physician, who was a gastroenterologist, investigated her large bowel and then said that the blood tests were due to a self-limiting condition, with no treatment being required. The patient remained unwell. The ESR on subsequent testing remained high, as did the serum proteins. The GPs again made a referral to the hospital, but this time to a haematologist. It was found that the lady was suffering from myeloma, and further opinion suggested that this had been present for some time.

It was held that, while untreatable long term, substantial

remission could have been induced had an earlier diagnosis been made. Causation was limited to about one year's loss of amenity and notwithstanding the gravity of the patient's condition the case was settled by the hospital for a relatively modest sum.

*Comment*: This case illustrates the general principle that a patient may be suffering from more than one condition. The high ESR was mistakenly attributed only to the temporal arteritis, and although the GP made an appropriate referral the consultant physician missed the diagnosis.

**Degeneration** in the joints results in *osteoarthritis*. It is almost inevitable as old age progresses. Like all types of degenerative disease it is caused by the change in growth pattern, in this case the ability of the cartilage of the joint surfaces to repair itself adequately. Not surprisingly, the weight bearing surfaces of the large joints are particularly prone to osteoarthritis. The hip and knee are the commonest sites, followed by the shoulders and then the joints of the feet and hands. No joint is immune however, and the facet joints of the back, even though they have limited weight bearing and allow only a small range of movement, may also become involved with degenerative change. Osteoarthritis is an insidious process, increasingly common as the years go by. Diagnosis is mainly made on the history and examination. Investigation is rarely necessary unless surgery is being considered, although tests may be undertaken to exclude other types of arthritis. Once diagnosed, the condition is managed by general advice including weight loss and muscle strengthening exercise together with anti-inflammatory preparation and painkillers. With appropriate management it may be many years (if at all) before a patient requires surgery or becomes seriously disabled by the condition.

NICE Guidance for diagnosis of osteoarthritis: *"Diagnose osteoarthritis clinically without investigations if a person is 45 or over and* has activity-related joint pain and has either no morning joint-related stiffness or morning stiffness that lasts no longer than 30 minutes."

Particularly in the elderly patient, osteoarthritis is so common that the diagnosis is rarely missed but treatment may give rise to problems and significant medical errors. This is because the treatment requires medication that if not carefully supervised may cause the patient significant problems.

**Iatrogenic** disease can occur with anti-inflammatory drugs that are used for both osteoarthritis and rheumatoid arthritis. *Rheumatoid arthritis* (described below) is usually treated with steroids or disease modifying anti-rheumatic drugs. These are powerful drugs – many of them are also used as chemotherapy in cancer patients. They should be under specialist supervision. Osteoarthritis, however, is usually treated by the general practitioner using **n**on-steroidal **a**nti-**i**nflammatory **d**rugs (NSAIDs). Although these have fewer side effects than steroids they must still be taken with care. Elderly patients are vulnerable to gastric erosion causing significant bleeds, a recognised side effect of NSAIDs. They should not be prescribed to any patient with a history of active peptic ulceration. The NICE guidelines recommend that for prolonged administration the patient should be given protective treatment by a proton pump inhibitor, for example Losec, (omeprazole) to protect the gut.

### Case report
A 28-year-old man presented with joint pain. After treatment with simple analgesics, and then anti-inflammatory drugs, he was referred to a rheumatologist. The rheumatologist was unable to provide any further diagnosis or treatment and advised that the patient should be kept on the lowest effective dose of anti-inflammatory preparation. This was done as a repeat prescription from the GP. Over the course of two years, however, the patient repeatedly exceeded the recommended dose. The GP surgery subsequently acknowledged that prescriptions had been issued over and

above the recommended amount. The inevitable happened, and the patient developed a gastric ulcer. This required hospitalisation, and while undergoing bed rest the patient developed a deep vein thrombosis and pulmonary embolus. It was argued that these latter complications would not have occurred but for the requirement for hospitalisation and the patient was awarded substantial damages.

*Comment*: this case illustrates the risk of prolonged administration even of a drug that can be obtained over the counter at a pharmacy. Although the patient had knowingly exceeded the dose, it was considered that there was no case of contributory negligence because the drugs had been issued on prescription from the doctor.

**Rheumatoid arthritis** is an example of disease caused by an autoimmune process. It is also common, although not as common as the degenerative type of arthritis. This pathological process causes inflammation in the synovium (the lining of the joint spaces) and as with any other inflammation this produces pain, raised temperature, redness and swelling around the joint. Rheumatoid arthritis tends to affect the joints of the hands rather than the weight bearing surfaces, although any joint may become involved. It can be a crippling condition and is particularly severe when it affects the young. Patients with rheumatoid arthritis should be referred by the general practitioner to a consultant rheumatologist. Blood tests are used for the final diagnosis of rheumatoid arthritis and the ESR (erythrocyte sedimentation rate) is usually raised. This test should be done in every case where rheumatoid arthritis is suspected or even a possibility. A more specific investigation is the test for Rheumatoid Factor, an antigen involved in the immune process, which can be found in the blood. (It is usually abbreviated on the biochemistry form as RF or RA latex.) The rheumatoid factor is not invariably raised, however, and patients may still exhibit rheumatoid arthritis, even in the presence of a normal rheumatoid factor.

*NICE Guidance for suspected Rheumatoid Arthritis.* The doctor should offer to carry out a blood test for rheumatoid factor in people with suspected RA who are found to have synovitis (inflamed joints) on clinical examination. Refer for specialist opinion any person with suspected persistent synovitis of undetermined cause. Refer urgently if the hands or feet are affected, if more than one joint is affected or there has been a delay of three months or longer between onset of symptoms and seeking medical advice. Refer urgently any person with suspected persistent synovitis of undetermined cause, even if their blood tests show a normal acute-phase response or negative rheumatoid factor.

**Metabolic** disease may cause gout, an abnormality of the metabolism caused by uric acid. This is a breakdown product containing nitrogen and is normally present in the blood in small quantities. If the concentration rises the uric acid can precipitate out in the joints in the same way as a kettle furs up in hard water districts. Uric acid crystals within the joint cause excruciating pain that can come on within a matter of minutes and be extremely incapacitating. The diagnosis is easily made clinically and confirmed by assessing the urate level in the blood. Gout is usually so obvious that medical mistakes in respect of diagnosing the condition are unlikely, but as with osteoarthritis the prescription of powerful medicines may allow errors to arise. In particular, allopurinol (which is given as a preventative for gout) should not be given to patients in the acute phase of the condition as it may actually make things worse. This is specifically contraindicated by the manufacturers and a prescription in this situation would undoubtedly be considered negligent.

**Infection** in the joints is septic arthritis. It is fortunately rare, but the diagnosis should be considered in a patient with worsening joint pain who also develops signs of generalised illness. Carpenters and plumbers, who often kneel while working, are susceptible to penetrating injuries around the knee joint. Septic arthritis may however occur after any event that allows bacteria into the bloodstream, such as a complicated delivery.

**Case report**
A 30-year-old lady gave birth to her third child. During labour she had suffered a tear that needed repair. The day after the delivery she had pain in her hip joint. Her doctors at the hospital had initially said that this was due to the uncomfortable position she had to adopt while the repair was being undertaken. She was discharged from hospital even though feeling unwell. Over the succeeding days the pain in her hip got worse and she developed a temperature. She telephoned the GP practice ten days after the delivery and the receptionist recorded that the patient was getting worse and could not walk, noting that she was in tears over the telephone. She requested a home visit and the GP attended her at home and recorded: "Pains in left groin since giving birth. Radiates down left leg to knee. Worse on walking. On examination pain in groin on passive and active hip flexion and rotation. No neurovascular deficit. Epidural site normal. No leg swelling or tenderness. Tenderness in groin. No bruising. Prescribed Tramadol Diclofenac." The GP followed the previous advice of the hospital doctors in attributing the pain to an uncomfortable position. It was only after some further days had elapsed that the patient attended hospital and was found to have a septic arthritis – infected hip joint. The joint had been destroyed and at the early age of 30 she required a total hip replacement that will need revision in 10 or 15 years. The general practitioner was found to be negligent.

*Comment*: This case illustrates the danger faced by general practitioners of becoming over-reliant on a diagnosis made by hospital doctors, particularly when there has been a significant time lapse. In this case the GP failed to reconsider all the possible pathology and hence a differential diagnosis including septic arthritis. He had assumed that the pathology arose from trauma and relied on the "groin strain" as diagnosed by the hospital anaesthetist, even though common sense would indicate that groin strain would be highly unlikely ten days after the relatively minor discomfort of the lithotomy position during an episiotomy repair.

**Trauma** may cause fractures or dislocations. A *fracture* may be defined as a break in the continuity of a bone. This may seem obvious, but like a break in, say, a piece of furniture the extent may be very variable. Similarly, the effects on the patient may be of greater or lesser severity. The cause of a fracture is the application of force greater than that which the bone can bear. The force required to break a bone is however very variable and can be influenced by pre-existing osteoporosis or its less severe form, osteopenia. *Osteoporosis* is discussed in the section on spinal disease. It is defined as a reduction in the mineralised content of the bone. Effectively, this means that the hardness of the bone is reduced and it is, therefore, more liable to fracture. This may be seen either on x-rays or on the DEXA scan which is a type of simple radiography used for mass screening, particularly in middle aged women, to see if they are developing osteoporosis. Clinically, osteoporosis is demonstrable as an increased tendency of the bones to break. (Experienced pathologists performing post-mortem examination will assess the degree of osteoporosis by their ability to snap a rib between the thumb and fingers of one hand.) Osteoporosis therefore causes an increased susceptibility to fracture. It is, however, only a susceptibility, and may be considered a normal age change. The fracture of a bone in a patient with osteoporosis is nearly always precipitated by another event, usually a fall. In the elderly the Colles fracture of the wrist and the fractured neck of femur are familiar examples to casualty doctors and orthopaedic surgeons. Tens of thousands of elderly people, particularly women, are at risk of fractures. The drug companies are keen to promote medication to reduce osteoporosis. The government is keen to reduce the expense of such treatment. The balance lies somewhere in between, but at present it is unlikely that a doctor failing to provide such treatment would be found negligent, on the basis that not all doctors provide the treatment. This may change.

The natural process of healing of bone takes about six weeks. Repair starts with a blood clot round the ends of the bone. This then becomes organised to form a fibrous scar. This fibrous scar gradually becomes calcified, forming a callus. At the end of the six weeks the bone is usually up to adequate strength. A process of re-modelling then continues and after a period of some months (depending on the age of the patient) the bone may be indistinguishable on x-ray from the appearance of a bone that has never been fractured. This process applies where there is no significant displacement. The behaviour of a fracture, however, is often influenced by the site of the fracture and particularly by the degree of displacement of the bones in the original injury. Bones which are not readily displaced and are best left alone to heal themselves include the fingers, toes, ribs, pelvis and collar bone. In the latter case, there may be significant displacement, but the re-modelling process usually allows restoration of function. Other bones, and particularly those undergoing a range of movement, may require reduction (i.e. setting) and fixation to allow the fracture to heal with good positioning of the fractured bone ends. Reduction and plastering is common in the wrist and some bones of the foot. Other bones may require not only reduction but also operative fixation, either closed or open. Various techniques including wiring, plating and nailing are available to the orthopaedic surgeon for fixation.

Except in the case of missing a tumour that has caused a pathological fracture, doctors are not of course responsible for the fracture itself. They may however be found negligent if the fracture is missed. Even so, damages may be limited to relatively modest sums for pain, discomfort and loss of amenity, particularly in cases where the fracture heals without any intervention. In other cases, a delayed diagnosis may cause significant complications because there is a limited time available for fixation, after which the final result is likely to be less satisfactory. Should a clinical negligence case proceed this far, this issue is likely to give rise to considerable controversy between opposing expert orthopaedic surgeons.

**Case report**
A 52-year-old lady slipped on ice while running for a bus. Immediately after the accident she was able to weight bear but this was painful. She delayed seeing her general practitioner (who was on holiday) but then saw a locum who made a diagnosis of soft tissue injury and referred her to a physiotherapist. The physiotherapist suspected a fracture and referred her to an orthopaedic surgeon, for which the patient paid privately. The orthopaedic surgeon organised an MRI (more expense for the patient) that revealed no abnormality. Six weeks later she remained in pain and attended a casualty department where a plain x-ray revealed a fractured head of tibia. By this stage the fracture (which was undisplaced) had started to heal. The patient claimed for pain, discomfort and loss of amenity, not only due to the fracture but also due to back pain, which, she claimed, had arisen because of her difficulty in walking. She was awarded damages based on the unnecessary professional fees she had incurred and for additional pain.

*Comment*: This case illustrates that in some cases, the more sophisticated imaging technique of MRI will fail to detect what, a few weeks later, was detected on a plain x-ray film. This case is also salutary in that the "victim" was awarded damages of £8,000. Each side had incurred costs estimated in excess of £25,000; the claimant's solicitor has since retired.

**Pathological fractures.** Literally, of course, all fractures are pathological and mainly due to trauma. The term pathological fracture is rather confusing, referring to a fracture that is *not* due to trauma. This type of fracture may occur when the continuity of a bone is eroded, usually by cancer. In the case of unsuspected primary cancer elsewhere a pathological fracture due to a secondary tumour in the bone may be the first indication of the primary tumour. In other cases the cancer may have arisen as a primary tumour of the bone itself.

**Case report**
A man in his mid-30s, occupied in heavy manual work, attended his GP with pain in the upper part of the thigh. He was referred for physiotherapy, but this had little effect. He attended again about two years later. Examination revealed no abnormality but the patient continued to complain of pain. He was once again referred for physiotherapy but defaulted after two sessions, saying the physiotherapy actually made his pain worse. On a third occasion, nearly 5 years after the initial presentation, he was again referred for physiotherapy. The physiotherapist recognised the previous history of unsuccessful treatment and arranged an x-ray. Before this could be undertaken, however, the patient went on holiday. While he was away he slid down a water chute into a swimming pool. This was hardly a traumatic event but nonetheless resulted in a fracture of his femur. An x-ray revealed an osteosarcoma in the upper part of the femur. Because the pathological fracture had allowed dissemination of the tumour cells an extensive amputation was necessary, involving the entire hindquarter.

The patient sued the general practitioner on the basis that, after the first physiotherapy had been unsuccessful, he should have been referred for x-ray on the basis of undiagnosed bone pain. It was agreed that had this been done the surgery (while still necessary) would have been less extensive and the patient would have been fitted with an artificial limb and still able to continue with some type of work. The case was settled for a substantial sum.

# Skeletal Problems – Joint Pathology & Fractures

**Dislocations** do not involve loss of continuity of an individual bone. They are considered together with fractures because they nearly always result from trauma although they are really problems within the joints. A dislocation is defined as a disruption of a joint and means that the normal surfaces of the two bones of a joint are no longer in their correct relative positions. The ease with which a joint may dislocate often depends on range of movement normally present at the joints. In other words, joints with the greatest range of movement have the greatest potential for dislocation because of the requirement to have a lax capsule. The shoulder joint is particularly vulnerable to dislocation, particularly as the capsule may be torn after the first traumatic incident and fail to heal properly. Although it is possible for 'heroic' treatment on the touchline to treat a dislocated shoulder, this is a risky procedure because unless the reduction is performed under proper conditions it is possible to cause nerve damage, resulting in muscle wasting – raising the question of who exactly is the hero! Should this occur the enthusiastic Good Samaritan doctor might well find himself on the wrong end of a negligence claim.

In addition to congenital dislocations of the hip, as described above, juveniles are also susceptible to a particular type of

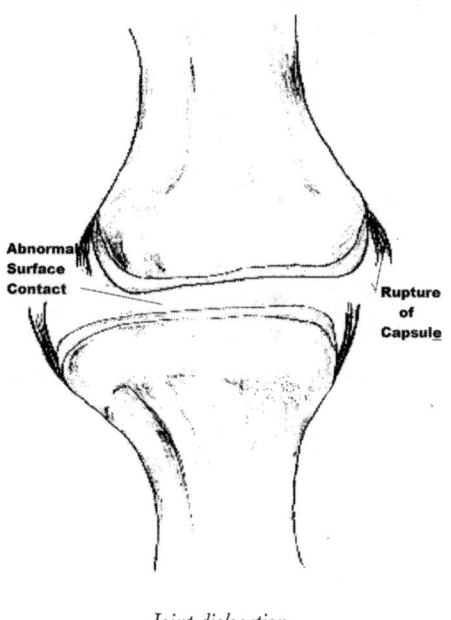

*Joint dislocation*

dislocation. A *slipped epiphysis* may be considered as a type of dislocation occurring within a joint. The head of the femur stays in contact with the acetabulum (socket) all the time, but during periods of active growth there is a vulnerable part, the epiphysis, between the head of the femur and the rest of the bone. Because this is an area of softened tissue it is vulnerable to trauma and displacement can occur. This requires operative treatment. Another area of vulnerability in growing adolescents is the point at which the patellar tendon attaches to the tibia. It may cause a condition known as Osgood-Schlatter's disease, where the point of attachment, a lump, just below the knee, is exquisitely tender. The treatment is rest.

**Case report**

A 14-year-old boy attended the general practitioner because of pain in his right leg. He was actively engaged in sport, having been encouraged to do this because he was overweight. The general practitioner recorded "Pain right leg. Osgood-Schlatter's." There was no record of the findings on examination, and no record of the history of onset of the pain. The patient (and his parents) accepted the diagnosis and he ceased any sporting activity. The pain remained. After six months the parents requested a consultant opinion, and (reluctantly) the GP made a referral. Two months later the child was seen by an orthopaedic surgeon who arranged an x-ray. A slipped femoral epiphysis was diagnosed. This required surgical intervention and it was considered that the outcome was significantly less favourable than would have been the case had the operation been performed earlier. Expert evidence suggested that he would need a hip replacement in early middle age. The child was awarded significant damages.

*Comment*: This case illustrates failure to consider a sufficiently wide differential diagnosis. The GP was correct in thinking that Osgood-Schlatter's disease can cause lower limb pain in adolescents, but he failed to consider slipped femoral epiphysis. In addition, an adequate clinical examination would have shown that Osgood-Schlatter's (typified by tenderness over the knee) was unlikely to have been the diagnosis here.

Other soft tissue injuries may occur to the *tendons*. These are vulnerable structures where muscles form attachments into the bone. Rupture can occur in the upper limb, where the biceps tendon may snap, but an area of particular concern is the Achilles tendon, which not only operates at a significant mechanical disadvantage, but also has a poor blood supply. This can allow the normal resilient elastic tissue to be replaced with fibrous tissue, particularly in the older patient. Rupture can occur without warning, often in association with sudden plantar flexion in springing upwards on the ankle. Typical events are stumbling from a curb or attempting a jump during a game of tennis.

**Case report**
A 24-year-old man serving a prison sentence was playing football when he felt a sudden pain at the back of his left foot. He was unable fully to weight bear. As is usual in HM prisons, he was unable to see a doctor directly but allowed only to go via a nurse, who recorded: "came to HCC after sustaining injury to right ankle/Achilles area whilst playing football today. On examination no apparent swelling as yet but complains of not able to fully weight bare (sic). Diagnosis: probable soft tissue injury." The patient was given advice and told to go back to his cell and rest, and avoid any further strenuous activity for six weeks. Six weeks later he duly returned, this time seeing a nurse and then a doctor who noted that he was still unable to weight bear. The doctor undertook a proper examination, detecting a deficit in the Achilles tendon. He was referred to an orthopaedic surgeon, but by this stage the tendon had shortened and repair was

unsatisfactory. He was eventually successful in bringing a claim against the Home Office.

*Comment*: In addition to the clinical aspects of the case, this history illustrates the difficulties faced by prisoners who, while theoretically entitled to the same health care as if they were at liberty, are in fact significantly constrained and have access only to such facilities as the prison governor thinks fit. In this case the nurse had failed to consider (or was unaware of) the possibility of Achilles tendon rupture.

The effects of fractures and dislocations are not limited solely to the immediately local disruption. *Complications* will depend on the surrounding damage. A bone end may damage an artery and a relatively straightforward fracture can, as a complication, sometimes require the amputation of a limb for this reason. Fractures involving the nervous system are particularly prone to complication. Fractures of the spine are discussed in the section on spinal injuries. Skull fractures, if depressed inwards, are an obvious threat to the integrity of the brain. This may be either because of direct trauma caused by the depressed bony fragments of the skull or because of the bleeding associated with the fracture. Occurring as it does within the confined space of the skull such a bleed (haematoma) may compress the brain and cause extensive damage. The consequences of complicated fractures and of head injuries have considerable legal significance, but fortunately these are rarely a source of error on the part of the treating doctors – the effects are all too obvious. Unfortunately, other errors in managing problems with the musculo-skeletal system may still occur, as the above examples show. The injuries which may result from these errors may be significant.

Chapter 5

# BACK CONDITIONS

There are few people who have not had a 'bad back' at some stage in their lives. The average GP may expect to see at least one new case a week, and will probably be issuing prescriptions or certificates for many more patients with a long-term problem. Health and Safety Executive figures for the UK in 2018 indicate that 2.2 million workdays were lost due to back pain.[1]

The treatment of patients with a painful back is usually straightforward, but there are some conditions which may be missed. If this occurs the effects may be devastating. Over the time under consideration there were nineteen cases of claims or potential claims associated with back problems. Of these, two thirds consisted of a single condition – compression of the cauda equina nerves causing incontinence and loss of sexual function.

To look at these cases in detail we need to consider the back from a scientific point of view by study of anatomy, physiology and pathology. We can then look at the medical management (history, examination and investigations) and any guidance on treatment.

BASIC MEDICAL SCIENCE

**Anatomy.** It is worthwhile reminding ourselves what we actually mean by 'the back'. In a sense it is the biological equivalent of the chassis on a lorry. Just as the chassis will hold together the front and back wheels, the engine, driving mechanism and cab, so the spine connects the front and back limbs which provide movement. These connect to the control mechanisms – represented by the head.

When we refer to the front and back limbs we are, of course, referring to the original plan in four-footed animals. In humans these are the arms and (only two!) legs.

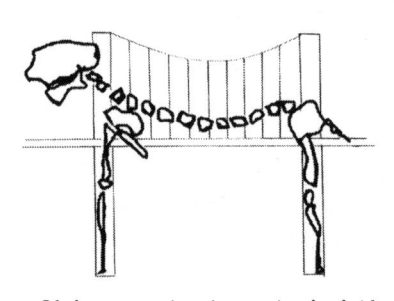

To the left is a simplified, and somewhat fanciful, diagram of a four-footed animal showing the spine connecting the front and back limbs and the head and acting as a bridge. The individual bones of the spine (vertebrae) are found in a series of segments. These segments are characteristic of nearly all animals except the most primitive and the spine provides a good example of these, consisting of a repeating pattern of bone, nerves and muscles.

*Skeleton as engineering – animal v. bridge*

A *vertebra* consists of the main *body* with bony projections. At the rear the *laminae* form a channel protecting the bundle of nerves (spinal cord) which passes along the length of the spine. At each level, nerves pass out through gaps between the bones to supply the parts of the body associated with that particular level. In the lumbar area (low back) the nerves run together to form the sciatic nerve to the legs. Bony projections provide attachments for the soft tissues (muscles, ligaments and tendons) which hold the whole structure together and provide movement.

The nerves do not line up exactly with the bones at each level because the spinal cord of nerves is shorter than the column of bones. This means that the nerves corresponding to the lower few vertebrae are bunched together and pass downwards before they exit from the bony canal. This bundle of nerves resembles a horse's tail and is described by the Latin, *cauda equina*. Among their other functions, the nerves in the cauda equina supply the sphincters (valves) to the bowel and bladder. They also supply sensory function to the so-called saddle area, and the external genitalia – penis or vulva.

A typical vertebra is represented in the diagram below as a cross section (that is, as if cut through horizontally). The bone is seen in isolation only when studying the remnants of the skeleton. In life the bony vertebra is surrounded by soft tissue – mainly a large amount muscle. In more familiar terms, the vertebra is the piece of bone to be found in the middle of a chop in the butcher's – we would soon complain if this consisted only of bone! The bony projections at the side provide attachments for the muscles around the bones, and so the functioning back consists of a column of bone and muscle. It is this muscle which allows the spine to work properly as a unit (and also cause a lot of its problems).

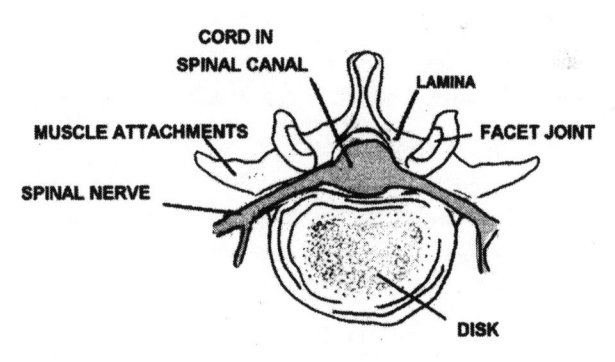

*Vertebra in cross-section*

**Physiology.** How does it all work? The first diagram above shows the back as a bridge-like structure between the two sets of limbs on a four-legged animal. Seen as a piece of civil engineering, this works well. The problem with humans is that after a few months of age we no longer move on four limbs. This erect posture causes all sorts of problems and we need to recognise that the spine is not fully adapted to this situation, which is comparatively recent in evolutionary terms. This is why back problems are so common. Consider first the vertebral bodies. If we try to make a stack of small bricks, like those that young children play with, we can probably

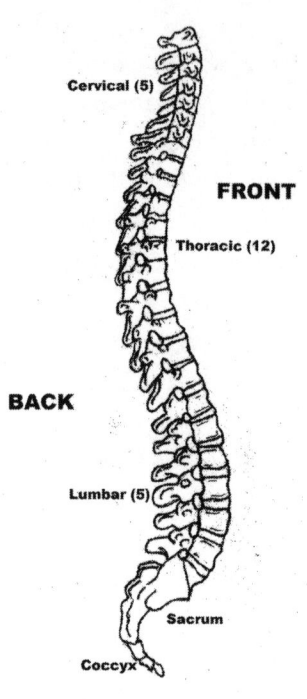

*The spine from the side*

make a stack of twenty or so if we are careful. In the case of the human back, however, note that there are significant curves. The diagram above right shows the stack of building blocks – the vertebral bodies – from the side as if the body is facing the right hand side of the page. We can see that there is a forward curve in the neck, a backward curve in the thorax (chest) and another forward curve in the abdomen before we get down to the curl represented by the tail – in humans called the coccyx. Even if we remained completely still such a stack would be unstable. Add to this the fact that we are required to move, bend, lift and do all the functions required of this flexible 'chassis', then it becomes clear that a pretty clever control mechanism is required.

Each spinal segment contains a nerve arising from the central

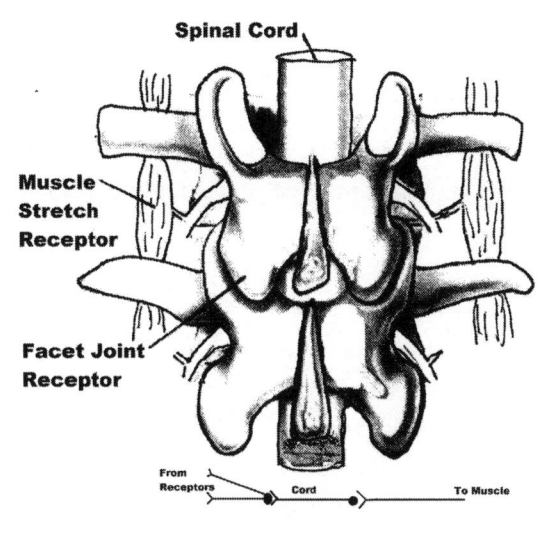

*Spinal reflex arc*

bundle of the spinal cord. This nerve contains input and output fibres to and from the muscles. The nerve output *to* a muscle is easy to understand – it makes it contract. The input *from* the muscle is more complex, but is really a sensing mechanism to see how far the muscle is being stretched. More information is provided from sensory fibres in the facet joints, so this bunch of muscle surrounding the backbone has the capacity both to measure position and to provide movement. This gives us the potential to control the stability of the spine at each individual muscle layer between the vertebrae. Again resorting to our engineering analogy, this is a servo system.

The muscles and joints at each level of the back are constantly providing information to the spinal column which in turn gives output to the muscles, enabling the whole structure to stay stable and functioning. All this happens without any conscious effort.

Given this ever-present muscle tension, how are the forces transmitted? Between each vertebral body and its neighbour there is a disc. The disc is rather like a cushion, with a squashy middle and a firm elastic outer rim which is a bit like a tyre. This arrangement means that the disc provides a shock absorber for forces between two vertebral bodies. The other point where movement can occur is between the facet joints which, as shown in the diagram of the cross-section, lie away at the side of the vertebral body, close to where the spinal nerve emerges.

In summary then, the human spine is a complex structure connecting the head with the upper and lower limbs. It is a stack of bones held together by muscles. These are controlled by a complex reflex nerve mechanism. There is a nerve at each level which exits between the vertebral bodies. The nerves supply the muscles between the vertebrae and are also formed into longer projections to supply the trunk, upper and lower limbs. Movement between the individual vertebrae is at the discs and facet joints.

PATHOLOGY

Considering how complex the spine is, it is hardly surprising that things may go wrong. This can happen in different ways in the different tissues. Trauma or degeneration can cause sprains to the muscles, damage to the nerves, bones and joints, and ruptures of the disc. Add to this the possibility of tumours and infections which can occur in the spine as in any part of the body. In short, the spine is a vulnerable structure.

**Herniated discs** due to degeneration or trauma cause problems when the outer part of the disc (the fibrous ring) gives way and allows the jelly-like substance of the nucleus to force its way through. Damaged discs are certainly a cause of low back pain but it has to be said that the pathology is not always clear because the same sort of pain may be due to a muscle sprain or to inflammation in the facet joint. When a disk does herniate it is, not surprisingly, painful. Just as importantly, if the bulge occurs in a position where it can start pushing on the nerves then there will be loss of nerve function. If the bulge is at the side of the disc, pushing onto the nerve as it exits between the vertebrae, this may cause sciatica. A central disc prolapse may push onto the more vulnerable nerves in the lower back causing compression of the cauda equina.

**Sprains** are caused by relatively minor trauma to a muscle, usually when it is overstretched. This tends to produce tearing of a few fibres within the muscle. There is nothing to see on the outside, but the muscle will no longer work properly. As a protective reflex the adjoining muscles go into spasm, providing 'nature's splint' to allow for repair of the damaged tissue. When there is a sprain the patient complains of pain and stiffness and on examination the immediate area becomes hard and tender.

**Fractures.** Like any other bones, the bones of the spine can fracture. The human spine is generally resistant to trauma because of the strength provided by the supporting soft tissues. Fractures of the pedicles of the cervical (neck) vertebrae can occur in high velocity whiplash injuries, but these are rare compared with the more usual whiplash injury which is due to muscle sprain. The most common fractures in the spine are crush fractures of the vertebral body due to osteoporosis. They may occur with very little trauma and are much more common in the elderly. The road sign indicating elderly people (as seen for example outside a nursing home) typically shows a bent figure, the common view of elderly people having rather bent spines. The underlying pathology is degeneration, although lack of exercise and excess alcohol are other important factors.

**Nerve compression** can be caused by a ruptured disc – often called a slipped disc although it does not really 'slip' anywhere. Pressure on the nerves will also happen if there is arthritis in the facet joint. Arthritis in any joint causes pain and swelling, and in the spine the swelling can push on the nerves. A compressed nerve will cause pain, and if bad enough will start to cause loss of function. This can start as numbness which may be noticed by the patient who complains of loss of sensation or paraesthesia (tingling). If the motor nerves become involved then foot drop will occur, with the patient's gait affected by a dragging foot. A person can live with these effects of sciatica, but if a large rupture of a disc cuts into the cauda equina then the nerves to the lower part of the pelvis are damaged. This has catastrophic consequences with incontinence and loss of sexual function

CLINICAL ASSESSMENT – THE DOCTOR'S JOB

**History.** When assessing a patient with new back pain the doctor should first enquire as to whether it started gradually or suddenly, how long the pain has been there and whether there is a history of injury. The severity of the pain, and whether it is associated with stiffness or relieved by movement should be clarified. Importantly, questions should be asked as to any associated symptoms such as numbness and weakness or problems with the bowel and bladder. (Equally importantly, the doctor should refer the patient for immediate specialist help should these symptoms occur.) He should enquire as to past medical history, particularly if there has been a previous back pain, and check for any past cancer, even if this may have been some years ago.

**Examination.** The doctor should check for any abnormality in shape, particularly loss of lumbar lordosis (the inward curve) which may occur with the muscle spasm of mechanical back pain. Tenderness should be checked, by (gently!) thumping down the back with the end of the closed first. The patient should be asked to get up onto the couch, and the ease or difficulty with which this is done should be noted. The doctor should then check for muscle wasting, reduced power or loss of sensation in the legs and test the reflexes at the knees and ankles. Scratching the sole of the foot checks the plantar response – whether the toes go up, or down as normal. (Traditional doctors' folklore states that plantar responses are checked with the sharp end of a tendon hammer by the GP, or the key of a Bentley by the private orthopaedic surgeon!). Finally but importantly, straight leg raising – abbreviated to 'SLR' in the notes – may cause muscle pain on the affected side.

If patients (or their solicitor) are concerned that things have gone wrong then the first step will usually be to get medical records. The record of the history and examination may not show all the details mentioned above, but any positive findings should have been noted together with negative findings with respect to normal bowel and bladder function, straight leg raising and reflexes. Clinical features of particular concern – sometimes known as 'red flags' – include widespread neurology, the patient being generally unwell, and non-mechanical pain. (This is a constant pain which is present irrespective of movement). Other red flags include night time pain, chest pain and pain that worsens when the patient is lying flat. Pain occurring in a patient under 20 or over 55 years is also of concern – there could be a malignancy somewhere.

**Investigations.** By this stage, the doctor should have an idea of the severity of the pain and any associated features, together with the duration of the symptoms. He should have formulated (if only in his mind) a list of the possible diagnoses – the differential diagnosis. Depending on these conclusions it may be necessary to order investigations. Many patients think they need an x-ray if they have been suffering from back pain; it is even a condition of some insurance policies that claims for back pain will only be paid if an x-ray has been taken. In fact, a plain film taken of a patient with backache does not usually help the doctor to reach a diagnosis –

the Royal College of Radiologists actually advises against plain films as a first investigation because the investigation involves a high radiation dose and is only useful in suspected fractures. From the point of view of a general practitioner consulted by a patient for the first time, the most useful investigation is actually a blood test – the erythrocyte sedimentation rate (ESR). This provides a useful screening tool and also has the important feature of being cheap and quick and easy to perform. The reason for doing this test first is that a patient with an abscess, other infection, or primary or secondary cancer is likely to have a raised ESR. In practice the vast majority will have a normal ESR, but it is important to eliminate these rare but dangerous items from the differential diagnosis. In cases of persistent back pain, where the diagnosis cannot be elaborated except by imaging, it is then usually necessary to proceed to more sophisticated imaging techniques either by computerised tomography (CT) or magnetic resonance imaging (MRI). Depending on local protocols, in the UK these investigations are often available only after specialist referral.

**Management.** As in any other branch of medicine, the first step in management is to try and establish a diagnosis. The next step is treatment. In the case of common back pain, it has to be said that the description of the commonest recognised 'diagnosis' is particularly imprecise. If an examination candidate were asked to make a diagnosis in the case of a patient with, say, abdominal pain and said: "The diagnosis is abdominal pain." he would fail his examination. In the case of the back, however, it is accepted that "*Low back pain with or without sciatica*" may be regarded as a working diagnosis – this is the description given in the NICE Guidance![2]. The condition is sufficiently common to be almost invariably abbreviated in the records to "LBP". At first sight this may seem a remarkable example of unscientific thinking – Dr Botchup at his worst – but in reality it is a pragmatic way of dealing with a common problem. The human back is not well adapted for the erect posture and is therefore mechanically inefficient. This in turn allows minor trauma and degenerative change to occur in the joints, discs and muscles, although it is often the case that the exact trigger for the pain, in terms of strict pathology, cannot be identified. This mechanical back pain is the most common complaint of "bad back", even though the patients may say they are suffering from a slipped disc. Examination usually reveals spasm of the muscles over the lower back. This causes the typical pain and stiffness of the bad back which most people have experienced, for example after unaccustomed gardening or physical exertion. The condition is not usually accompanied by any signs or symptoms of nerve entrapment and the patient may be otherwise fit. There is often a history of trauma although this may be limited to unaccustomed exercise. The condition may be treated with anti-inflammatory preparations, muscle relaxants and rest and should subside within a few days.

**Case report**
This case arose from a complaint made to the General Medical Council, GMC. A middle-aged man consulted his general practitioner. The (entire!) note of the first consultation read: "LBP. Brufen". A month later, when the prescription was finished, the next consultation read: "ISQ. Add paracetamol." This pattern continued for nearly a year, the general practitioner providing increasing doses of more powerful anti-inflammatory preparations and additional analgesics. After this time the patient, who was suffering from increasing pain, consulted another general practitioner while he was on holiday. This practitioner took a proper history and conducted an examination. This revealed that the patient was a heavy smoker. On direct questioning he admitted to occasional episodes of coughing flecks of blood. He was tender on firm palpation of the thoracic vertebrae. The initial blood test revealed an elevated ESR. The practitioner immediately ordered a chest

x-ray. Within days it was confirmed that the patient was suffering from lung cancer with a secondary cancer deposit in a vertebra.

When questioned by the GMC Fitness to Practice Panel the respondent general practitioner had, with some apparent indignation, provided the defence that the patient had not complained of cancer. He had complained of backache. The doctor is no longer practising.

*Comment*: Although the commonest cause of backache is simple mechanical low back pain this can never be assumed. It is for this reason that proper history taking and examination should be done for every patient presenting with a new backache. Had this been done in this case, the history of smoking and coughing blood would (or should) have been elicited. It is likely that even in the early stages there would have been some tenderness on palpation over the vertebrae. A blood test would have shown an elevated ESR. While it may not have been possible to treat the lung cancer (a civil claim may have been unrealistic) the case demonstrated an appalling level of ignorance on the part of the treating doctor.

Because low back pain is so common, and also because 'low back pain' may actually be regarded as a working diagnosis, it is unfortunately all too easy for the doctor to fail to consider a proper differential diagnosis. While other possibilities are usually much less likely, the history and examination should always be undertaken with other possibilities in mind. Even if the clinical assessment shows nothing untoward, many doctors consider that a simple blood test will help eliminate any serious diagnoses. It is important to consider a full differential diagnosis on first presentation. There are some conditions which cannot wait.

**Tumours** within the bone are fortunately uncommon in comparison with simple back pain. The history may reveal non-

## Back Conditions

mechanical pain, night time pain, or pain away from the lower back – the thoracic spine in particular. These 'red flags' should be investigated, and as indicated above a blood count may confirm (or hopefully eliminate) other suspected diagnoses. Secondary cancer, in the bone but starting in the thyroid, lung, kidney, breast or prostate must be considered and properly investigated – imaging may help here. Paget's disease (an abnormality of bone growth although not strictly a tumour) is usually associated with chemical abnormalities. Raised calcium and abnormal enzymes can easily be assessed by a blood test done at the same time as the ESR. If any of these conditions look possible an immediate referral should be made – failure to do so would be negligent.

**Fractures** may be an obvious consideration if there is a history of severe trauma but even minor trauma may cause compression fractures in the elderly, and particularly postmenopausal women who may have osteoporosis. If the patient with back pain says she has lost height this would justify a plain x-ray. Osteoporosis may be diagnosed by a Dexa scan, which measures the bone density of the os calcis (heel bone). It is important to make this diagnosis because medical treatment is available to improve bone density.

**Cauda equina** syndrome is caused by a central disc prolapse pushing on the nerves in the spinal canal before they exit from the channel between the vertebrae. These are the lower lumbar and sacral nerves, particularly important because they supply the sphincters to bowel and bladder and the sensory supply to the genitalia. Permanent damage to these nerves can cause double incontinence and loss of sexual function – a devastating incapacity. Although the syndrome is rare it must always be borne in mind, which is why the history should include brief questions as to bowel and bladder function. Even if these are normal, a history of bilateral sciatica may indicate that there is a central disc prolapse and would justify an emergency MRI examination or as a minimum an immediate referral for specialist opinion.

**Case report**

A 27-year-old supermarket assistant attended her general practitioner with a complaint of low back pain radiating down her left leg. The GP noted that there had been a previous episode of sciatica two years previously. He recorded "LBP and sciatica again. BMI++. (a cryptic record that the patient was overweight) Advice." In a subsequent statement he said that he had asked the patient about bowel and bladder symptoms and been told that there were none. The next day the patient returned. The GP recorded that the pain was the same but that the sciatica now also had pain in her right leg. No further advice was given and analgesics were prescribed. The patient took the next day off work, but that evening she found that she had been incontinent of urine and noted that she was numb over the saddle area. Because it was the weekend she waited until the Monday. She then telephoned the general practitioner but could not get an appointment. She attended the local casualty department where it was recorded that she had a three-day history of bilateral sciatica, incontinence of urine, numbness over the saddle area, and laxity of the anal sphincter. An MRI scan showed a central disc prolapse L5/S1. She was admitted for emergency surgery. This was partially successful in that the sciatica was relieved and she regained control over her bladder. She remains with partial numbness over the saddle area and diminished sexual function.

*Comment*: This case illustrates the gradual progression of a central disc prolapse causing a cauda equina syndrome, which eventually proceeded to being nearly complete and to some extent irreversible. The GP had mistakenly assumed that this was a further episode of sciatica since she had suffered from a similar condition which had resolved on a previous occasion. It was alleged that the progression to bilateral sciatica should have been seen as a significant warning sign of a progressive lesion. Even though there were no complaints of bowel and bladder disturbance on the initial consultation she should have been warned to be aware of these and to seek immediate medical advice should these symptoms develop. She was awarded more than a quarter of a million pounds in damages.

**Nerve entrapment** problems affecting the nerve roots (rather than the cauda equina) may cause sciatic pain in one leg. This may be caused by a disc prolapse towards the side of the vertebrae, rather than centrally as in the cauda equina. Other causes of entrapment may be an arthritic facet joint causing swelling to narrow the channel as the nerve exits the bony spinal canal. Clinically, nerve entrapment is associated with back pain, although the pain in the leg is often worse than the back pain itself. As well as pain there may be numbness or paraesthesia (tingling). Straight leg raising will stretch the nerve root, and may cause an increase in, or reproduce, the pain. The ankle reflex may be absent on the affected side. In contrast to cauda equina syndrome, where nerve damage may be permanent within a very few days, sciatic nerve root compression may resolve if the source of the pressure is relieved. This may happen spontaneously, either because the degree of herniation of a disc may reduce with rest or because treatment may resolve muscle spasm. For this reason, if the symptoms are resolving on review, no referral is needed for some weeks. After this, however, specialist assessment should be undertaken for detailed imaging and consideration of surgery.

If surgery is considered appropriate this is done to relieve the pressure on the nerves due to a prolapsed disc. In a *laminectomy* procedure the surgeon removes part of the bone of the vertebra which forms the protective arch. This allows the spinal cord to move back slightly, relieving the compression from the disc. It is also possible to remove the disc itself (discectomy) and fill the gap with chips of bone, effectively fusing two vertebrae together. Before considering surgery it is worth remembering that the spine is already a finely balanced mechanism, vulnerable to change, and any surgery is likely to alter the anatomy. This may, in turn, produce further degenerative change and muscle spasm. While many patients are delighted with the results of their spinal operation it has to be said that a number wish they had never gone near a surgeon. Unfortunately, the results of the operation cannot be guaranteed. From a medico-legal point of view, provided the risks have properly been explained, a 'failed' back operation does not automatically represent negligence.

**Infection**. Although not common, infections in and around the spine cause increasingly severe problems, or even death, if they remain undiagnosed and untreated. Infections may occur outside the lining of the spinal cord (epidural abscess) within the cord (very rarely) or within the bone. The large bulk of bone which constitutes the spinal column increases the opportunity for circulating bacteria to lodge and cause an infection. This is more likely to happen in patients who are immune-compromised or who abuse intravenous drugs. Tuberculosis is uncommon but is on the increase particularly in some ethnic groups. Infections may be suspected by the presence of 'red flags' in much the same way as spinal tumours. The ESR is likely to be raised. The pain may be in the thorax. It may be constant rather than related to movement. Diagnosis is confirmed by imaging. Depending on the nature of the infection treatment may be with antibiotics, or a combination of antibiotics and surgery.

> **Case report**
> A 45-year-old Indian businessman attended his general practitioner with back pain. There was no history of trauma and the patient was otherwise healthy. He was advised to take over-the-counter analgesics. He attended again one month later and the general practitioner requested a plain

x-ray. This was reported as normal. Three months after the initial presentation the patient started to feel generally ill and to lose weight. The GP diagnosed a "flulike illness" and recommended the patient to take more paracetamol, which he was already taking because of the pain in his spine. As this GP had provided little by way of assistance the patient did not attend again. Six months after the initial presentation, while still feeling generally ill and in pain from his back, the patient went to visit his family in India. While there he consulted another doctor who immediately requested an MRI. This demonstrated significant erosion of one of the lower thoracic vertebrae by tuberculosis. The patient was admitted to hospital in Mumbai and the orthopaedic surgeons fitted a metal frame and support between the thoracic and lumbar vertebrae to prevent an imminent collapse of the spine. The patient was started on antituberculous treatment. He was subsequently operated on again, this time to fuse the damaged vertebrae with a bone graft. Happily, in spite of the 'near miss' which could have led to his being permanently wheelchair-bound, he made a full recovery.

*Comment*: This case shows the importance of being on the alert for developing signs. It also demonstrates that plain x-ray films, particularly early in the condition, are not always helpful. This is because standard radiography will not demonstrate any alteration in the bone until about fifty percent of the calcified material has been lost. It is likely that an ESR, had this been done in the early stages, would have been more helpful. Although the first GP in the case had mismanaged the patient, his fortunate recovery meant that causation of injury was limited. The difficulty of obtaining evidence from the Indian hospital compounded the litigation difficulties and the case was abandoned.

The NICE Guidance[2] on back pain was published in November 2016. Entitled *"Low Back Pain and Sciatica in over 16s: Assessment and Management"*, it reflects predictable Government policy over a condition which causes the loss of tens of millions of work days every year. As discussed above, the working assumption is that low back pain is mechanical but the Guidance starts in the very first paragraph with a firm warning: *"Think about alternative diagnoses when examining or reviewing people with low back pain, particularly if they develop new or changed symptoms. Exclude specific causes of low back pain, for example, cancer, infection, trauma or inflammatory disease such as spondyloarthritis. If serious underlying pathology is suspected, refer to relevant NICE Guidance on: Metastatic spinal cord compression in adults, Spinal injury, Spondyloarthritis, Suspected cancer."*

The remainder of the Guidance addresses the presumptive diagnosis of a non-specific back pain, with the implication (albeit unstated) that this is due to a variety of minor degenerative changes, in turn due to the unfortunate fact that the human spine is something of a failure in terms of evolutionary advance. The Guidance provides for strong psychological support – always important where chronic pain is concerned – and actively dissuades practitioners from a variety of treatments such as acupuncture, homoeopathy and similar remedies.

From the point of view of the aggrieved patient who has been suffering from back pain for months or even years, the question to be asked is "Could my doctor have done more?" With the important exceptions of the more severe conditions discussed above, the answer is, unfortunately, probably not.

REFERENCES

1. http://www.hse.gov.uk/statistics/causdis/msd.pdf
2. https://www.nice.org.uk/guidance/ng59

Chapter 6

# THE BREAST

Diseases of the breasts cause significant problems, and problems lead to medical errors. Over the time under consideration there were sixteen cases concerning the breast. Of these, fifteen were mis-diagnosis of cancer. The general practitioners were liable in all but three of these missed breast cancer cases.

BASIC MEDICAL SCIENCE
**Anatomy.** It almost goes without saying that the breasts are glandular structures on the anterior female chest. Interestingly, the size of the breasts depends largely on the fat content rather than the glandular tissue – big breasts do not always mean a well-fed baby! The glandular tissue itself consists of lobules – clusters of milk producing cells – linked by branching connecting ducts. As discussed in the section on pathology, glands have a high growth rate and cell turnover. As a result, the growth process can go wrong, allowing tumours to develop. Breasts are apparently represented in the male only by the nipple, but men also have vestiges of glandular tissue that may develop under the influence

of hormones. If this happens, there is a relatively high risk of tumour development.

**Physiology.** The function of the breast is, of course, to produce milk for the infant. Lactation (milk production) occurs with the change in hormone levels at the time of birth. Lactation may also (rarely) be induced by physical stimulation of the nipple. Human milk has evolved to the point where it is the ideal food for growth, and infant feeding may continue for many months. A type of malnutrition called kwashiorkor occurs in underdeveloped countries. It affects young children at the time of birth of the next child in the family because they are suddenly weaned from breast milk and switched to a diet too low in protein. The threat of kwashiorkor means that in some countries women may be breastfeeding for a substantial part of their reproductive years.

**Pathology.** The main areas of concern for pathology affecting the breast are tumours and, to a lesser extent, infection. As in most tissues, tumours that occur in the breast may be either benign or malignant. (Remember that 'tumour' simply means lump – by no means all tumours are cancers.)

The commonest benign tumour is fibroadenoma – a mixture of glandular tissue and fibre. Fibroadenomas are the most frequent breast tumours in adolescents, with the incidence decreasing with age. Generally, they appear before the age of 30 years. Over the course of their lives, 10% of women will have a fibroadenoma. Fibroadenomas are usually hormone-dependent, and so change according to the stage of the menstrual cycle.

Malignant breast tumours are the commonest type of cancer for women in England and Wales. There are about forty thousand new cases diagnosed each year and eleven thousand deaths. Breast cancers start as clusters of uncontrolled growth in the cells lining either the tubes (ductal carcinoma) or the milk-producing lobules (lobular carcinoma). Like all malignant tumours, the cells have the capacity to grow uncontrollably, first invading locally and then spreading to other parts of the body. Ductal carcinoma represents 80% of cases and may at first be limited to the duct, so-called carcinoma in situ. If not picked up early it will spread. Invasive ductal carcinoma (IDC) is the most common form of invasive breast cancer.

Breast cancer develops insidiously, and if untreated progresses through what are known as 'stages', all of which have a different prognosis. If we examine the notes of a cancer patient there will usually be correspondence from an oncologist (cancer specialist) describing this staging of the disease. Cancers are staged using the TNM system (**t**umour, **n**odes, **m**etastases), based on the size of the tumour, whether or not the tumour has spread to the lymph nodes in the armpits, and whether the tumour has metastasised. Large size, spread to nodes, and metastasis have higher staging numbers and a worse prognosis.

Prolonged breastfeeding makes a difference to the chance of acquiring breast cancer because breastfeeding is to some extent a protective factor against cancer development. It is thought that the modern trend for formula feeding in the so-called developed countries is likely to produce an increased incidence of cancer. Other associated risk factors include obesity, smoking, and (controversially) the use of the contraceptive pill and hormone replacement.

**Epidemiology.** Family history is a highly significant factor in the risk of breast cancer. At the time of writing at least three specific genes have been identified, giving an increased risk of the development of the disease. Inheritance of these genes provides such a strong likelihood of the development of cancer that some vulnerable women elect to have bilateral mastectomy purely because of this risk.

CLINICAL ASSESSMENT OF BREAST LUMPS –
THE DOCTOR'S JOB

**Signs and symptoms.** In the case of breasts, the woman herself should share the doctor's job. Women are strongly encouraged to check their own breasts regularly, and many breast cancers are first detected by the patient feeling a lump. Others are detected on routine examination by a doctor or nurse. Some early cancers may be detected by mammogram (x-ray) before a lump is detectable.

**History** taking should include questions about previous lumps, both in the patient and in her immediate family. A woman presenting with a lump should be questioned as to its duration, and whether it has persisted throughout the menstrual cycles. Many breast lumps are benign fibroadenomas or cysts, but a lump that is present throughout the menstrual cycle and continues unchanged into the next cycle must be regarded as cancer until proved otherwise.

**Examination** of the breasts should be performed systematically in six movements, using the side of the hand and rolling the breast tissue between the examining hand and the chest wall so as to detect any lumps. The examination should assess the breast as four separate quadrants, with additional palpation (feeling) of the 'tail' of the breast up into the armpit and the palpation of the sixth area using two hands to feel behind the nipple. When a clinician detects a lump it should be assessed for size, density and mobility. A cancerous lump is usually harder and firmer than benign breast lesions such as fibroadenoma, although the 'feel' of a lump can never be relied on to reach a diagnosis. Lumps may be immobile and tethered either to surrounding breast tissue or to the chest wall. They may cause nipple retraction. Both these signs are ominous. Pain usually only develops in the later stages of the disease.

**Case history**
A 49-year-old woman presented to her general practitioner. She had previously had a breast lump investigated at the local clinic and this had been found to be a benign fibroadenoma. She was aware of breast problems and regularly examined herself. She had found a small lump in the lower part of the left breast. The GP notes read: "L I B. Previously seen in clinic. Benign lump. OE fibroadenoma. Reassured."

Not surprisingly, the lady accepted her GPs reassurance, notwithstanding the continuing presence of the lump. Some 10 months later however, after discussing the problem with a friend who was a nurse, she re-attended the practice and saw a different practitioner. She was immediately referred to the breast clinic and it was found that the lump was malignant. Happily, she underwent successful surgery but required radiotherapy and chemotherapy. The prognosis is now good.

*Comment*: The GP notes did not indicate that a proper systemic examination had been performed, because the site of the lump was not recorded. The findings were not described, the clinical record being limited to a diagnosis – which in any event turned out to be wrong. This lump remained "unexplained" and the fact that the woman had previously been diagnosed with a fibroadenoma was irrelevant. She should have been referred under the two-week rule. The woman brought a claim against the first general practitioner. This was clearly indefensible. Damages were relatively limited given that it was accepted that surgery would have been necessary in any event, but the award covered the additional pain and discomfort and loss of amenity necessitated by the more extensive surgery and the additional chemotherapy and radiotherapy, together with the anxiety caused by the poorer prognosis.

**Investigation.** On a mammogram, breast cancer usually shows as a lighter shadow with fine spikes radiating from the edges. Mammography is carried out as a mass-screening program for otherwise asymptomatic women. It may also help in staging where a lump has been identified. In nearly all cases a fine needle aspiration biopsy must be performed to indicate the histology of the lesion.

**Management.** It is axiomatic, and taught to first year clinical medical students, that no woman should have an undiagnosed lump in the breast. It follows from this that any doctor consulted by a woman with a lump in the breast must search for an explanation. Provided clinical examination does not indicate a hard tethered lump, skin changes or one-sided discharge or nipple retraction, referral may be delayed until after the next menstrual period. In this situation the woman must be made to understand that further examination is essential. If (and only if) at a second examination a few weeks later the lump is definitely absent or significantly smaller then the woman may be reassured. In all other situations an urgent referral to a specialist breast clinic must be made. Almost invariably, a biopsy will be required. This can be done by fine needle aspiration biopsy or more definitively by excision biopsy. The doctor must not, at the first consultation, provide reassurance which may prevent the woman from returning. If the lump persists the referral should be done with sympathy and qualified reassurance (because many breast lumps still turn out to be benign) but the woman should be left in no doubt that specialist assessment is essential. All district hospitals have a dedicated breast lump clinic and it is expected that a significant proportion of women referred to these clinics will have benign breast disease. This does not however permit a general practitioner simply to reassure the woman unless there are definite clinical grounds to indicate that a lump is benign – usually because the lump is absent or smaller after the next period. It should also be made clear that a history of benign breast disease in the past does not indicate that a new lump may be regarded as benign. A new presentation must be treated as such and if in any doubt a referral must be made.

*NICE Guidance.* The suggestions for management of breast cancer as proposed by NICE are mainly those described above. The guidelines provide for a 'referral pathway' to a specialist unit for an appointment within two weeks. A woman aged 30 or over with an *unexplained* breast lump should be referred. "Unexplained" for the purposes of the guidelines refers to symptoms or signs that have not led to a diagnosis being made by the healthcare professional in primary care after initial assessment including history, examination and any primary care investigations. In women aged over 50 discharges or nipple retraction should prompt a two-week referral. Skin changes at any age that are suggestive of cancer should similarly prompt referral. The first Guidance for suspected cancers was published in 2005 but was updated in 2015 to include new recommendations; these are essentially "catch all" alternatives for situations not previously covered. These include two-week referral for "other changes of concern" in patients over 50, and an unexplained lump in the axilla for patients over 30. In addition, a *routine* referral should be considered for patients under 30 with an unexplained breast lump.

It has to be said that these guidelines are by no means foolproof, providing as they do a considerable degree of latitude for the general practitioner. Breast cancer under the age of 30 is uncommon but not unheard of. Nevertheless, according to the Guidelines a woman under 30 will not get a two week referral unless she has skin changes – by which stage any cancer is likely to be quite advanced. The difficulty here is that the NICE guidelines are based not only on what is good for the patient but also what is good for the country. NHS resources simply will not allow enough clinics to be staffed to see any patient with a lump within two weeks. The Guidelines provide that *unexplained* lumps need referral, but the extent to which a lump may remain unexplained will depend on the doctor's assessment. This, in turn, will depend on precise history taking regarding any change with the cycle, and careful examination. The reality is that a combination of a tired or overworked doctor together with the inevitable risk of human error means that some patients with cancer may still be missed. Worse still is the lazy doctor who simply opts for the most likely possibility – Dr Botchup again. If this happens a woman with a potentially curable condition may face an early and unnecessary death.

**Treatment.** Ideally, if a breast cancer occurs it will be detected in its early stages. These cancers are often found by routine mammography or because the woman is self-examining; she has then attended the general practitioner promptly and a referral has been made. In these cases it is usually possible to preserve the breast, and a 'lumpectomy' may be performed. If the tissue around the lump is clear on microscopic examination, and there are no lymph nodes involved, this may be all that is required. Some centres will advise additional treatment in the form of radiotherapy or chemotherapy. More advanced cancer will require removal of all the breast tissue – mastectomy. If there is any doubt, most women (and surgeons) will prefer a mastectomy to the risk of terminal cancer. Breast cancer is unfortunately so common that a large number of operations are performed. There is however at least some benefit from this – research has allowed evidence-based protocols to be developed for working out the best treatment for each patient. Very rarely, as in the case of Mr Ian Paterson, a surgeon will take it upon himself to depart from these protocols. Working at a hospital in the Midlands, Mr Paterson regularly undertook operations which were later shown to be unnecessary. Some of the operations he did undertake, including the so-called 'cleavage-sparing mastectomy' were inadequate. Women who had been subjected to this surgery later died, probably unnecessarily, of their cancer. While this had nothing to do with the referring general practitioners, this sad story does indicate that a combination of arrogance and incompetence can occur even at the level of senior surgeons. Mr Paterson was sentenced to 20 years in prison.

If detected early breast cancer carries a reasonably good prognosis. If detected late, it can metastasize, commonly spreading to bone. This carries a poor prognosis and breast cancer is unfortunately still a common cause of mortality in women in the developed world.

**Case history**
A 45-year-old lady presented to her general practitioner. She was on regular breast screening, because her mother and an aunt had both developed breast cancer at a relatively early age. She had been seen in a breast clinic one year previously and after mammography had been told that there was no problem. The GP notes read: "patient reviewed. Lump at lower left quadrant right breast. Due for annual review mammogram. Seen last year in breast clinic. On examination? fatty tissue or ? lumpiness very periphery of right breast. Review the first week after bleeding. Patient thinks changed and smaller" The patient denied having been told to return. She moved from the area and thought no more of the matter until she developed bone pain. Sadly, this was due to multiple metastases. Despite surgery, chemotherapy and local radiotherapy to bony deposits she remained significantly ill and was within a few months of death. Although the general practitioner stated in defence that he had requested the patient to return, it was considered that as the patient had a high degree of awareness of breast cancer this information was not imparted properly. Given the circumstances of the claimant and her relatively young age, the general practitioner's defence organisation made an admission and the case was settled for a substantial sum.

*Comment*: This case illustrates the problem of relying on screening. Screening should be seen as a first stage in a process designed to produce early diagnosis. By definition screening is intended to apply only to people who are asymptomatic. If the patient presents with clinical signs or symptoms then any screening conclusion is irrelevant and in this case the lady should have been immediately referred to a breast clinic because of the presence of an undiagnosed lump, irrespective of any previous negative findings on mammography screening.

**Case history**
A 32-year-old lady consulted her general practitioner. He recorded: "CO: Lump in breast. Hx: one month history, two small lumps in right breast. No change with cycle. No previous breast problems or family history breast cancer. Examination right breast 1x1cm right upper quadrant and 0.5 x 0.5cm above right nipple. Discrete. Mobile. Fluctuant. Comment: happy to observe breast lump". In her statement, the patient said that the practitioner had told her that the fact that the lumps were easily felt and mobile indicated that they could not be malignant. She felt reassured and although the lumps persisted she did nothing further for more than a year. She finally became concerned because of the persistence of the lumps and consulted the practitioner again. This time she was referred. She had mammography and fine needle biopsy, and it was found that one of the lumps was cancerous. Because of the history, and the possibility of spread, she required mastectomy and radiotherapy followed by chemotherapy. Happily, she was pronounced free of cancer, but had undergone considerably more radical treatment than would otherwise have been necessary had she been referred when the lumps were first detected. The case was settled for a significant sum to compensate for the surgery which would otherwise have been unnecessary and the anxiety arising from the finding that the cancer had advanced to a further stage.

*Comment*: The Doctor in this case had taken (and recorded) a reasonably good history and examination. On the basis of these clinical findings he had formed the opinion that the lumps were benign. Unfortunately, reliance on the clinical characteristics of the lump (discrete and mobile) did not mean that they could be deemed to be fibroadenomas. He had recorded that there was no change with the cycle, indicating that the lumps could not be written off as benign. This was another case where the NICE guidelines relied on clinical opinion, and the clinical opinion was in error.

OTHER PATHOLOGY

**Infections.** Like nearly all tissues the breasts are susceptible to infection. This is more likely during breastfeeding when mastitis can occur. This starts as a tender, hot, reddened area of the breast, and the infection may be sufficiently severe to cause a fever. The underlying problem is cracked skin, allowing the entry of skin bacteria, commonly staphylococci. The treatment advised is the antibiotic flucloxacillin and adequate painkillers. The woman should be advised to continue breast-feeding or to express the milk if breast-feeding is too painful. Mastitis does not normally require hospitalisation and is treated with oral antibiotics in primary care. If the condition progresses then the infection will go beyond inflammatory change and produce an accumulation of dead bacteria and white cells – pus. This is an abscess. If there is uncertainty as to the possibility of abscess formation it is possible to attempt treatment with high-dose antibiotics if these are given intravenously. This may allow a sufficiently high dose to penetrate the infected tissue and reach a concentration sufficient to overcome the infection. If pus has formed, however, then the damage is done and surgery will be required. The adage: *"never let the sun go down on undrained pus"* still applies, and the patient needs to be admitted to hospital for incision and drainage of the abscess.

**Case history**
A 32-year-old woman gave birth to her second child and decided to breast-feed. This was successful, but within five

days she developed significant tenderness over the left breast, together with a fever. She consulted her general practitioner who made a diagnosis of mastitis and prescribed oral flucloxacillin. She was able to express milk (as recommended) and within five days the condition had resolved. She then recommenced breastfeeding, again successfully. One week later she developed a second episode of mastitis in the same breast. The doctor again recommended expressing the milk and prescribed antibiotics. On this occasion the treatment was unsuccessful. She remained unwell with a low-grade fever and the condition of the breast deteriorated, eventually forming an abscess. The doctor's note at the time read, "Indurated area of breast now pointing. Abscess. Admit." The lady was admitted to hospital as an emergency. An attempt was made to treat the condition with intravenous antibiotics but ultimately she required incision and drainage, with a resulting scar and misshapen breast. The lady brought an action against the GP on the grounds that she should have been admitted to hospital on the first episode of mastitis, and that intravenous antibiotics would have treated the initial infection more effectively and prevented a recurrence.

It was argued on behalf of the general practitioners that the treatment plan, which she claimed should have been followed, was made very much with the benefit of hindsight, and that oral antibiotics would have been the treatment of choice by a responsible body of opinion. The development of the abscess (which is different from mastitis) could not be predicted. The case against the general practitioner was discontinued.

*Comment*: This case illustrates the application of the Bolam principle. (See the later chapter: Putting Things Right). While some doctors may have arranged admission on the first infection it was appropriate and rational (and is standard treatment to be found in textbooks) to treat the original episode of mastitis with oral antibiotics. The development of a breast abscess could not be foreseen, and the scarring which resulted from the operation would have occurred in any case since once the condition had progressed to abscess formation surgery became inevitable.

In summary, diseases of the breast are relatively common and cause significant problems, not only in terms of the direct pathology but also because of the psychosexual and social implications. Unfortunately, these diseases may still be a source of medical errors.

## Chapter 7

# GASTROINTESTINAL PROBLEMS

The gastrointestinal tract – usually called bowels or simply gut – is a tube up to thirty feet long starting at the mouth and ending at the anus. It has nine different sections, fulfils multiple functions, and has lots that can go wrong. Over the ten years under consideration there were more than twenty cases involving complaints and claims against general practitioners. As may be expected in such a complex system, the conditions giving rise to complaints varied widely, ranging from toothache to terminal cancer. In particular, cancers of the lower bowel were still regularly missed by general practitioners, often in the face of glaringly obvious signs and symptoms.

BASIC MEDICAL SCIENCE

The anatomy, physiology and pathology of different parts of the gastrointestinal tract will be described in more detail according to its different organs. Here is the overall picture:

**Anatomy.** From above downwards these different organs

comprising the gut consist of the mouth, oesophagus (gullet), stomach, small bowel (consisting of duodenum jejunum and ileum), large bowel (consisting of colon and rectum) and finally the anus.

**Physiology.** The function of the gut is to take in the food and drink which the body can then use for energy and repair. The food is broken down in a series of digestive processes and then passes across the gut wall into the blood vessels. From here it is processed in the liver. This is a process of absorption (extraction). What remains within the gut is passed out as faeces after a transit time varying between several hours or more than a day. The action of the bowel proceeds without conscious effort apart from swallowing and defaecation but may vary, particularly under psychological influences. The gut has no *direct* connection with the bloodstream. Although materials pass both into and out of the gut into the blood this is either across the wall of the organ concerned or through a duct. There is always a separation between the blood, which should be sterile, and the contents of the gut that contain bacteria over most of its length.

**Pathology.** As with any complex tissue, the different organs of the gastrointestinal tract are susceptible to many forms of pathology. The areas where problems occur in terms of doctors' errors and medico-legal issues are mostly confined to tumours and infection, although immune reactions may be responsible in some cases. Alterations of the spontaneous action of the bowel may occur under psychological influences, producing diarrhoea or constipation – so called irritable bowel. A particular problem with the gut is that if it becomes inflamed, producing pain, that pain is not necessarily localised to any specific part of the gut, or even to an individual organ. If the source of inflammation is confined to the bowel itself, the pain is usually referred to the midline. The pathology underlying this clinical presentation can make diagnosis difficult.

MANAGEMENT AND DIAGNOSIS – THE DOCTOR'S JOB
When considering problems from the gastrointestinal tract, it is important for the doctor to remember that these organs share the same body cavity with a number of different systems. (See the diagram on page 117). This means that pain felt from the oesophagus is often indistinguishable from pain from the heart. Similarly, pain from what is apparently a stomach problem could be due to an aortic aneurysm. (The aorta is the large blood vessel passing from the heart down through the chest and abdomen. See the chapter on circulation for further discussion.) For this reason patients with complaints which they think comes from the gut must be assessed carefully, and a broad differential diagnosis borne in mind. Cancers are not necessarily evident in the early stage and must always be borne in mind. Bowel cancer is sufficiently common to justify screening, and in the UK patients over 60 are offered routine tests for faecal occult (hidden) blood. A positive result should lead to colonoscopy with, hopefully, early detection of any cancer.

**History.** The doctor should enquire as to any precipitating or relieving factors. He should ask about the site of the pain, but for the reasons explained above this is not always reliable. The history should include questions on any medications taken, particularly anti-inflammatory preparations such as ibuprofen or even aspirin. These can cause gastric erosion. Alcohol consumption should (tactfully) be assessed. If the patient complains of difficulty in swallowing the doctor for should ask whether this applies to solids or liquids. Questions should be asked as to any change in bowel habit (constipation or diarrhoea) and any sign of bleeding. Blood from the lower bowel shows up as red in the stool. Bleeding from higher, from the stomach or duodenum, appears as changed blood which is black. Any relevant family history should be obtained because there is a genetic predisposition to some types of bowel cancer.

**Examination** will as usual be influenced by the history. As a minimum, where abdominal problems are suspected, the patient should be asked to lie on the couch in as relaxed a way as possible. Using the flat of the hand the abdomen is felt in all four quadrants. The liver may be palpable on the upper right. The kidneys may (just) be palpable in the loins. Masses may be felt in the lower part of the abdomen, although these need to be quite big before they can be felt. Although potentially unpleasant for the doctor and embarrassing for the patient, rectal examination should normally be carried out if abnormalities of the gut are suspected. Genital examination is not always undertaken, but if there is any doubt as to the origin of symptoms then palpation of the testes and inspection of the penis in the male, and vaginal examination in the female, are necessary. For these intimate examinations, the presence of a chaperone is highly recommended.

**Investigations** into gastrointestinal problems that can be done by the GP will usually include routine blood tests. A *full blood count* will detect anaemia if there is a chronic gastrointestinal bleed. It will also show a raised white count if there is any infection. Abnormalities of the kidneys may present as abdominal pain and may be assessed by *urea and electrolytes*. *Liver function tests* look at the liver enzymes. If there is any abnormality of the liver there is a tendency for enzyme levels to be raised and for these to spill out from the liver and into the bloodstream where they are detectable on a venous blood sample. Blood tests may be taken in the doctor's surgery and should be processed the same day at the local hospital. These blood tests are usually all done together and may appear in the GP notes abbreviated as "FBC, U&E and LFTs". In the case of suspected infection the doctor may request the patient to provide a stool sample. Only a small smear is required. It is sent to the laboratory for examination under the microscope and for bacteriology. The stool may also be examined for occult blood.

Other investigations of the gut are usually hospital-based. Endoscopy using a fibre-optic instrument will allow direct visualisation of the upper part of the gut (gastroscopy) and the lower part of the gut (colonoscopy). Only the middle part, the small bowel, is inaccessible for direct inspection. Happily this is the area which causes the least problems, and tumours of the small bowel are almost unknown. Because of the development of endoscopes imaging by barium x-ray is now carried out less frequently. Imaging from outside the body is also effective as magnetic resonance imaging, although this is not routinely available in all cases.

The diagram below shows the various parts of the gut. Because they are all different, both in terms of anatomy and in function they have different pathologies and cause different problems for the patient when things go wrong. It is useful to consider each part of the gastrointestinal tract separately, although in the living person digestion is of course a continuous process.

**The mouth** is the first part of the gastrointestinal tract. It contains the tongue which is supplied with special senses (taste buds) which help to discriminate nice from nasty food. This is not just of interest to "foodies" – the capacity to distinguish between different foods has evolved as a survival mechanism. Another powerful discriminator of taste is in the nose – the sense of smell is as important as the sense of taste. Once food or drink is in the mouth any liquid is swallowed straight away. Anything more solid needs to be broken down before it can be swallowed. This is of course done by the teeth. While it is perfectly possible to survive with dentures (or even no teeth at all) these impose restrictions on

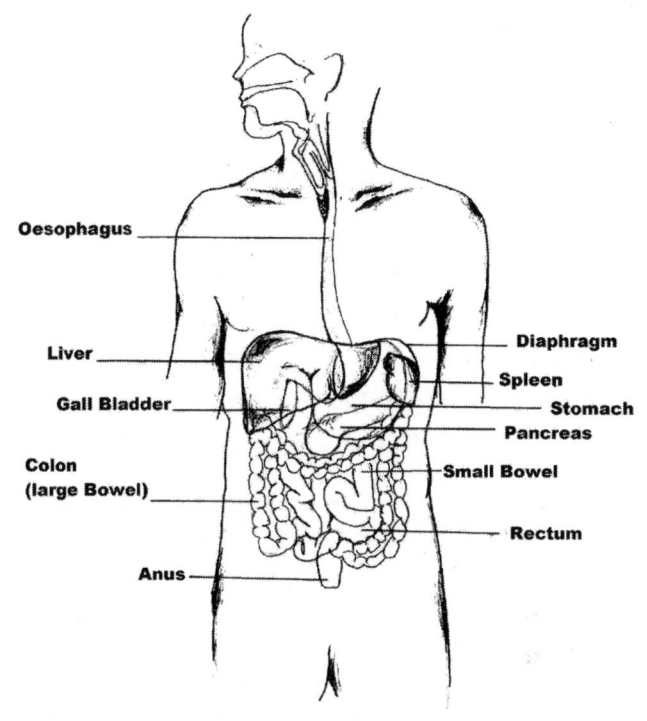

*The gastro-intestinal tract (gut)*

the type of food which can be tasted and enjoyed, or even eaten. It is far preferable to keep one's own teeth for as long as possible. Problems occurring with the teeth tend to fall into two groups depending on the age of the patient.

**Dental caries** (decay) is caused by acid formation due to the action of bacteria on dietary sugar. The acid dissolves away the hard tissue of the teeth and the bacteria then attack the soft tissue. This softening process eventually allows bacteria to get to the centre of the tooth, the pulp, which can then get infected and cause an abscess within the jaw. This is the commonest cause of tooth loss in the younger patient, leading to the requirement for complex (and expensive) restorative dentistry. While in theory crowns and bridges are available on the National Health Service, the time involved and the laboratory costs effectively preclude this type of treatment except as an act of charity on the part of the dentist – a relatively rare occurrence. This means that the patient is obliged to pay a significant amount to have his or her appearance restored. In turn this places a significant burden on the dentist who is likely to be treating a critical patient with high expectations.

**Case history**
A 27-year-old girl had an unfortunate childhood from a dental point of view. She had been brought up in an area where there was no natural fluoride in the water and her parents had not only failed to provide her with fluoride supplements, but allowed her a plentiful supply of sweets. As a consequence she had multiple unsightly restorations in her front teeth. She attended her dentist, who said that he would provide six crowns for upper front teeth, and furthermore that he would do it on the Health Service. The procedure was carried out in two relatively brief sessions, the first being to prepare the teeth and take an impression, the second being to fit the crowns. Although the patient was initially satisfied because of her improved appearance, she found it difficult to clean the crowns and after a few weeks one of them became dislodged. She went back to the dentist who re-cemented the crown and "patched up" a defect in the remaining tooth. A few weeks later the same thing happened to another crown. She made a complaint, via the Dental Practice Board, and after an examination by another dental surgeon appointed by the regional dental service it was determined that all six crowns were deficient. The dentist was ordered to repay her fees, and a substantial withholding was made against him. Because the teeth had already been prepared, she required completely new crowns and attended a (private) dental surgeon for these to be completed. She subsequently claimed the cost from the first dental surgeon, and after some negotiation with his insurers this was paid.

*Comment:* This case illustrates the diversity of remedies which an aggrieved patient has available. The patient had initially expressed dissatisfaction through NHS procedure and obtained an independent assessment as to the dentist's failings. This did not produce any direct satisfaction, but armed with this information she was able to bring a successful case for compensation to the extent of being awarded special damages to pay for treatment to remedy the position.

**Periodontal disease** tends to affect the older patient. This is another chronic infective process. It damages the supporting tissues of the teeth, where the hard tissue of the tooth is attached to the bone as a fibrous joint. The condition occurs through poor oral hygiene although individual susceptibility plays an important part. If the condition is allowed to progress the teeth will become so loose that they get painful and have to be extracted, or even fall out by themselves.

**Impacted wisdom teeth** present a problem in the late teens and early twenties. The wisdom teeth – which are the last teeth to erupt (i.e. come through) – are something of an evolutionary throwback. The jaws have become smaller over the generations but the size of the teeth has not changed, so the wisdom teeth do not have room to grow properly into the mouth and come up at an angle. This itself does not matter, but when food starts to impact and the gums around the incompletely erupted teeth get inflamed, then the patient experiences pain. Surgical removal of impacted wisdom teeth is among the commonest operations in the western world. When removal of wisdom teeth is necessary this can be a relatively simple matter in the dental chair, or may require complex surgery in theatre under general anaesthetic. Deciding on the exact treatment plan may sometimes present difficulties when wisdom teeth removal becomes necessary:

**Case history**
A 26-year-old lady, a nurse in a hospital outpatient clinic, had recurrent problems with a wisdom tooth. As was customary at the time she made an informal approach to a consultant oral surgeon who offered to remove the tooth, saying that this could easily be done under local anaesthetic in the dental chair. In the event, this extraction proved to be more complex than had originally been thought and it was necessary to drill part of the jawbone away to allow removal. Although the precise details of the accident were never determined, it is thought possible that the drill had slipped and damaged the lingual nerve. This is a large nerve supplying sensation to the tongue, and lies just on the inside of the jaw immediately to the side of the wisdom tooth. The tooth was removed, apparently satisfactorily, but when the local anaesthetic wore off the patient's tongue remained numb, and has been numb ever since. From a medico-legal point of view, the patient had clear grounds for a claim, because it is recognised surgical technique that the lingual nerve should be identified and protected prior to any instrumentation likely to cause damage. In this case, however, the nurse was employed in the clinic of the doctor concerned. Perhaps wisely, she let the matter rest!

*Comment*: This case provides an example of a practitioner who was too ready to undertake a procedure for a nursing colleague, probably as something of a "favour". It turned out to be nothing of the sort, and illustrates the danger of undertaking a surgical procedure without full and proper prior assessment.

**The oesophagus** is the tube between the mouth and the stomach. It is supplied with sensory nerves in its upper third. Beyond this there is no sensation of having swallowed the meal and the onward passage of the food is automatic. The oesophagus has to run down through the chest and pierce the diaphragm before it enters the stomach. If this hole in the diaphragm gets stretched the stomach can protrude and slip up into the chest – a condition described as hiatus hernia. This in turn allows the valve between the lower end of the oesophagus and the stomach to leak. The acid contents of the stomach go up into the oesophagus (**gastro-oesophageal reflux disease** – GORD) and cause pain because the oesophagus has not got the protective lining to cope with the acid. The lower end of the oesophagus has a generous blood supply. The veins around the lower part of the oesophagus can become subject to back pressure in the presence of liver disease. They form so-called oesophageal varices which can be a source of a catastrophic bleed if they rupture. If the patient complains of difficulty in swallowing the doctor should always consider oesophageal cancer.

*NICE Guideline.* Oesophageal cancer is relatively unusual but very difficult to treat if diagnosis is delayed. The recommendation is to offer urgent direct access for upper gastrointestinal endoscopy (to be performed within 2 weeks) to assess for oesophageal cancer in people: with dysphagia (i.e., difficulty swallowing) or aged 55 and over with weight loss and with either upper abdominal pain, reflux or dyspepsia (indigestion).

**The stomach** is, strictly, an expansion of the gastrointestinal tract between the lower part of the oesophagus and the beginning of the small bowel. (The term 'stomach' is often loosely and incorrectly applied to the abdomen as a whole, but the stomach is really only part of the gastrointestinal tract – though a very important part.) It acts as a reservoir allowing food to be held in a part-digested state and released slowly into the small intestine where the absorption occurs. This allows us to eat only a few meals a day, rather than engage in constant grazing. The food has already been broken down by the teeth and within the stomach it is exposed to strong acid which is secreted by the glands lining the stomach. It is this acid which can cause oesophagitis and is also responsible for both gastric ulcers and duodenal ulcers if things go wrong. The tendency for ulcers to develop is increased by a bacterium called Helicobacter Pylori which can live in the upper part of the digestive tract. This can be tested for in cases of suspected duodenal ulceration. The stomach may also develop cancer, which must be borne in mind when abdominal pain is being considered, particularly when weight loss or bleeding is also present.

**Case history**
A 55-year-old man developed gradual central abdominal pain. Initially he ascribed this to 'indigestion' because it improved when he took over-the-counter antacids. As these became less effective he consulted his general practitioner who prescribed more antacid medication. Again, this gave some relief, but only for a matter of months. Eventually the general practitioner referred him to a local hospital where he underwent gastroscopy. This was reported as normal, and the source of the pain remained undiscovered. Stronger antacid medication was by this time being taken regularly. It was not until the patient started to feel generally ill and to lose weight that further investigations were undertaken. Abdominal MRI revealed the presence of a gastric cancer which had, unfortunately by this time, spread widely within the abdomen. Within weeks of diagnosis the patient was terminally ill and died in the local hospice.

*Comment*: This case illustrates the difficulty of diagnosis of some gastrointestinal conditions. Although the working diagnosis clearly pointed to an upper gastrointestinal problem the first investigation (gastroscopy), was negative. Unfortunately, the fact remains that gastroscopy is not perfect and some false negatives are inevitable. Assessment of the operative notes indicated that there had been no demonstrable fault in technique. The fact that the cancer had been missed did not constitute a breach of duty.

# Gastrointestinal Problems

**The small bowel** is the part of the gut where the breakdown process of the food is completed and absorption occurs. The mixture of broken-down food and acid passes into the first part of the small bowel, the duodenum, and then to the jejunum and ileum. In the duodenum it receives an injection of juices from the pancreas. The pancreas is a large gland lying on the left side of the abdomen. The juices which it secretes contain enzymes. These are specialised chemicals, like catalysts, which allow the food to be broken down into its constituent molecules or particles. Very simply, the protein which we eat (meat, fish, eggs etc.) is broken down into amino acids. The carbohydrate which we eat (bread, rice, potatoes etc.) is broken down into sugars. Once the food constituents have been broken down to these small molecules they are able to pass out through the gut wall into a specialised part of the circulation, the hepatic portal vein, and on to the liver where further chemical changes take place.

**The gall bladder** also provides an injection of fluid into the duodenum. The bile is produced by the liver and passes into the gallbladder where it is stored until it is needed. Bile is produced from breakdown products of the blood, and is a powerful emulsifying agent, allowing fats to be broken down to small particles so that they too may be absorbed into the circulation. Because the gallbladder receives this concentrated fluid from the liver it may produce stones if some of these chemicals precipitate out. These stones may cause inflammation (called cholecystitis) which is both painful and can spread to adjacent structures, notably the pancreas. Cholecystitis can be treated with antibiotics but removal of the gallbladder (cholecystectomy) is often required.

**The pancreas** produces the digestive juices. Inflammation of the pancreas causes an increase in the enzyme amylase, which spills over into the blood and can be detected on routine testing. Pancreatitis produces excruciating pain. Cancer of the pancreas also occurs. It tends to present late – that is, the patient and his doctor may be unaware of the condition until he is seriously ill and possibly only a few weeks from death.

*NICE Guideline*: in relation to cancer of the pancreas the Guidelines state: *"Consider an urgent direct access CT scan (to be performed within 2 weeks), or an urgent ultrasound scan if CT is not available, to assess for pancreatic cancer in people aged 60 and over with weight loss* **and** *any of the following: diarrhoea, back pain, abdominal pain, nausea, vomiting, constipation or new-onset diabetes."* The significant feature here is the weight loss, accompanied by some or even all of the other conditions. Since these are all relatively common, and not necessarily indicative of cancer, it is the weight loss which is important – but this can (and usually does) occur in many other cancers. Add to this the fact that weight loss is often deliberate through dieting. This accounts for the difficulty in diagnosis of pancreatic cancer, and so some delay is usually inevitable. Because of this delay in diagnosis the patient – or more often, those administering his estate – may consider that the doctor should have made the diagnosis earlier. With the benefit of hindsight it is often possible to identify a delay but this is usually only a few weeks. By this stage the patient's death is probably inevitable. From a practical point of view, any damages awarded in a case in clinical negligence would be limited to pain and suffering over these few weeks. Any causation associated with death would be defensible. Given the difficulty involved in bringing a case, pursuing an action where death has occurred due to cancer of the pancreas is generally inadvisable.

**The liver** is a large organ at the upper right part of the abdomen and is responsible for producing the biochemical changes that are the final stage in turning the diet into useful chemicals needed by the body. Energy-rich sugars may be released directly into the blood under the influence of insulin, or stored in the liver as glycogen. The building blocks of protein, amino acids, may not be stored but may be changed, in the case of some amino acids, so that their availability at sites of growth may be regulated. Fat metabolism is also controlled by the liver, with some types of fat being removed and triglycerides and cholesterol being allowed to enter the blood. This process is important for energy production but also causes problems because too much fat and cholesterol can lead to the development of atheroma. (See the chapters on Heart & Circulation for details of arterial disease).

Pathology in the liver is relatively common, either as infection or tumours. Cancers may arise directly in the liver, so-called primary liver tumours. More commonly, because there is direct blood flow from a large part of the gut to the liver, tumours from other structures within the abdomen may be carried to the liver where they form secondary tumours.

Hepatitis (infection of the liver) is caused by viruses. Hepatitis A (spread by contaminated water) and hepatitis B (spread by contaminated body fluids) are significant causes of pathology in the liver. Hepatitis C is similarly acquired from infected body fluids, although a greater quantity of these is required. A common cause is sharing needles by intravenous drug abusers. All three of these hepatitis viruses are difficult to treat, often resulting in chronic hepatitis, which in turn can be a precursor to primary liver cancer.

Alcohol is broken down in the liver, but the liver can only do so much. In the event of a determined and long-term assault via the bottle the liver will eventually give up the struggle and the unfortunate drinker will succumb to cirrhosis. This in turn may reduce the flow of blood through the liver, with increased blood pressure in the hepatic portal vein producing oesophageal varices and sometimes piles. Cirrhosis also leads to liver cancer.

**Case history**
A 56-year-old professional man came under the care of the local hospital, having been referred for routine surgery. Blood tests were undertaken to assess his general health, and it was found that he had raised liver enzymes. This did not prevent his elective surgery, but the GPs were informed of the incidental finding of abnormal liver function and it was suggested that this should be investigated. In the event the GPs did nothing. Several years later the patient developed obstructive jaundice and was found to have liver cancer. Further investigation revealed that he also had Hepatitis C, and on direct questioning he admitted to intravenous drug abuse some 25 years previously. By the time of diagnosis the liver cancer had progressed to the point where it was untreatable and he died within a matter of months.

*Comment*: This case demonstrates the importance of taking a detailed history, even though this may cause some embarrassment. Had the patient been asked if he had ever used intravenous drugs, he would probably have answered in the affirmative, but was unlikely to volunteer this. The presence of hepatitis could only be determined by specifically asking for Hepatitis C antigen, but a valuable clue was missed when the GPs omitted to investigate the abnormal liver function tests, as had been suggested. It was therefore difficult to defend liability on the part of these general practitioners.

**The appendix** is a blind duct at the junction of the ileum and the caecum – the connection of the small and large bowel. It is of no use whatsoever in humans, other than as a source of income to private surgeons. In some animals it is a part of the bowel where the food may exposed to bacterial decomposition to allow further nourishment to be extracted. The problem with the appendix in humans is that it may become infected, and the infection may cause it to burst. The question of chronic (i.e. long–term or 'grumbling') appendicitis is a matter of dispute among surgeons, and although an acute appendicitis is often obvious, it may mimic other conditions such as irritable bowel or diverticulitis. Delayed diagnosis may allow the appendix to rupture and cause peritonitis (infection of the cavity of the abdomen). This can be fatal.

**Case report**
A 28-year-old lady consulted her GP who recorded "Abdo pain. Central. Intermittent two weeks. Bowels open regularly. No blood." The GP went on to conduct abdominal examination noting that the abdomen was soft, and there were no masses. There was no enlargement of spleen, liver or kidneys. Rectal examination was not undertaken. A midstream urine sample was sent to the microbiology laboratory and a blood count for inflammatory markers (erythrocyte sedimentation rate, ESR) and white count was requested. The patient was given advice and a provisional diagnosis of bowel spasm. The urine sample was reported as normal, but the blood test revealed an elevated ESR (25 mm/h) and a white count of 15,000. Both of these were abnormal, indicating an inflammatory process due to infection. For reasons which were never explained, these results were annotated "normal" and filed. The patient attended two days later, still in pain, and was given further advice on the assumption of bowel spasm. One week later she attended the casualty department where, after further detailed history taking and examination, a CT scan was ordered. This revealed inflammatory change around the appendix which by this time had ruptured. The patient required an extensive laparotomy and a prolonged period in hospital. Fortunately she made a good recovery.

*Comment*: The GPs in this case had done all they could reasonably have been expected to do up until the clerical error which occurred when the result was filed. This was however indefensible. It was concluded that the patient would have required surgery in any event (albeit not so extensive) and the case was settled for a relatively modest sum.

**The colon,** commonly known as the large bowel, starts at the caecum in the lower right part of the abdomen which is next to the appendix. It then goes straight up, passes across to the left just below the diaphragm and then passes down to the rectum. The function of the large bowel is to extract fluid from the gut contents. This fluid has been taken in as part of the diet and added to by the secretions of the pancreas. The dietary contents can only pass through the small bowel, where absorption occurs, if the mixture is in a fluid state. Once the contents have reached the colon, however, this fluid needs to be conserved. If the colon is inflamed or does not function properly then the patient develops diarrhoea because the bowel contents pass through the colon without all the fluid being absorbed. The colon invariably contains bacteria, notably Escherichia Coli, in vast quantities. In normal circumstances these are harmless, but a change of species of bacteria (as in *travellers' diarrhoea*) may have unfortunate consequences. In extreme cases diarrhoea can lead to dehydration which is of particular concern with some types of infection (e.g. cholera) or in the very young or the very old who are more susceptible to dehydration. Normally, the function of the colon proceeds without conscious control. Extreme emotion, however, such as a sudden shock, may produce a rapid increase in function and can occasionally cause incontinence. The susceptibility of the colon to psychological influence may also manifest itself as the so-called *irritable bowel syndrome*, where the function may vary between episodes of constipation and episodes of diarrhoea.

Although cancers are relatively common within the colon, the commonest pathology apart from infection is diverticular disease. This occurs when the pressure in the colon causes small projections to occur. The lining of the colon herniates through the muscle to form little pouches on the outside of the structure. These are so common in the elderly as to be regarded as almost normal, but are a significant cause of pain if they become infected (diverticulitis). Another important cause of inflammation within the colon is ulcerative colitis. This condition, together with Crohn's disease, is a cause of *inflammatory bowel disease*. Taken together these conditions form an important part of the consideration of abdominal pain, particularly when rectal bleeding is present. Crohn's disease is distinguished from ulcerative colitis by the fact that it may involve any part of the gut, rather than just the colon. Treatment is by surgical removal of the affected section of the gut, preferably re-joining the ends, but if this is not possible the patient may end up with a colostomy and a bag on the skin of the abdomen. Inflammatory bowel disease and diverticulitis are important considerations in the differential diagnosis when considering abnormalities of the colon.

**Case report**
A 21-year-old female student consulted her general practitioner at the university student health surgery. The GP recorded "Diarrhoea. Advice". No other history was taken and no examination was performed! Two weeks later the student returned, and although the GP conducted examination (of a sort) the note was limited to the entry: "ISQ. OE. NAD. Imodium." (Imodium is medication which reduces the action of the large bowel. It is useful for travellers' diarrhoea). One month later the patient again attended the general practitioner, who noted that she was taking her final exams. His diagnosis on this occasion was "IBS" (irritable bowel syndrome). No further examination was undertaken and no specific questions were asked regarding anxiety, which was the presumed underlying cause. A month after this, the student returned to her home town and consulted her previous general practitioner. A detailed history was taken, and the GP noted that the patient had been suffering from diarrhoea for upwards of three months. She had lost two stone in weight. There was no evidence of untoward anxiety about her studies. A stool sample was sent to the laboratory and this did not reveal any abnormal pathogenic bacteria.

The GP also undertook blood tests which revealed a high ESR, indicating underlying inflammation. He made an urgent referral to a gastroenterologist. In the meantime the patient was overtaken by events and suffered an acute bowel obstruction, with total constipation and faeculant vomiting. She required emergency surgery to relieve the colonic obstruction which had been caused by Crohn's disease. She had a temporary colostomy but this was ultimately reversed and the condition managed by alteration of diet and provision of medication.

A case was brought against the student health doctor. It was considered that while the initial (presumed) diagnosis of simple infective diarrhoea had been reasonable, the continued assumption of varying diagnoses without proper history taking examination and investigation represented substandard practice. It was further considered, after taking expert advice from a gastroenterologist, that earlier treatment would have avoided the need for surgery. The case was settled for a significant sum.

**Cancer of the colon.** The most potentially serious condition of the colon is cancer. Whereas cancer of the small bowel is very unusual, bowel cancer is quite common and as many as one person in twenty may acquire the condition. If bleeding occurs into the upper part of the bowel, usually the stomach, the blood is itself digested and releases iron. The faeces become black as the digested blood is formed into the stools. When the colon bleeds, however, fresh red blood mixes with the stools. While bleeding can occur from haemorrhoids, in a patient over 40 this should never be assumed to be the case. An early cancer will produce only small amounts of bleeding. This is however detectable by special reagents and is the basis of the faecal occult blood screening test. Cancer may also cause a change in bowel habit, which may either be diarrhoea or constipation depending on the site and shape of the cancerous growth. Confusingly, bleeding and alteration in bowel habit are also caused by many other conditions and so bowel cancer is often misdiagnosed or diagnosed late. Because most of the blood coming from the gut passes through the liver, tumours in the gut will often spread to the liver and this may actually be the first point where abnormalities are detected.

NICE Guidelines for colorectal cancer specify: *"Refer adults using a suspected cancer referral pathway (for an appointment within 2 weeks) for colorectal cancer if: they are aged 40 and over with unexplained weight loss and abdominal pain or they are aged 50 and over with unexplained rectal bleeding or they are aged 60 and over with: iron-deficiency anaemia or changes in their bowel habit, or tests show occult blood in their faeces."* This Guideline is, unusually, unequivocal about the requirement to refer. The guidelines go on to suggest that a doctor should consider referral in patients with a rectal or abdominal mass, or those adults aged under 50 with unexplained abdominal pain, change in bowel habit, weight loss or iron deficiency anaemia. As stated previously, the Guidelines are only guidelines, but in recommending consideration of referral for patients whose symptoms could well be due to bowel cancer, it may be argued that a doctor failing to make such a referral would have a difficult defence. He would certainly find that the burden of proof had shifted, and he would need to explain why he had *not* made a referral.

### Case history
A 50-year-old man presented to his general practitioner complaining of a few months intermittent rectal bleeding. The doctor took a reasonable history, noting "blood streaking stool". He then conducted examination, including rectal examination, and noted "Abdo exam. LK2S, no masses. PR: piles. Advised." The patient went away, reassured, but about a year later saw another general practitioner in the same practice noted that he had weight loss. Full blood count revealed marginal anaemia. He was referred for colonoscopy and a cancer was found in the descending colon. Fortunately, this was operable, but the patient required more complex

surgery and also needed chemotherapy and radiotherapy. He brought a case against the first doctor. Although it was considered that there had been no impact on his survival time, the additional pain discomfort and loss of amenity attracted a moderate settlement.

*Comment*: This case illustrates the obvious but sometimes-forgotten fact that there is no reason why a patient should only have one pathology. In this case the haemorrhoids were *likely* to be responsible for the bleeding, but 'likely' is not enough. The possibility of another source of bleeding should have been borne in mind, and a referral made.

In summary, the complexity of the bowel and the variety of the associated pathology may allow significant medical errors to be made. While these may sometimes be no more than a nuisance, in many cases failure of diagnosis and proper management can be fatal.

Chapter 8

# THE GENITOURINARY SYSTEM

Because they are close together anatomically the kidneys and bladder, together with the male reproductive organs, are traditionally described as the genitourinary system. (The female reproductive system is considered separately – in this book by the section on gynaecology.) During the time under consideration there were four cases of cancer of the kidney; all but one of these represented failure on the part of the GP. There were two cases of bladder cancer. Bladder cancer is actually more common than kidney cancer. Because it presents with bleeding it is more difficult to miss but one of these was still missed by the GP in question. There were two cases of neglected prostate cancer and two cases of testicular tumour. Substandard treatment was found in all of these.

URINARY SYSTEM V BOWELS
The urinary system is responsible for maintaining the correct concentration of chemicals in plasma, including the removal of

waste products. The main waste product is urea, which is formed in the liver from the breakdown of amino acids. At this stage it is as well to make an important point. Because urine and faeces both require a visit to the lavatory, there is a tendency to consider the two together. For social purposes this may well be true, but when considering the physiology things could not be more different! The urine is a sterile fluid produced by a precisely balanced and controlled process which allows exactly the right amount of unwanted salts to pass into the kidney together with breakdown products from metabolism. Faeces, on the other hand, is simply that part of whatever we eat which has never properly passed into the circulation and so remains within the infected bowel to be passed out as waste.

BASIC MEDICAL SCIENCE

**Anatomy.** The two kidneys lie on the back wall of the abdomen, just below the lowest part of the ribs. Each is about the size of a slightly flattened fist. From the kidneys, urine passes down the ureters into the bladder. The bladder is in the pelvis at the lower part of the abdomen, sitting in front of the rectum and, in the female, in front of the vagina and uterus. The bladder connects to the outside world via the urethra, which for obvious reasons is longer in males. The bladder itself is capable of great expansion, from its shrunken empty state holding only a few millilitres to its fully expanded state which can be a litre or more. The wall of the bladder is muscular. The lining of the bladder has a specialised type of cell, described as transitional epithelium.

**Physiology.** The kidney is sometimes described as a filter, producing urine from the blood passing across it. This concept is inaccurate. Better to understand the function of the kidney is to consider two possibilities for removing unwanted rubbish from a house. It is possible (and probably usual) to go round the house with a black bag collecting all unwanted material. This may be likened to the "filter" analogy. Another method of cleaning the house, however, would be to strip the entire contents of every room and put them into a skip in the drive. After this the contents of the skip are inspected and those items which are required are put back into the house, leaving the rubbish behind. This is the best analogy for considering the way in which the kidney actually works. The output of the heart is about five litres of blood per minute. Of this, about a quarter goes straight to the kidneys. The kidneys therefore have a very generous blood supply and are capable of producing more than twenty litres of urine per day – about five gallons! Most of this is, of course, recovered – hence the skip analogy. Each kidney consists of over a million *nephrons*. At the first part of the nephron the blood flows through a fine mesh (the glomerulus) and most of the liquid element of the blood, containing water, salts, amino acids and sugars, passes into the *tubule*. The fluid at the first part of the tubule is therefore potential urine, but during its passage through the tubule it is subjected to a lot of changes. Firstly, an active process removes (or should remove) all the sugar and amino acids. If there is so much sugar present – as in diabetes – that the system cannot cope, then some of the sugar will remain and spill over into the urine. This must always be seen as abnormal. Amino acids are the 'building blocks' from which proteins are formed. While amino acids may pass into the fluid in the tubule, whole protein should not. If any protein passes into the tubule, this is because there is some damage present at the glomerulus. Protein in the urine is therefore another abnormality. The presence of protein and sugar in the urine can easily be tested in the doctor's surgery and should be recorded in the notes. As well as reabsorbing these essential nutrients, the kidney operates a process of fine adjustment to balance the sodium and potassium content of the blood.

Finally, a greater or lesser quantity of the water is absorbed, depending on the fluid requirements. This gives rise to an important point regarding general health. It is a matter of experience that if one drinks a great deal then one passes more urine. The opposite applies, and if we drink less, then we pass less urine. Against this, the amount of waste produced remains about the same, including a product called urobilinogen which is derived from breakdown of the blood and has the characteristic green-yellow colour. If we are not producing much urine then the urobilinogen becomes more concentrated, so the colour of the urine will vary according to the level of hydration. One practical point arising here is that we should drink enough to ensure that the urine is never more coloured than pale straw. Darker yellow usually indicates failure of fluid intake!

**Pathology.** The genitourinary system is subject to many types of pathology including infection, degeneration, autoimmune problems, metabolic problems, tumours and toxicity. Some, but not all, of the pathological changes are considered here under the individual organs. The kidneys may also be damaged by pressure changes, and a high arterial blood pressure will exacerbate any renal problems. Back pressure (obstruction) to the flow of urine out of the kidney will also produce chronic failure.

CLINICAL ASPECTS OF KIDNEY DISEASE –
THE DOCTOR'S JOB

**History.** Renal problems are not always evident. Tumours, including malignant tumours, may grow to considerable size without producing symptoms. Renal failure, even at very high concentrations of blood urea, makes the patient feel generally ill but is not painful. This is one of the reasons why renal function testing forms (or should form) part of a standard screening test in almost all patients under investigation. If kidney disease is suspected, the patient should be questioned about difficulty in passing urine and the amount and frequency. The presence of frank blood (haematuria) is usually volunteered by the patient, but haematuria may be microscopic and so not obvious, though it may be found on testing in the doctor's surgery. Nocturia (where more than one third of the daily output is passed over the eight hours of night), may represent obstruction by a large prostate gland. Of course, things are never simple and nocturia can also be expected after an evening's beer drinking! Unexpectedly large volumes may be indicative of renal disease but can more often point to diabetes. A complaint of odour from the urine may indicate infection, as may cloudiness on inspection.

**Examination** may reveal an enlarged kidney in a thin patient, but the kidneys are not always palpable (able to be felt). Similarly, it is not always possible to feel the bladder although in cases of obstruction it may expand to be felt as high as the patient's navel. More information is usually obtained by dipping the urine with specially prepared reagent sticks. These will give information as to the presence of glucose, ketones, nitrates blood and protein as well as measuring specific gravity and pH (acidity). If protein is present it may be the first clue to kidney disease. Sugar may indicate diabetes. Urine dip testing is an instance where what is strictly an 'investigation' should for practical purposes be considered part of standard clinical examination, and should be carried out in the doctor's surgery if kidney problems are suspected. If an infection is likely, usually indicated by the presence of white cells and nitrates in the urine, a specimen may be sent for laboratory culture to assess the infecting organism and the likely antibiotic sensitivity.

**Investigation.** As well as analysing the urine, if kidney disease is suspected the doctor should send off a blood sample. Analysis of the venous blood levels of albumin (a protein normally found in the blood) and creatinine allow an estimation of the efficiency of the filtration process taking place in the glomerulus. Decrease in the glomerular filtration rate (GFR) indicates whether kidney disease is present and if so, how severe. Kidney problems are initially dealt with by a physician called a nephrologist. After referral, investigation in hospital will usually be done by imaging and if necessary biopsy. Initial imaging investigation is done with ultrasound. Plain X-ray films are often not helpful, although 'KUB' (**k**idney **u**reters and **b**ladder) is still requested and may be the first indication of stones forming in the kidney or bladder. X-ray imaging with injected contrast has to some extent been superseded by more sophisticated imaging techniques, either CT scan or MRI, which may provide information without the need to inject potentially toxic material. Some types of renal disease are amenable to therapy, notably those associated with an autoimmune process, and where it is helpful to be aware of the histology renal biopsy may be undertaken. This can be done with a core sample taken straight through the skin, although the procedure is invasive and by no means free of risk.

**Case report**
A 56-year-old man was under routine surveillance for blood pressure. Every year the GP (or his nurse) took routine screening blood samples, including lipids (for cholesterol) urea and electrolytes (for kidney function), and liver function tests. These routine tests demonstrated slightly raised lipids, for which the patient was given dietary advice. They also demonstrated the rise of the enzyme alkaline phosphatase. This enzyme can arise either from liver or from bone where it may be an indicator of increased turnover or of erosion. No action was taken although the alkaline phosphatase remained raised over several years. The patient then developed a lump on his jaw. Because he had a dental phobia dating from his childhood he attended the GP. The GP referred him to the

dentist anyway, who told the patient his teeth were fine and the lump on the jaw was nothing to do with him. No action was taken for a further year, at which point the patient became generally ill and started to lose weight. The lump on the jaw had spread down into his neck. He was referred urgently to a head and neck surgeon, and it was found after x-ray investigation and referral to a general surgeon that the lump in the jaw was in fact a secondary cancer deposit from a tumour on the kidney. In spite of surgery to the jaw and removal of the kidney accompanied with chemotherapy, the patient gradually deteriorated and, sadly, died. The patient's family brought an action against the general practitioner, primarily for failing to act on the lump in the jaw. Expert advice suggested that the GP's action was reasonable in this respect as referral to a dentist was acceptable. Perhaps surprisingly, the dentist himself was not criticised. The GP was, however, held liable for having ignored the raised alkaline phosphatase over many years. Not surprisingly, the GP's defence organisation contested this vigorously, but was ultimately persuaded that an abnormal result, particularly when persistent, should not have been ignored. Had the reason for the raised alkaline phosphatase been pursued, the renal tumour would have been discovered earlier. The case was settled in favour of the patient's estate.

*Comment*: The battery of tests done in this case, taken here as part of surveillance of a patient with high blood pressure, is routine. This sort of screening process is really a fishing expedition for detection of any abnormality. It is not a test done to check for a specific condition on the doctor's differential diagnosis. Even so, a laboratory result outside the expected values, particularly when persistent over time, demands an explanation. It is significant that the renal function tests in this case remained normal throughout. This is because there is a large reserve in renal function and there is no reason why a tumour in one kidney should affect the overall function of the kidneys as a whole. This case demonstrates the difficulty of diagnosis, but also the obligation of a reasonably competent doctor to find the cause of an abnormality on screening, even in the absence of symptoms.

**Renal Failure** describes the inability of the kidneys to clear the blood adequately of waste products. The concentration of waste products in the blood gradually rises as the kidney is unable to clear them. This can easily be tested in venous blood. Raised urea and creatinine (a breakdown product from muscle protein) are the indicators of renal failure. Hospital laboratories have an automated process for testing blood samples, and the average laboratory will process hundreds of samples day with the request: "*U&Es and creat*", representing a routine screening test for renal function. This is part of the standard screening process when taking bloods, and so frequent is the request that the request for urea and electrolytes is often pre-printed on the laboratory form.

Acute (i.e. sudden) renal failure is, as the name implies, a rapid event. We cannot live without kidneys for more than a few days and a patient who suffers sudden kidney failure due to infection or other toxic effect will require urgent dialysis. On the other hand, chronic kidney disease (usually abbreviated to CKD), may be present for some years before the patient requires extensive treatment. Urea and creatinine rise inexorably in chronic renal failure and if the patient does not die of something else first a point eventually comes where intervention is required. This is renal dialysis. It is done either by an external machine, or by running fluid into the peritoneal cavity and removing it after a few hours together with the waste products (peritoneal dialysis). It goes without saying that this treatment is extremely inconvenient. It is also far from ideal, because neither method is perfect. Most patients on a dialysis program want desperately to receive a donor kidney. This can, of course, only be provided when the original owner of the kidney has died, unless one has a compatible relative to provide a kidney. (In this situation it should be remembered that

The Genitourinary System

there is plenty of renal function in a healthy person and the donor can survive perfectly well on the one remaining kidney). Renal transplantation has its own difficulties because the new kidney may be recognised by the immune system as being 'foreign'. No matter how near the match, the body may still tend to reject it. For this reason immune-suppressant drugs are provided, but these may also suppress the beneficial effects of the immune system so the patient becomes susceptible to infection.

*NICE Guidance.*[1] The preamble to the Guidance recognises the difficulty in recognising early chronic kidney disease, saying: *"CKD is usually asymptomatic, but it is detectable, and tests for CKD are simple and freely available. There is evidence that treatment can prevent or delay the progression of CKD, reduce or prevent the development of complications, and reduce the risk of cardiovascular disease. However, CKD is often unrecognised because there are no specific symptoms, and it is often not diagnosed or diagnosed at an advanced stage."*

Although the Guidance does not specifically say so – NICE usually tries not to scold – the door is open for doctors' errors if the Guidance is not followed. Dr Botchup will find it inconvenient, but testing for chronic kidney disease should be offered to people with and of the following conditions:

- diabetes,
- hypertension,
- acute kidney injury,
- cardiovascular disease (ischaemic heart disease, chronic heart failure, peripheral vascular disease or cerebral vascular disease),
- structural renal tract disease,
- recurrent renal calculi or prostatic hypertrophy,
- multisystem diseases with potential kidney involvement for example, systemic lupus erythematosus (an autoimmune condition affecting multiple systems),
- family history of end-stage kidney disease,

- hereditary kidney disease
- patients in whom routine urine dipping (for whatever reason) haematuria is detected.

This guidance implies a great deal of testing, but that is against a background of the testing itself being relatively cheap, whereas if kidney disease is allowed to develop and require treatment the outcome is very expensive. NHS treatment of patients with kidney disease costs about £1.5 billion per year. While some of the above conditions – trauma or family history, for example – obviously cannot be treated, conditions such as diabetes and hypertension should be brought under as good a control as possible. Once the general practitioner has referred the patient to hospital the Guidance provides well documented evidence-based pathways. Regular blood pressure monitoring often devolves on the general practitioner who is then responsible for sharing the care of kidney patients and plays – or should play – an important part in preventing progression to end-stage (serious) renal disease.

**Case report**
A 45-year-old man attended his general practitioner with a complaint of feeling tired all the time. The doctor took a general history which suggested that the man had personal problems, including trouble at work and within his marriage. He then undertook routine examination and (some) investigations. The blood pressure was 165/95. The potassium (an electrolyte controlled by the kidneys) was slightly elevated. There were also marginal elevations of the urea and creatinine. On review with these results, the feeling of 'tired all the time' was ascribed to anxiety and no further action was taken. Some two years later, the patient had moved house and consulted another general practitioner. Further routine screening tests were done. These showed significant deterioration of renal function and he was referred to a nephrologist. The underlying cause of the renal failure was degeneration and could not be treated, but the

patient's blood pressure was controlled and he was put on a programme of regular monitoring. In spite of this the condition deteriorated and he needed twice weekly dialysis and was put on the waiting list for a transplant.

*Comment*: This case demonstrates the difficulty of detecting and managing renal disease in a patient who is not obviously ill. The presentation of 'tired all the time' is often abbreviated in GP notes to 'TATT' – showing how often it is the patient's only complaint! On this occasion the general practitioner had done all the screening tests necessary. None of these was spectacularly elevated but taken together warranted investigation for chronic renal disease. It is probable that dietary control and blood pressure monitoring at the first opportunity would have slowed the progression of chronic kidney disease. From the litigation point of view, breach of duty on the part of the general practitioner was established by reference to NICE Guidance. A nephrologist gave a causation opinion to the effect that on the balance of probability the deterioration would have been prevented, but because it was to some extent an inevitable the case was settled for a relatively modest sum.

THE BLADDER

**Pathology.** Because the urine is formed from the blood it is normally sterile. It may, however, happen that the urine becomes infected. Because of the shortness of the urethra in females this is commonly encountered in young women who have recently become sexually active, when bacteria may be forced back into the bladder – a condition knowingly described by student nurses as 'honeymoon wee'. In males and in children, however, a finding of infected urine must be seen as abnormal. Chronic infection within the kidney (pyelonephritis) will produce infected urine and this should be investigated.

NICE Guidance.[2] *"Urinary tract infections are caused by the presence and multiplication of microorganisms in the urinary tract. A urinary tract infection can result in several clinical syndromes, including acute and chronic pyelonephritis (infection of the kidney and renal pelvis), cystitis (infection of the bladder), urethritis (infection of the urethra), epididymitis (infection of the epididymis) and prostatitis (infection of the prostate gland). Infection may spread to surrounding tissues (for example, perinephric abscess) or to the bloodstream."*

The guidance goes on to define different groups of patients requiring different clinical management. Adults over 65 years old with a urinary tract infection require full clinical assessment. Men with an upper urinary tract infection need full investigation by a urologist. In contrast to nephrology, urology is a surgical speciality; there may be an obstruction which may be amenable to surgical treatment. One exception to the requirement for investigation is that patients with an in-dwelling urinary catheter may be expected to have bacteria in the urine; treatment with antibiotics is not always necessary. The Guidance specifically states that it is important to avoid over-use of antibiotics in order to prevent emerging resistance.

**Case report**
A 45-year-old man attended his general practitioner complaining of dysuria (pain on micturition) and after dipstick testing of the urine he was prescribed an antibiotic. Three months later the same situation occurred. The patient had repeated visits to the general practitioner over a period of four years, and on each occasion the urinary tract infection was empirically treated with antibiotics. He then saw another general practitioner who arranged for an ultrasound examination. This suggested that stones may be present. The GP wrote to a hospital specialist: "I would be grateful if you would see this 41 year-old gentleman as soon as possible... past history of urinary tract infections...ultrasound scans confirms a right calculus..." The specialist arranged x-ray imaging with contrast. The report read: "control radiographs demonstrate a large stag horn calculus in the right kidney...

the right kidney appears to be functioning but not excreting well". The patient required a nephrectomy. (removal of the kidney). It was claimed that he had suffered from general malaise and debility over an unnecessarily long period. The management by the general practice was held to be indefensible, but a causation expert instructed by the general practitioner's defence organisation produced evidence to suggest that the nephrectomy would have been necessary in any event. The case was therefore settled for a relatively modest sum.

*Comment*: This case illustrates the principles of the NICE Guidance. Many GPs would treat a 'one–off' urinary tract infection in a man without further investigation. Repeated infections, however, need follow-up to ascertain the cause. In this case, the GPs ignored the repeated infections which were caused not by an opportunistic lower urinary tract infection, but by the kidney stone harbouring persistent bacteria.

**Cancer** of the bladder is a well-recognised problem. Among other causes, it is due to certain chemicals (particularly some dyes) concentrating in the urine, a consideration which, historically, gave rise to issues of employer's liability. Bladder cancer typically presents as painless bleeding into urine – haematuria. This should be contrasted with bleeding into urine accompanied by pain, which – paradoxically – is usually due to the less dangerous condition of cystitis. Painless haematuria should always be investigated. Bladder cancer is commoner in the older age groups and if detected early is usually successfully treated. It follows from this that any patient who has had a demonstrable haematuria, particularly when it has been shown that the urine is sterile, should be considered to have bladder cancer until proved otherwise.

NICE Guidance on bladder cancer[3] advises referral for people using a suspected cancer pathway referral (for an appointment within 2 weeks) for bladder cancer if they are: "*aged 45 and over and have: unexplained visible haematuria without urinary tract infection, or visible haematuria that persists or recurs after successful treatment of urinary tract infection, or aged 60 and over and have unexplained non-visible haematuria and either dysuria or a raised white cell count on a blood test.*" Consideration for non–urgent referral for suspected bladder cancer is recommended in people aged 60 and over with recurrent or persistent unexplained urinary tract infection.

**Investigations** of bladder problems are initially carried out by analysis of the urine. Commercially available plastic sticks are simply dipped into the urine. The sticks have reagent patches to show various abnormalities as described above. Some types of sticks, particularly those used for routine testing, will not show the presence of very small quantities of blood (microscopic haematuria) and special sticks are required to this. If abnormalities are suspected, referral to a urologist should be made and the inside of the bladder can be seen directly by the cystoscopy. Using a fine fibrotic instrument the inside of the bladder can be inspected through the urethra – this can now done in the outpatient department, and with the patient awake. Tumours may be biopsied or even removed completely and when treatment has been completed the success of the treatment can be monitored by repeat cystoscopy.

**Case report**
A 56-year-old lady presented to her general practitioner complaining of blood in her urine. She denied any discomfort on micturition. Routine testing confirmed the presence of blood and protein. The GP diagnosed a urinary tract infection and prescribed antibiotics. Six months later, the lady presented again, complaining that the bleeding had persisted. Again she had no other symptoms. The GP proposed a further course of antibiotics but on the patient's

insistence arranged a hospital referral. Cystoscopy revealed the presence of a bladder tumour which was, fortunately, removed via the cystoscope. The lady subsequently remained well on follow-up. She complained to her local NHS organisation (then the Family Practitioner Committee) who found that the GP had been in breach of his terms of service. He was required to adhere more closely to his contract, but there was no withholding of fees. The patient then consulted a solicitor. Expert advice suggested that the GP was likely to be found in breach of his duty of care, but in terms of causation the patient had not been in pain and her life expectancy had not been reduced. It was therefore decided not to proceeds with a claim.

*Comment*: This case illustrates the danger of treating painless haematuria as an infection. From a litigation point of view, the case also demonstrates that a dissatisfied patient has a number of remedies, but that a breach of terms of service may not necessarily result in a successful claim in tort. (See the chapter on Putting Things Right for further details).

THE MALE REPRODUCTIVE SYSTEM

**Anatomy & Physiology** The *testes* are in a pouch of skin hanging outside the body. This location makes the testes vulnerable to injury but it provides a lower temperature for the organs. This is necessary for healthy sperm production. From a clinical point of view, it also has the advantage that unlike the ovaries the testes are easily accessible for examination. The testes produce the germ cells, the DNA-containing spermatozoa. They are also exocrine glands producing testosterone, a hormone with multiple functions such as maintaining libido, stimulating sperm production, maintaining muscle strength and mass and promoting healthy bone density. The *epididymis* is a tightly coiled tube connecting the rear of the testis to the *vas deferens*. The vas is palpable and easily accessible for the minor surgical procedure of vasectomy, an operation designed to render males permanently sterile although otherwise capable of sexual intercourse. The vas deferens passes through the upper part of the scrotum and continues into the *prostate gland*. This gland produces the bulk of the fluid which forms the seminal ejaculate. It is situated behind the pubic bone and just below the bladder. Unlike the testes, this gland is not easily accessible either for examination or for surgery, although useful information can be obtained by feeling through the wall of the rectum on digital examination. The urethra (tube from the bladder) passes through the prostate gland. This renders surgery of the gland even more complex.

**Pathology.** In common with most structures undergoing rapid cell turnover, the testes and prostate gland are susceptible to cancers. Testicular cancers can be particularly important in medico-legal considerations of quantum (how much the damage is worth!), occurring as they may do in the younger age group. Although certain types of testicular cancer were previously notorious for their poor prognosis, improved treatment has resulted in greatly improved cure rates, although the treatment may render the patient sterile. Benign cysts may form in the epididymis and may sometimes reach a spectacular size.

In the prostate, benign prostatic hypertrophy (usually abbreviated BPH in the notes) is a condition affecting men with increasing age. Cancer of the prostate is among the more common cancers. The testes, the epididymis and the prostate are susceptible to infection which may be sexually transmitted, although this is not always the case.

CLINICAL CONSIDERATIONS – THE DOCTOR'S JOB

**History and Examination** The patient with testicular problems may complain of pain or of a lump. The testes should be firmly palpated to assess for lumps. A mass on the body of the testis must be assumed to be cancer until proved otherwise. A mass distinct from the testes is probably an epididymal cyst, but 'probably' is not enough – it still requires referral by the GP for further investigation. Ultrasound is then the investigation of choice.

**Case report**
A 24-year-old man attended his (female) GP who noted: "Testicular lump, worried – noted lump in left scrotum in shower – not changed recently – more prominent in shower. On examination both testes smooth/uniform and not enlarged. Small pea-sized lump posterior and separate to testes. Non-tender. Too small to transilluminate. Patient reassured – asked to report any further lumps or further change." The patient was initially reassured, but about a year later was reading an article in a men's health magazine advising that a testicular lump should be investigated. He re-attended the GP. On this occasion he was referred for investigation and ultrasound and the biopsy demonstrated a cancer. By this stage it was found that the cancer had spread, and he required not only surgery to remove both testes, but extensive chemotherapy. This precluded him from providing sperm for banking. The therapy gave him a good chance of survival, but expert causation opinion suggested that the treatment would have been much less severe, and sperm banking could have been made available, had the GP made a referral on presentation. The case was settled for a large sum in favour of the Claimant.

*Comment*: The doctor had undertaken a conscientious examination and written a reasonable clinical note. She had, however, formed the wrong conclusion, because it is not clinically possible, particularly with a small lump, accurately to determine the nature of a mass within the scrotum. Referral should have been made for further investigation.

Benign prostatic hypertrophy (BPH) is almost universal in the older age groups. It may cause difficulty in micturition, or occasionally complete urinary retention. An earlier complaint may be nocturia. Men complaining of difficulty in micturition, or even any change in their usual pattern of micturition, should have a digital rectal examination (DRE). Failure to do this, even if accompanied by a tinge of embarrassment, is negligent. On examination, the prostate may be felt as a smooth elevation about the size of a hen's egg towards the front of the rectum. Enlargement may be expected in the older man, but any hardness or irregularity suggests cancer.

Each year in the UK about 47,000 men are diagnosed with prostate cancer and about 11,000 die from the disease. The most common age of diagnosis is 65 to 69. The prostate releases a chemical into the bloodstream, prostate specific antigen (PSA), which is an indicator of cell activity within the gland. The normal level is about 3.5 units. It may be expected to rise to about 4.5 units at age 70 and 6.5 at age 80. Patients with prostate cancer may have a PSA level of more than 1000. As tumour markers go, PSA is a useful test, but there is considerable controversy about its use for screening men who have no symptoms. The problem is that if a high level is found then this will (or should) lead to the next stage. This is a rectal examination often followed by prostate biopsy. Biopsy is by no means a casual procedure and may turn out to be completely normal. At present there is no clear policy but GPs may offer a test provided these limitations are made clear: about 3 in 4 men with a raised PSA level will not have cancer. The PSA test can also miss about 15% of cancers.

NICE Guidance for Prostate cancer. *"Refer men using a suspected cancer pathway referral (for an appointment within 2 weeks) for prostate cancer if their prostate feels malignant on digital rectal examination. Consider a prostate-specific antigen (PSA) test and digital rectal examination to assess for prostate cancer in men with: any lower urinary tract symptoms (such as nocturia, urinary frequency, hesitancy, urgency or retention) or erectile dysfunction or visible haematuria. Refer men using a suspected cancer pathway* referral *(for an appointment within 2 weeks) for prostate cancer if their PSA levels are above the age–specific reference range."*

**Case report**
A 58-year-old man attended his GP several times over the course of two years. His complaint was that he was running to the lavatory a lot, particularly at night, and having difficulty in obtaining or maintaining an erection. He had been prescribed a diuretic for treatment of blood pressure, and the GP ascribed his symptoms to a side-effect of this medication. No examination was undertaken. Some time later the patient attended the general practitioner complaining of severe backache. Examination revealed tenderness on firm palpation of the lumbar spine. The GP undertook a series of blood tests and found that the PSA was significantly elevated. He referred the patient for further investigation and it was determined that he had a prostate cancer which had, unfortunately by this time, spread to bone. He was subjected to radiotherapy and chemotherapy, but unfortunately succumbed to the advanced cancer.

*Comment*: While the diuretic could indeed have been responsible for the symptoms, the GP had 'ruled out' the possibility of an abnormality within the genitourinary system without any justification for doing so. A male of this age should have had, as a minimum, a PSA blood test undertaken once he started to complain of any symptoms referable to the genitourinary system. While GPs (and patients) do not welcome a digital rectal examination this can be a life-saving part of the examination and should be undertaken in any cases of doubt or in the event of a raised PSA.

**Treatment of prostate cancer.** Once biopsy has been done and the cancer staged the urologist will usually discuss new cases with a multidisciplinary team (MDT) to determine the best outcome. Treatment options range from surgery through radiotherapy, chemotherapy, and in non-aggressive cases simply watchful waiting.

As a final word of warning, and considering genitourinary problems as a whole, it is worth remembering that some people, particularly in the older age groups, are reluctant to discuss or be examined for what Monty Python referred to as 'the naughty bits'. This may lead to some doctors also being hesitant in their clinical assessment. It is worth remembering the words of the superb clinical teacher, the late Dr John Davies OBE, whose favourite remark in this situation was: "Come on, we're all grown up. Tell him to get his pants off!"

REFERENCES

1. https://www.nice.org.uk/guidance/cg182 (Chronic kidney Disease)
2. https://www.nice.org.uk/guidance/conditions-and-diseases/urological-conditions/urinary-tract-infection
3. https://www.nice.org.uk/guidance/ng2

Chapter 9

# NERVES

This chapter looks at medico-legal issues involving the nervous system. The title is "Nerves" because although from a medical point of view nerves are involved in two different branches of medicine, psychiatry and neurology, there is a lot of overlap. Looking at the two together is unconventional but helps to give a clearer insight into both types of condition.

During the period in question there were nine cases where it was considered that a diagnosable psychiatric condition had been mismanaged. Some of these involved physical brain pathology as well as psychiatric disturbance – examples of the overlap. Psychiatric illness (usually depression) occurred as a result of mismanagement of other conditions and was found in a wide variety of cases, often resulting in damages for causation of injury.

As distinct from psychiatric problems, claims for purely neurological conditions involved brain tumours, epilepsy and meningitis. There were fifteen cases.

**Neurology** is the branch of medicine dealing with nerves, not in their functional sense as in 'the mind' but simply as anatomical structures which are liable to trauma, tumours, infection, and degenerative change – as usual, the thousand shocks that flesh is heir to. The traditional way of studying medicine in terms of anatomy, physiology and pathology holds good.

**Psychiatry.** These patients' problems are different. The study of mental health does not easily fit into the traditional concept of medicine. Fitting psychiatric diagnoses into the traditional Western study of anatomy, physiology, pathology and clinical medicine can seem like forcing a square peg into a round hole. This view is understandable – in many societies mental health is seen not as a medical problem but as a cultural or even religious one. Another problem – almost exclusive to psychiatry – is that people who are suffering from mental health problems are often seen as objects of derision and may be reluctant to seek help. Even so, people who are mentally ill and who consult their doctor (or who are obliged to see one) should have the benefit of the same basic clinical management. As always, this must consist of history taking, examination, diagnosis and then treatment.

**Case report**
A 23-year-old supermarket cashier consulted her general practitioner because of a hand tremor. The GP initially conducted a good clinical examination, noting that the tremor was intermittent and not incapacitating. There was no obvious indication of any psychiatric issues. He made a diagnosis of benign tremor and did not arrange further referral or investigations. The tremor continued. Three years after the initial event the patient suddenly developed an acute psychiatric episode, with visual hallucinations and hearing voices. She was admitted to a mental hospital where drug treatment was tried. Because this was unsuccessful she was then sent to a neurologist. A CT scan revealed a brain tumour. Happily this was benign and amenable to

> surgery. The operation relieved both the psychosis and the tremor. She sought advice concerning liability on the part of the general practitioner. It was considered that the acute psychiatric episode was managed properly. Arguably, the earlier diagnosis of benign tremor was inappropriate, since this was, in retrospect, likely to have been due to the brain tumour. Nonetheless the diagnosis was considered to have been reasonable at the time. The action was discontinued.

This slightly unusual case illustrates the relationship between neurology and psychiatry. Of course, many psychiatric conditions occur in patients where the anatomy of the nervous system is apparently normal, and it is often not possible to find the cause. The underlying problem may still represent some abnormality within the brain. This may however be at microscopic or biochemical level and the mechanisms are not fully understood – particularly where the biochemical pattern has occurred as a result of learning and upbringing.

## STRUCTURE AND FUNCTION OF THE NERVOUS SYSTEM

**Anatomy.** Macroscopically, that is at the level easily visible to the eye, the nervous system is traditionally considered to be divided into the *central* nervous system and the *peripheral* nervous system. The central nervous system consists of the brain and spinal cord. These are vulnerable structures and are all encased within bone. The brain lies within the vault of the skull. It is covered in membranes known as the meninges. The outer membrane, the *dura mater*, as the Latin name implies, is a relatively tough layer (*ie* durable). The inner membrane has a spider's-web-like arrangement of blood vessels and so is described as the *arachnoid mater*. The spinal cord lies behind the arches of the vertebral bodies in the spine. Its structure has been described more fully in the section on the back. The peripheral nerves extend from the central nervous system to all parts of the body. In the chest and abdomen the peripheral nerves are arranged so that there is one nerve for each spinal segment to supply that part of the body. In the head and in the limbs the segmental nerves from several levels fuse together to form the nerves supplying the limbs or the head and face. Peripheral nerves are easily visible, the sciatic nerve being the largest (and longest) and supplying the leg. It is about the thickness of the little finger. As the nerves approach the extremities they divide into smaller and smaller branches to the point where the nerves supplying the skin and muscles are invisible to the naked eye.

Microscopically the nerves consist of individual *neurones*. All neurones have the same basic structure, a cell body and a filament called the *axon*. There the similarity ends. Some nerves have a very long axon, so the nerve cell supplying sensation to your big toe, for example, will have its cell body within the spine and the axon then extends nearly a metre. Some neurones have sheaths of protective cells. The sheath consists of a protein called myelin. Other neurones, particularly those within the brain, have very short connections to other nerve cells. Nerve connections are called *synapses*. The synapse is really the point at which the nerve does its work. A nerve is arranged to receive a chemical stimulus (neurotransmitter) at one end and can release another – possibly different – neurotransmitter at the other end. This may be a connection to another nerve cell at a synapse, or may be a motor endplate on a muscle fibre. Within the brain and spinal cord the nerve cells are supported by a structure of specialised connective tissue called glial cells. These cells are significant because unlike the neurones, they are capable of growth and repair – and therefore (unfortunately!) tumour formation.

**Physiology.** Nerve cells work by having a cell membrane with an electrical charge. In the normal state the membrane acts as an insulator but if it changes its conductivity then a current will flow. The passage of this current then causes the next section of the nerve to change its conductivity. In this way an impulse will pass from one end of the nerve to the other, where it may then release a tiny amount of neurotransmitter. In a sensory nerve the stimulus may be sound, heat, light, pressure or even pain – the source of the senses. This sensory input goes to the central nervous system where the signal is 'processed'. The motor nerves receive the output from this process and may initiate movement. Other nerves may stimulate glands to produce secretions, although these are also triggered by other chemicals – hormones. Some, hormones (notably adrenaline) will have an overall stimulatory effect on the central nervous system.

These signals to the central nervous system combine with information which is already stored there – the memory. This processing within the central nervous system is what governs the response to any given stimulus. Neurotransmitters released at synapses may be either stimulatory or inhibitory. Synapses may alter at microscopic level to form different connections. These changes occur at specific parts of the brain and form the basis of learning and memory. The nerve cells in the brain transmit impulses along a series of synapses which are sometimes described as "logic gates".

So much for a look at the rather complicated anatomy and physiology of the nervous system. Now consider what it does. In a sense the brain works like a computer and so we can use an analogy with computers (with which most of us are at least vaguely familiar) when trying to understand how the brain functions.

At its simplest, the computer may be considered to have at its centre the central processing unit or CPU. Before information gets to the CPU, however, it has to get into the box. In the case of the computer this is via a mouse, keyboard, scanner, microphone or digital camera. This goes in as electronic information and is processed. Processing means changing the information in some way (the program) and mixing the information with information that is already stored on the computer (the memory) and then providing some sort of output. In a computer the output may be a screen image, printed image, music or speech. If the output is connected to electric motors then robotic movement can be produced.

So much is familiar in computers. With some imagination it is possible to consider that the human body actually acts in a similar way. Our senses (touch, sight, hearing, smell) provide the input. The brain provides the central processing unit. The analogy is at its most important here, because the information from our senses is integrated by the program into our previous experience (the memory) and produces the outcome. This means that what a person says and does in a given situation depends not only on the situation itself but also his experience and learning.

This analogy gives an outline of the way that psychiatry can be compared to a piece of electronic equipment. How far can this analogy be taken? Consider the brain as containing a program. It is this programming which forms the basis of psychiatry, and consists of the conscious and unconscious memory.

**Case report**
(For a change, this one is from a Dr Sigmund Freud.) A 24-year old man consulted Dr Freud. He had an unusual complaint in that he became sexually aroused in the presence of high-heeled shoes, to the extent that even passing a fashionable shoe shop would cause an embarrassing erection. (Men wore very tight trousers in 19th-century Vienna.) Under hypnosis Freud discovered that as an infant the patient had been cared for by a nurse who had 'soothed' him by stroking the front of his diaper with her shoe. Freud concluded that this had provided a masturbatory stimulus, and the learned response had persisted into manhood. The patient was helped by further hypnosis, with counter suggestion.

This classic case illustrates the effect of learned response in terms of apparently bizarre behaviour. While simplistic, it is likely that many psychiatric conditions stem from learning processes in early childhood.

**Memory.** In the middle of the last century some American scientists conducted a rather strange experiment.[1] They took some primitive worm-like creatures called planaria. These were chosen because they have a nervous system – but a very primitive one. The scientists put the worms in a tank with a light on one end and put food next to the light. After a few days the planaria learned in some way that the food was associated with the light and moved to that end of the tank when the light was turned on. These 'trained' planaria could be distinguished from 'naive' planaria because they swam towards the light, whereas new entrants into the tank did not at first do this. The next stage in the process was to take some of the 'trained' planaria, mince them up and feed them to some of their brothers and sisters. Interestingly, it was found that these 'cannibal' planaria, when introduced into the tank, immediately swam towards the light. They had not previously been 'trained' and the only explanation was that

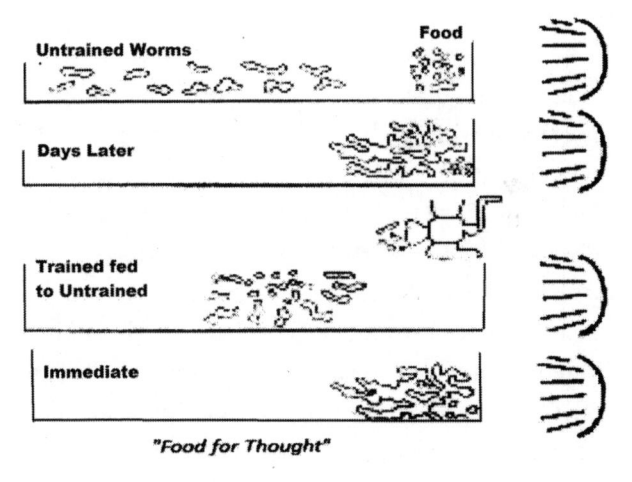

*"Food for Thought"*

*Learning in worms*

in eating the 'trained' planaria they had somehow acquired their knowledge of where the food was! What does this mean? Simply (but importantly) this experiment showed that memory is based on a chemical process and may directly influence behaviour.

Where does this conclusion leave us in considerations of psychiatry? One theory is that any response made by humans whom we classify as 'mentally abnormal' can ultimately be explained in terms of chemistry within the brain. This forms the basis of a possible classification of mental disorder into organic or conditioned. Organic disorders are those due to oxygen deprivation, abnormalities or degeneration of the tissues, or the chemical effects of alcohol, drugs or poisons. Conditioned abnormalities still have a chemical basis but arise from a faulty learning pattern.

The first case history described above, where the patient had both neurological (tremor) and psychiatric (hallucinations) symptoms shows that the causes of neurological problems and the causes of psychiatric illness may be difficult to disentangle; this of course means that there may be a significant source of doctors' errors. Even so, most conditions coming to the attention of the neurologist may be considered by the usual classification of pathology. That is, congenital or acquired, with the acquired conditions being considered under the headings of infective, degenerative, neoplastic and the rest. Some neurological cases may be considered first, and the rest of this chapter will then be devoted to psychiatric problems.

NEUROLOGY – THE DOCTOR'S JOB

**History.** Neurological conditions may produce symptoms of numbness, weakness or incoordination. Headache is another important presenting complaint, as is confusion. Full neurological assessment, as taught to medical students, will occupy about an hour of the doctor's time. It is unrealistic to expect this to happen in the average GP surgery, or even in a busy hospital clinic. The nature and extent of the examination will therefore be influenced by the complaint.

**Examination.** Classically, the cranial nerves are assessed first, this examination involving vision, eye movement, smell, taste, and movements of the tongue and face. The peripheral nerves are examined by checking the limbs for tone and power. Coordination may be assessed by a variety of clinical tests including the "finger to nose" test where the examiner repeatedly moves his or her hand while asking the patient rapidly to touch the nose and then the examining hand in alternating movements. Sensation is assessed by testing for both blunt and sharp stimulation. Full examination requires this to be done for every dermatome (segmental nerve). Patients with a headache should be asked about its onset (sudden or gradual), its severity, and the history of previous headaches.

Accurate history taking, followed by careful examination, should usually allow the differential diagnosis to be narrowed to the point where investigations may be indicated. In the past, neurological assessment was something of an esoteric occupation. The advent of CT and MRI has, however, made the neurologist's task much easier. Public awareness of *stroke* is increasing through the government campaign FAST — the acronym used as a mnemonic to help detect and enhance responsiveness to the needs of a person having a stroke. The acronym stands for **f**acial drooping, **a**rm weakness, **s**peech difficulties and **t**ime to call emergency services. Stroke may be due either to a bleed or to its antithesis, lack of blood due to a clot. The latter is more common, but the final diagnosis must be made by CT scan because using clot-dissolving drugs on the presumption of an infarct, where the condition is in fact due to haemorrhage, would be disastrous — the bleed would become worse. Most district hospitals now have a stroke unit able to provide urgent diagnosis and treatment.

**Case report**

A 19-year-old apprentice left work early due to sudden severe headache. He returned to his flat. His flatmate later said that he appeared confused and disorientated. The next day, accompanied by the flatmate, he attended the local GP emergency clinic. The GP recorded that the patient had vomited but made no note as to the sudden onset of the headache. Examination of pulse and blood pressure and the fundi (back of the eyes) was said to be normal. The GP made a diagnosis of viral headache and advised paracetamol. The next day the patient remained seriously ill and his parents came to collect him from his flat. His father later said that he appeared disorientated. They attended the patient's registered doctor who conducted a brief history and examination. This time the doctor found tenderness over the face. There was no recorded description of the onset of the headache, although the patient stated that, had he been asked, he would have clearly indicated to the doctor that this had come on extremely suddenly. The GP made a diagnosis of sinusitis and the patient was reassured, but two days later he became severely disorientated with fluctuating levels of consciousness. He was taken by his father to the accident and emergency department where he was investigated by CT scan and a subarachnoid haemorrhage diagnosed. He remains disabled, both physically and with learning impairment.

*Comment*: Headache is common in general practice and the skill lies in determining which headaches are serious. To do this a proper history must be taken. Subarachnoid haemorrhage classically starts with a sudden headache – often described as "thunderclap". Neither of the GPs had posed questions as to the onset of the headache. For this reason the serious diagnosis of subarachnoid bleed was missed. Had the diagnosis been made earlier the patient could have had emergency surgery to stop the bleeding and remove any clot; he would in all probability have made a full recovery. He was awarded substantial damages.

**Infection.** Headache due to infection is always a possibility, and in the above case, purely on a statistical basis, the first GP's diagnosis of viral headache could have been correct but for the history of sudden onset. Viral infections are relatively common and usually self-limiting. Bacterial infections, however, are more serious – meningitis. Particularly in young infants who cannot give a history or explain that they have a headache it is important to obtain as much information as possible by physical examination. The bacterium which causes meningitis circulates in the blood and causes a general illness which cannot to be distinguished from that of a viral illness such as mild flu. This bacterium has the tendency then to produce a haemorrhagic rash and to infect the meninges. This development can occur over the matter of a very few hours.

### Case report

The mother of a six month old boy took the infant to the GP saying that he was off his feed. The GP conducted a thorough examination, noting that the temperature was normal, and that there were no signs of infection in the ears nose or throat. Urine examination by dipstick failed to demonstrate infection. The GP made a diagnosis of viral infection but advised the mother to return in the event of the child worsening or failing to improve within two days. Unfortunately, about three hours after this consultation the child became unrousable. The parents took him to the casualty department where it was found that he had a non-blanching rash. (This is a rash which does not disappear when seen through glass pressed against the skin). A diagnosis of meningitis was made and penicillin commenced immediately, but notwithstanding this rapid treatment the child continued to deteriorate and, sadly, died. The NHS Health Authority held an investigation into the actions of the general practitioner, but it was found in that his history taking and examination had been reasonable in the circumstances, given the natural history of the progression of meningitis. The parents also sought legal advice but were advised that the difficulties of litigation would probably cause considerable additional stress and would in any event achieve little by way of damages. Nothing can compensate for the death of a child.

As well as stroke or infections, the structure of the nervous system may also be affected by a variety of different pathological 'shocks'. Alcohol may produce death of the neurones – another example of the crossover between neurology and psychiatry. Heavy metal poisoning (lead, mercury and arsenic) will also produce neurological symptoms of mental disturbance as well as numbness or weakness. Neurodegenerative conditions include multiple sclerosis, where the myelin sheaths of nerves break down, probably due to an immune response. The old name for multiple sclerosis was disseminated sclerosis – the condition being disseminated both in time and space. This meant that any part of the nervous system may be affected, producing weakness, sensory change or psychiatric problems or a combination of all of these; in addition, the condition may relapse and remit. Diagnosis should be suspected when a combination of otherwise unexplained neurological symptoms arises. The final diagnosis must be made by referral to a neurologist.

**Case report**
A 45-year-old lady consulted her general practitioner because of tingling in her hand. After careful examination the doctor advised that this was due to carpal tunnel syndrome – compression of the nerves at the wrist as they pass into the hand. He advised her to return if the condition did not resolve. The condition did resolve, but six months later the patient returned with numbness in one foot. Again a careful history and examination confirmed the numbness, which the doctor thought may have been due to posture. After a third consultation some months later, this time where the patient

said her grip had weakened, the GP made a referral to a neurologist. The neurologist was unable to reach a diagnosis but kept the patient under review. When he saw her three months later she had extensive numbness and investigation showed that she did in fact have multiple sclerosis. The patient went to her solicitor (who had previously been responsible for her house conveyance) saying she wished to sue the GP for not making the diagnosis earlier. I advised that the GP had followed a course which would probably have been followed by many other responsible GPs, and had made a referral in reasonably good time. I also pointed out that the neurologist, too, had failed to reach an immediate diagnosis. I privately advised the solicitor (so as not to distress the client) that causation would be negligible because her condition was in any event untreatable. Unfortunately, both the patient and the solicitor (who had no clinical negligence experience) were able to understand this and it was only after protracted conferences and correspondence that the patient was persuaded to let the matter rest and concentrate on coming to terms with her condition.

*Comment*: This unfortunate case illustrates the difficulty faced by GPs (and patients) with some transient neurological conditions. MS is of course a devastating illness in many cases and one can understand the patient's anxiety, which led her to blame the doctor. This case also illustrates the inadvisability of seeking legal advice in clinical negligence cases from a non-specialist solicitor.

PSYCHIATRY – THE DOCTOR'S JOB

The above cases involved serious neurological disturbance but all, to a greater or lesser extent, had ramifications extending to the patient's mental health. The possibility of mental illness should be borne in mind at every new consultation, because many conditions can present as mental disturbance. Conversely, mental illness can cause the patient to produce symptoms which may be unrelated to any physical pathology. For this reason the doctor should always try and determine if the patient has a mental disorder and if so which. If a psychiatric problem is suspected the doctor should assess the patient's emotions and attitudes and establish effective communication. The history taking will be governed by the presenting complaint but the background to mental health problems should include information as to occupation, home situation, family history (particularly of psychiatric illness) and personal history including difficulties such as current alcohol use, and abuse or violence in childhood. The mental health examination should include assessment of appearance for signs of self-neglect, the speech for spontaneity and logical content, the mood for depression or over-elation and the patient's perception including the possibility of hallucinations. Sophisticated tests may sometimes be used for intelligence assessment or, particularly in general practice, a brief screening questionnaire may be employed to check for depressive illness. An assessment should be made of the patient's insight into the understanding of his or her illness and possible need for treatment.

CLASSIFICATION OF PSYCHIATRIC CONDITIONS

As shown by the above cases the distinction between psychiatry and neurology may be blurred, but as a rough approximation many psychiatric conditions will be due to a learned response with no discernible pathology at tissue level. These conditions are usually considered as:

- Neuroses.
- Psychoses.
- Affective disorders.
- Personality disorders.

**Neuroses.** Most people know what they mean when they say someone is neurotic or "a bit over the top". The term is often used disparagingly but is actually fairly close to the 'official' psychiatric term. Broadly, it means that someone is acting in a way that is much exaggerated in terms of the response, but is at least based on rational principles. For example, someone with acrophobia – a phobic neurosis of heights – is at least basing their fear of heights on the rational supposition that they may fall and hurt themselves. Most people would agree that this reaction is completely different from, say, somebody who was psychotic and did not like heights because this put them at greater risk of being taken over by aliens. Neurosis may arise in many situations but for medico-legal purposes we may consider three important ones, namely pain disorder, anxiety and post-traumatic stress disorder.

**Pain Disorder** deserves careful consideration. This is because 'pain' itself is not a predictable sensation, but may vary according to the experience of the sufferer. By way of example, imagine two situations: Firstly, you are on holiday in a remote country. You are captured and held to ransom. You are told that in an hour your captors will return with a video camera to take a film of you being hit across the shins with a stick. The film will be sent to your family to encourage payment of the ransom. The second situation is that you are captaining your hockey team in the final. You run across and score the winning goal, just as a defender hits you across the shin with his stick. Consider these two imaginary scenarios. The actual blow with the stick is identical, but on reflection most people would agree that in the first situation it will be far more painful. In other words, pain is not a fixed quantity. This principle is important when considering legal claims, because the degree to which pain may be disabling is dependant very much on the circumstances of the sufferer. At one extreme, the claimant's circumstances may give rise to a situation somewhat cynically termed 'compensationitis'. This may be unfair on the claimant because someone who has a personal injury claim is not necessarily *pretending* to be in greater pain. A more accurate term is compensation neurosis, which is a description of the clinical situation of genuine victims of a medical accident whose recovery process is being complicated by litigation. These people are not liars. They genuinely *are* in greater pain because of the neurotic component of their pain. It may be very difficult to disentangle the essential component of the pain from the superimposed effect of the circumstances. It is by no means unknown for the defendant to produce expert psychiatric evidence to the effect that a large component of the claimant's pain is 'functional', with the implication that it should not count towards damages.

**Anxiety** is another type of condition which may give rise to neurosis. What is anxiety? One definition is simply an increased awareness of problems in the sufferer's environment which need to be solved. Problem solving is, of course, the basic function of any thought process in the sense that information comes in, is processed, and a plan of action determined. It is convenient to call the incoming problems 'stress'. While some people use the term stress to describe an unpleasant situation, a moment's thought indicates that if we have no stress at all life becomes intolerably boring. A certain amount of thoughtful activity is necessary for normal mental health, but if the stress gets past a certain point either in quantity or quality then we become anxious. The sensation of anxiety is really a warning system, to keep us on our guard. In times of heightened stress – with its implication of impending danger – a sense of anxiety is a valuable safeguard. Unfortunately, however, the human mechanisms for dealing with stress are thousands of years out of date. Consider the stress imposed on primitive man. He is in his cave with a fire burning and hears the cry of a woolly mammoth as it appears out of the forest. He has a choice either to run or to try to kill the animal. This is the basis of the 'fight and

*Anxiety*

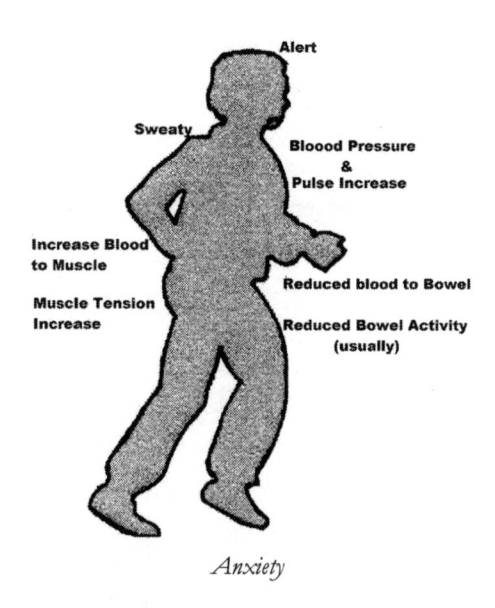

- Alert
- Sweaty
- Blood Pressure & Pulse Increase
- Increase Blood to Muscle
- Muscle Tension Increase
- Reduced blood to Bowel
- Reduced Bowel Activity (usually)

flight' reaction. It is mediated by adrenaline and related chemical transmitters. This causes the familiar bodily processes to enter the anxiety state, including increased wakefulness, increased pulse and blood pressure, sweating, tightening of the bowels and increase in the respiratory rate. All these are preparation for instant action. The problem in the twenty-first century, of course, is that stress very rarely requires intense physical activity as its solution – no matter how worrying the Income Tax demand, violence is unlikely to provide a solution. The reactions to anxiety are often likely to cause more harm than good in the form of blood pressure and increased heart attacks. We are considering mental health here, however, and the effect of repeated stress in causing anxiety may lead to an anxiety neurosis, whereby even the slightest stress may promote an exaggerated anxiety reaction. Anxiety itself can be disabling, but is often a precursor to frank depressive disorder (see below).

**Post-traumatic Stress Disorder** (PTSD) is a relatively new diagnosis as neuroses go. It is found more often in lawyers' offices than in doctors' consulting rooms. It is a neurosis caused by exposure to extreme stress, and causes the patient to react in typically abnormal ways. To make the diagnosis of PTSD the trauma should have been severe and violent. The manifestations of the disorder include recurrent vivid flashbacks of the situation, often with exaggerated consequences. Signs of anxiety may predominate, or may progress to frank depressive illness with severe withdrawal. Another important feature in making the diagnosis is that long after the event the individual will (quite irrationally) take steps to avoid the site of the incident, often taking a long detour to bypass the area where the trauma occurred. When genuine post-traumatic stress disorder has occurred it is a significant and disabling condition. The diagnosis does, however, require the criteria outlined above as determined by a psychiatrist. Lawyers' attempts to claim compensation for PTSD after what amounts to no more than a nasty surprise on the part of the client are generally viewed with some scepticism.

**Case report**
A 20 year old Swedish girl was a student at the Slade School of Art (a Department of University College London) in 1942. Her house was bombed during the Blitz. Although she was not physically injured she was severely traumatised mentally, her condition being diagnosed in those days as 'shell shock'. She was admitted to Friern Barnet psychiatric hospital – then known as Colney Hatch lunatic asylum. She stayed there for 30 years. At this point, allegedly because of an enlightened treatment plan but in reality to save money, moves were made to rehabilitate patients in her condition and move them into the community. This was done with various forms of therapy, including art therapy. Most patients in this situation produced childlike scrawls. Miss Jensen (her real name) produced paintings to match those of the Impressionists, some of which now grace my home. After this prolonged period of institutionalisation it was not possible to move the lady into the community. She died some years later.

**Affective Disorder.** *Depressive* illness is the commonest mental health problem encountered in general practice and not surprisingly is frequently encountered when considering medico-legal issues. A patient who has suffered a medical accident may well end up not only with the consequences of the accident itself, but with the addition of depressive illness. It is worth considering the mechanism of this because the pathology here is more complex. The classic psychiatric approach to depression was to consider the condition is having two different causes, one 'endogenous' and the other 'reactive'. An endogenous depression would occur with no apparent reason, although there was often a family history. The reactive depression occurred as a result of repeated stressful life events. The underlying pathology in these two types of depressive illness may at first sight appear very different, but it is possible that there is a common underlying cause. This is the amount of neurotransmitter at the synapses. Any thought process starts with a stimulus being provided to the brain – but this can be a requirement for a decision. The clinical effect here is the application of stress. Provided it does not progress to anxiety neurosis (as discussed above), or on to frank depression, then stress is a normal reaction. Most of its effects, however, prepare the body for 'fight and flight' and represent an appropriate reaction in Stone Age man. Unfortunately, the 21st century threat consists of a disciplinary warning at work or a demand from the Inland Revenue. Fight and flight is inappropriate here (or at least futile!) but the physiological response remains the same. If this requirement for 'processing' becomes too great, it is probable that the neurotransmitters responsible for the thought processes become depleted. To return to the previous analogy, the computer crashes. This causes the patient to desist from active thought, and ultimately to desist from any further action, resulting in withdrawal. A depression results. Incapacity due to medical mismanagement will come into the same category. Protracted litigation and the possibility of having to give evidence in court may also produce long-term stress which again can lead to frank depressive illness. Clinically, depression consists not merely of feeling sad. It may also take the form of fatigability, lack of energy and loss of libido. Physical illness may also occur including muscle pain and an alteration in bowel habit – irritable bowel.

**Case report**
A 58-year-old man, known to have been a smoker for many years, attended his general practitioner because of a persistent cough. The general practitioner noted the smoking history and the cough. He conducted careful physical examination but could find no abnormality in the chest. He appropriately ordered a chest x-ray. The radiologist reported the chest film: "there is a 2 cm area of increased density in the right upper lobe. Malignancy cannot be excluded." Based on this report, the GP informed the patient that he was suffering from lung cancer, that the lesion was inoperable, and he was suffering from a terminal condition. The patient (who had also considered this possibility) went away and put his affairs in order, giving away a considerable amount of money and quitting his job. Several weeks passed during which, not surprisingly, he became significantly depressed. Then the cough improved and the patient did not feel at all ill. He re-attended the general practitioner who, this time, sent him to a chest physician. After investigation it was determined that the abnormal finding on the chest x-ray was in fact benign and likely to be the result of a previous infection. The patient sought advice about bringing an action against the general practitioner on the basis of inappropriate diagnosis and false information. The patient had suffered considerable financial loss and he had also become significantly depressed. He based his claim on both these causes of injury. The claim was eventually settled without going to trial, albeit for a relatively small sum on the basis that he was advised that a Court would not look favourably on a claim by a patient because he did *not* have cancer.

*Comment*: The GP in this case had clearly made an error. Misinterpretation of the x-ray result may have been a genuine misunderstanding on his part but there is also the possibility of *schadenfreude* – described by some people as 'playing God'. His inappropriate advice had caused an intolerable amount of stress which spilled over into anxiety and then reactive depression. From the patient's point of view, in addition to his financial losses there was also a significant depressive element, not surprisingly directly attributable to the mismanagement on the part of the general practitioner.

Treatment of patients with depressive illness is usually carried out in general practice, not least because of the large numbers of patients requiring help. As mentioned previously, depressive illness is sometimes categorised as reactive or endogenous. The above case clearly describes a reactive depression which occurred purely because of stress and anxiety which in this unusual situation had been directly caused by the doctor's misdiagnosis. Once the error had been discovered the patient was provided with some counselling and within a short time his mental state, if not his finances, had recovered. In other cases, however, severe *endogenous* depression may occur in a patient who has, apparently, no stress or anxiety. The depression occurs out of the blue. In these situations it is also likely that there is an abnormally low concentration of transmitter substances. (The concentration may also be abnormally high, as in bipolar illness). On questioning the patient there is often a family history and it is likely that the abnormality is inherited. With this variety of depressive illness the patient will usually benefit from medication. The treatment object here is to redress the chemical imbalance. Antidepressant medication allows the re-accumulation of transmitter substances and can be very effective even in cases of severe endogenous depression.

Because of the possible different circumstances in which depressive illness may occur, the treatment methods are sometimes described as 'talk or tablets' as if the treating practitioners had to choose one or other alternatives. In practice, every patient must be assessed on his or her merits and the treatment provided accordingly.

**Case report**
A 35-year-old single lady, new to the area, attended her general practitioner at the time of her registration. She had previously suffered from significant endogenous depression and had been prescribed long-term antidepressants by a consultant psychiatrist. The consultation got off to a bad start when she introduced herself as Ms Smith (not her real name). The doctor retorted that she did not recognise that title, and she should choose between Miss or Mrs. Not surprisingly, the patient (who was at the time treated successfully with the antidepressant) responded somewhat angrily. The doctor then conducted a medication review and noted the antidepressant medication. Although the notes were available, including correspondence with the recommendation from the consultant psychiatrist, this GP declined to issue the antidepressant and told the patient that she did not need it. One week later the patient experienced severe suicidal thoughts. She retained sufficient insight into her condition to ask for help (from a different doctor) and was immediately admitted to a psychiatric hospital where she stayed for three weeks, having been restarted on antidepressants. Fortunately, she was restored to her former healthy mental state but had been exposed to significant risk by the action of the general practitioner who had failed to establish an appropriate rapport, failed properly to assess her mental state and failed to heed the previous history with the clear requirement for continuing antidepressant medication. Perhaps sensibly, the patient recognised that legal action would probably produce more stress than it would be worth and restricted her response to changing to another practice.

**Psychosis.** Psychosis is quite different from neurosis. It is the term we use when we think that people are, in common parlance, 'completely mad'. The main characteristics of patients who are psychotic are that they suffer from delusions and hallucinations. Hallucinations are the sensation of receiving some sort of sensory input which does not exist. These commonly take the form of hearing voices but visual hallucinations can also occur. Such hallucinations are not exclusive to psychosis and can also occur in organic conditions, as discussed below. Delusions, as distinct from hallucinations, are false ideas. The sufferer in this situation does not merely think he is Napoleon, he knows he is! All his actions are based on the delusion. Although the effect can provoke black humour, if the patient has a delusion to the effect that he is being persecuted then he may react appropriately – for him! Such paranoid delusions form the basis of one form of paranoid *schizophrenia*, and can be very dangerous for those around the sufferer. *Schizophrenia* is a form of psychosis but unfortunately it is a much misunderstood term, largely because of the incorrect use of the word in an American film made in the 1950s called The Two Faces of Eve. The term schizophrenia was used for Eve's split personality, which is actually a rare form of neurosis. The word has unfortunately stuck. The real meaning of schizophrenia, however, is not much clearer, because it comes from two Greek words meaning fractured diaphragm. The ancient Greeks thought that as the diaphragm was in the middle of the body (which it is), it must be the centre of the thought processes (which it certainly is not). When the thought processes became disturbed as in someone who was seen as mad they said this was because the diaphragm was broken. Hence the term. The causes of schizophrenia are not known, but one component thought to play a strong part is the learning process known as double binding. This may occur when, in childhood, a parent or other role model repeatedly tells the child to do one thing but by body language or other signals clearly implies a request to do something else. Schizophrenia is actually quite common in society. One manifestation is the 'simple' schizophrenic who has very little social function. Such people become tramps and bag ladies, and are among the most unfortunate individuals in society as they tend to be ignored by the support services. Other forms of schizophrenia depend on whether the illness is based on hallucinations, delusions or changes in affect.

**Case report**
A young general practitioner, new in his post, was asked by the district nurse to visit an elderly lady who was on long-term Modecate, but had declined her monthly injection which was due that day. (Modecate is a major tranquilliser used in the treatment of psychotic illness). The GP introduced himself and succeeded in establishing good relations. Mental state examination revealed a fully orientated patient with normal speech and awareness and no abnormal thought. The practitioner concluded that there was no justification for compulsory treatment under the Mental Health Act but arranged to visit again a month later. On the second visit the patient again greeted the practitioner politely, and initially entered into what appeared to be a normal conversation. Shortly after this, however, she apologised for entertaining the doctor in the kitchen, explaining that although they had been in the sitting room before this was now being invaded by laser beams from the neighbours and she did not want their conversation overheard. After some persuasion the lady agreed to resume her injections, after which the laser beams subsided.

*Comment*: This case illustrates some of the legal difficulties surrounding the management of mental illness generally, and compulsory treatment in particular. Forcibly to restrain a patient and give them an unwanted injection would be held by many to be a serious infringement of human rights. Unless there was a good reason it is unlikely that the provisions of the Mental Health Act would be fulfilled. On the other hand, stopping medication in some schizophrenic patients has led to innocent third parties being murdered. At present, there is no satisfactory solution in every case.

**Personality disorders.** *Personality* refers to individual differences in characteristic patterns of thinking, feeling and behaving. Characteristics such as introversion/extraversion, tolerance/intolerance, pessimism/optimism and so on, are of course present in all individuals in varying degrees. There is no clearly defined point at which an individual's personality can be described as a disorder, but from a practical point of view individuals with personality disorders such as narcissism and paranoia do not fit well into society. It is unfortunate that although an individual may sometimes be persuaded to alter his or her behaviour, the underlying personality remains. Because the personality determines behaviour, including criminal behaviour, personality disorders may be responsible for extremes of violence. From a medico-legal point of view this situation may cause occasional tragic consequences, because while a patient may be admitted for compulsory treatment the paranoid personality (which by definition is untreatable) is considered not to justify admission under the provisions of the Mental Health Act.

**Organic Disorders.** As well as psychiatric conditions arising from learned responses, there is also a group of organic illnesses affecting the brain and causing detectable pathology. These may present as mental health or learning issues. This broad group ranges from children who are brain-damaged at birth to those who suffer from dementia in old age. It may also include abuse of drugs or alcohol.

> **Case report**
> A 64 old lady was admitted to hospital under the care of the maxillofacial surgeons. She had sustained facial injuries after a fall and the casualty officer thought that she smelled of alcohol. On examination her voice was slurred and she appeared generally uncoordinated. It was determined that any further treatment would be postponed until the (presumed) effects of the alcohol had worn off. The next day

however, she remained confused and uncoordinated with slurred speech. She did not smell of alcohol and a tactful search of the area in the ward failed to reveal any bottles. It was only at this point that the senior surgeon appeared on the ward round. He took one look at the woman's eyebrows – which were thinned – and enquired of his juniors: "Have you checked the thyroid function?". Sure enough, the thyroxine levels were found to be almost unmeasurable. The lady had not been drunk – her apparent mental state confusion was due entirely to hypothyroidism which rapidly responded to treatment.

*Comment*: A constant theme throughout the failings quoted in this book is the failure to consider a differential diagnosis. This applies as much in hospital specialties as in general practice. It also applies to psychiatric and neurological conditions to the same extent as in any other illness.

The brain has a high energy requirement and functions only if supplied with glucose and oxygen. Deprivation of either for more than a very brief period can cause irreversible changes in the neurones. The time of birth is fraught with hazards, and oxygen deprivation during birth is likely to be the cause of retardation as a result of perinatal anoxia (lack of oxygen at around the time of birth). Brain tissue is almost unique in being unable to repair itself. Any damage still present by about six months after the accident is, to all intents and purposes, permanent. Such patients exhibit a wide range of learning difficulties, from the mild case where the child may not quite reach the likely genetic potential, to the more extreme case where the individual is completely dependent and incapable of leading a life on his own. Claims for brain-damaged children can result in awards of several millions of pounds and will be vigorously contested by the doctor's or Health Authority's representatives.[2] The frequent defence is that birth is, itself, a hazardous process. In order to prove liability (fault) the claimant must show that there was a departure from standard practice.

The successful claim will depend not only on establishing liability on the part of the hospital practitioners, but also demonstrating the degree of disability which has resulted, and proving that the disability was a result of the negligence.

*Degenerative change* may occur in the brain as in other tissues. Even in the absence of insult or trauma from drugs many people will gradually lose their memory. Indeed, the age of maximum intellectual capacity is about 19 years, the age at which most individuals in the developed world start university education. After this it is downhill all the way! Cerebral deterioration in old age is partly the result of degeneration but may also be influenced by heredity. The process is likely to be continuous. Alzheimer's disease, once diagnosed, is irreversible. The condition is unlikely to be associated with doctors' negligence, although there may be controversy surrounding medical opinion in support of disability allowance.

*Alcohol* plays an important part in Western society. Because alcohol is partly fat soluble, it influences the way nerve impulses are transmitted along the neurones in the brain. It is actually an inhibitory substance, but by 'inhibiting the inhibitions' it may give rise to a feeling of well-being. When used in this way in moderation it is unlikely to cause harm but if used regularly and to excess it can lead to dependence. This occurs when the chemical processes within the brain adapt to function in the presence of alcohol. Unfortunately this adaptation leads to a situation in which the brain cannot function adequately without alcohol. The patient has become alcohol dependent – an alcoholic. This in itself is not obviously or immediately incapacitating, because the patient may have learnt to live with a high level of alcohol and may indeed function at an acceptably high level. There is, however, a risk that the tissues may decompensate, with either liver disease or physical deterioration of the brain. Within limits, alcohol use is not only tolerated but considered normal in

Western society. The amount of alcohol consumed should be a standard part of a doctor's history taking in all but the most trivial conditions, since excess may affect many different parts of the body. Alcohol abuse may occur in depression. Such abuse is usually a *symptom* of depressive illness and is only rarely a *cause*. The clinical effects of alcohol abuse can include early dementia or liver failure due to cirrhosis or liver cancer. The 'morning pink elephants' as seen in the delirium tremens of alcohol withdrawal are the subject of occasional, if misplaced, humour. Physical effects of alcohol outside the nervous system include peripheral neuropathy and bleeding from the gastrointestinal tract (oesophageal varices).

*Illicit drugs* cause effects similar to those of alcohol. Psychotropic drugs change the way the brain works, often producing a temporary feeling of elation. Unfortunately this use can lead to habituation. Such drugs may actually cause less physical damage than alcohol (one of the spurious reasons advocated for the legalisation of cannabis) but may, nonetheless, cause changes in behaviour. Unlike alcohol the use of these drugs is considered antisocial and while the doctor may suspect their use, direct questioning on the matter is sometimes avoided – with occasional unfortunate consequences.

In summary, disease of the nervous system may come to the attention of doctors either as neurological or psychiatric problems, and sometimes both. Particularly in the case of psychiatric conditions, there is often a tendency to treat the patient as if their illness is in some way different. This can lead to errors, and the traditional steps of history taking examination and consideration of differential diagnosis are still the only safe route to patient care.

REFERENCES

1. J. V. McConnell *J. Neuropsychiat.* 3 (Suppl 1). S42 1962

2. Montgomery v Lanarkshire Health Board. UK Supreme Court 2015 [11]

Chapter 10

# CARDIOVASCULAR SYSTEM – THE HEART

The heart and circulation are together known as the *cardiovascular* system. They function as a single unit within the body but for descriptive purposes and when looking at doctors' mistakes, the heart will be considered as presenting its own problems, and the vascular system (blood vessels) will be considered later in its own chapter.

SUMMARY OF CARDIAC CASES

During a ten year period there were fifteen cases acute coronary syndrome (heart attack or threatened heart attack). All of these involved culpable negligence. There were three cases of cardiomyopathy (abnormality of the heart muscle) none of which was found to represent negligence. There were two cases of missed endocarditis (infection), where the doctor was found to be in error.

When looking at the heart for medico-legal purposes (or even for general interest) we must consider structure, function and

Cardiovascular System – The Heart

abnormalities – anatomy, physiology and pathology. We can then look at the clinical side of things (medicine and surgery).

**Anatomy and Physiology.** The anatomy of the heart was probably known long before its exact function. In popular folklore the heart was considered to be the centre of passionate emotions. This is probably because it was known to speed up in times of emotional stress. So what does it look like? The heart is roughly the size and shape of a large avocado pear sitting in the left side of the chest. The lining of the heart, in contact with the blood, is called the *endocardium*. The walls consist largely of muscle. You can feel the apex (the pointed end) as it beats, to the left centre of the chest. Like any sizeable muscle the heart has its own blood supply. This comes from the *coronary* arteries – so called because the ancient anatomists noted that these arteries encircled the top of the heart like a *corona* (Latin for crown). The heart is divided into left and right sides. Each of these sides has two separate pumping chambers one after the other, firstly the atrium and then the ventricle.

Heart muscle is unique in that, unlike skeletal muscle, it has a tendency to contract spontaneously. It also has a specialised conducting system to synchronise a wave of contraction. The pumping action is performed by the muscular walls of the heart which contract in systole and relax in diastole (pronounced sistolly and die-ass-tolly). These terms are important because they are also used to describe the phases of the blood pressure. A pump will work if it contracts against a valve. The valve allows one-way movement only, so that the repeated contractions cause an onward movement of fluid – in this case the blood. Considering the heart as a pump there is one valve for each chamber. Each side of the heart plays a different part in the circulation, with the right side of the heart pumping all the blood through the lungs and the left side pumping the blood through the rest of the body.

Beginning at the right side of the heart and following the order of the circulation, the valves are as follows:

- The *tricuspid* valve is between the right atrium and the right ventricle.
- The *pulmonary* valve is between the right ventricle and the pulmonary arteries. The blood then goes through the lungs and back to the left side of the heart.
- The *mitral* valve is between the left atrium and the left ventricle.
- The *aortic* valve is between the left ventricle and the aorta – the main output vessel to the body tissues. The blood returns from the body to the right atrium and the process starts again.

**Pathology.** Problems may occur with the lining, the valves and the muscle. The lining may be subject to bacterial infection, *endocarditis*. The valves can undergo degenerative change causing them to stiffen up or leak, causing valvular *incompetence*. The muscle may be affected by poor blood supply if the coronary arteries have *atheroma*, a waxy substance causing the arteries to narrow. Like any other muscle the heart muscle is subject to *ischaemia* if the coronary arteries have developed atheroma. The causes of atheroma are described later in the section on circulation. The muscle may develop other abnormalities (myopathy) which in the case of the heart is, not surprisingly, called *cardiomyopathy*. The individual fibres of the heart muscle contract spontaneously, but in order to produce the pumping action the muscle must contract in a coordinated fashion. The conduction system within the heart is responsible for this regular rhythm. This rhythm can be disturbed from a variety of causes and if this happens the situation is described by the Greek word, *arrhythmia*.

These are the main features of the pathology (things that can go wrong at tissue level) in the heart. So what effect can this pathology have on the patient? It will produce the symptoms of which the patient complains and the signs which, it is to be hoped, the doctor may find when he examines his patient. We can now consider the clinical presentation of this pathology.

**Cardiac ischaemia.** The most important cause of heart disease, certainly in the Western world, is build-up of atheroma in the coronary arteries. This may appear in clinical notes variously described (and abbreviated) as *coronary artery disease* (CAD), *coronary heart disease* (CHD) or *ischaemic heart disease* (IHD). These all mean the same thing – the blood supply to the heart is being compromised. *Angina* is often the first symptom of coronary artery disease. The full clinical description is 'angina pectoris', literally from the Latin 'squeezing of the chest'. The pain from cardiac angina is the equivalent of cramp in the leg muscles in peripheral vascular disease. It is a crushing central chest pain, often radiating to the left shoulder, the jaw or down the left arm. This is the classical description, but unfortunately many patients do not conform to the description. Some may have no pain at all, or only a vague discomfort until some crisis occurs. The central chest pain may radiate downwards into the epigastrium – the part of the abdomen between the lower end of the sternum (breast bone) and the navel. Occasionally the pain may only be felt as a radiation, the central chest pain being absent. Thus, for example, it may occasionally happen that a patient with angina first feels pain in the jaw – dentists beware!

> **Case report**
> A 67-year-old man was walking to a local bingo club. It subsequently transpired that this was the only form of exercise he took. It was also, later, apparent that there was a strong family history of heart disease. While hastening on his way he was observed to collapse. An ambulance was called but he was pronounced dead on arrival at the local hospital. Because he had not seen a doctor for some time a

post mortem was ordered by the coroner. It was found that there was moderately pronounced atheroma within all the coronary arteries, but that one of the coronary arteries had become completely blocked. A section of the atheromatous plaque had come away from the wall of the artery and was lying across the lumen (interior), forming a complete blockage and causing a blood clot to form.

*Comment*: Although there was no clinical negligence involved, this case is quoted here because it is, sadly, all too common. There may be no sign at all of extensive coronary artery disease, particularly in a patient whose coronary blood supply under normal circumstances (that is, not exercising) is apparently adequate.

Clinically, angina is described as stable or unstable. Stable angina is the equivalent of claudication. It comes on with effort and dissipates once the effort has ceased. This is because there is still some remaining flow within the coronary arteries and the products of the muscle metabolism, which are responsible for the pain, are gradually flushed out. It may be helped by the application of nitrate, often in the convenient form of glyceryl trinitrate spray. This allows the coronary arteries to dilate. By way of contrast, unstable angina may be unprovoked. It will last after the cessation of exercise and does not usually respond to application of nitrates. The presence of either type of angina is indicative of heart disease and requires urgent investigation. Angina itself is painful but not fatal; it does however point to the presence of atheroma. The risk here is that blood clots may also develop on the atheroma, or the plaques of atheroma may break off and lie across the vessel. This may produce a sudden complete blockage of one of the arteries – the fuel line is closed completely. In this situation the heart muscle, which depends on the regular flow of blood, becomes deprived of its nutrients. This is what happens during a *heart attack*.

# Cardiovascular System – The Heart

**Heart Attack: Myocardial Infarction.** There are several possible results of a heart attack. Firstly and most seriously, the damage to the muscle may cause an instant arrhythmia called *ventricular fibrillation*. All the muscles fibres contract independently, rather than being co-ordinated. A fibrillating heart looks like a bag of worms. Not surprisingly the pump produces no output. The patient will die in about two minutes, because there is no blood flow to the brain, unless the random muscle contractions can be stopped and allowed to start again in a proper co-ordinated way. This is the reason for giving an electric shock to a patient who has had a heart attack. Defibrillators are now becoming commonplace in many public places – the deficiency probably now lies in the small number of people trained to use them. If fibrillation does not occur, or if the fibrillation is treated, the heart muscle does not 'die' immediately. It can manage without a blood supply for about an hour. Emergency treatment in this situation is to unblock the artery by the so-called 'clot busting' drugs. Provided the patient can be got to hospital or a trained paramedic quickly enough the injection of streptokinase or a similar product can make all the difference between a scarred heart and one which sustains little or no permanent damage. If the clot remains then after about an hour the muscle dies and becomes 'stuffed' with inflammatory cells – infarction literally means stuffed. If this happens the dead muscle may rupture, usually about ten days after the event. The patient undergoes fatal failure as the blood pours from the hole in the ventricle and compresses the heart from the outside – a condition described as cardiac tamponade. The best result possible once an infarct has occurred is that the damaged muscle will form a scar, after which the patient may live for many years.

**Infection: Endocarditis.** Although atheroma – essentially, a degenerative process – is the commonest type of pathology within the heart, the tissues are also susceptible to infection. This is relatively rare, because the heart is plentifully bathed in blood containing white cells and these will keep infection under control. The parts of the heart which have a less generous blood supply, the valves, are more at risk of infection. This is particularly common if there is a predisposing condition which has damaged the valves. In the days before antibiotics, when rheumatic fever was quite common, the mitral valve often became inflamed and was susceptible to infection even after recovery from the rheumatic fever. A further problem occurs in patients who have an artificial valve. These valves are particularly vulnerable because of course they have no blood supply internally, relying only on the blood flow going past. If these patients get endocarditis it is usually because of a combination of factors, firstly the predisposing condition and secondly the presence of bacteria in the blood, *bacteraemia*. Even a cut or graze may allow bacteria to enter the circulation. A complicated childbirth may be a cause. Dental problems are another, and a patient with a known problem with the heart valves should be treated with care when dental extractions are undertaken; this may involve the administration of a single high dose of antibiotic just before the extraction. Patients with endocarditis will usually feel ill and have all the symptoms of a fever due to the circulation of bacteria and toxins in the blood. They may not complain of obvious heart symptoms such as shortness of breath or palpitations because the heart may be functioning relatively normally. They may, however, have a detectable murmur due to blood flow turbulence over the damaged valve. Blood tests will reveal the usual signs of infection – raised white count and high ESR. The blood may then be cultured for bacteria. A patient with endocarditis is at considerable risk, not only because the valve may be gradually destroyed, but because clumps of infected material (described as vegetations), may break off into the circulation, blocking small vessels within the brain and causing strokes.

Although endocarditis is rare, and indeed very much less common than it was in the pre-antibiotic era, it is so important that no doctor should fail at least to think of it. A patient presenting with an unexplained fever and who has a history of heart problems should be examined for murmurs, and if necessary blood tests should be taken to assess for inflammatory markers and cultured for bacteria.

**Case report**
A 38-year-old man was a keen athlete, participating in long distance running with his local club. He had been born with a slightly defective aortic valve and as he approached middle aged the decision was taken to replace this with an artificial one. The operation went well, and he was able to resume his former running activity. A few months later however he attended his GP saying that his exercise tolerance had suddenly decreased. He was also complaining of night sweats (a sign of fever) and feeling generally unwell. The GP attributed this to long-term effects of the operation and to 'stress'. Examination revealed a noisy heart valve but this was to be expected because the valve had been replaced with an artificial one. No other tests were undertaken. It was only after several weeks had elapsed that the patient attended the local hospital where routine blood tests revealed a significant inflammatory response, suggesting that blood cultures should be undertaken. These were positive. Further investigation revealed that the artificial heart valve was malfunctioning and requiring replacement. The case went to Court. There was a significant difference of opinion between experts. The expert retained by the claimant's legal team suggested that the GP should have undertaken blood investigations. The expert retained by the defendant doctors suggested that there was no logical reason to do this, and that a responsible body of opinion would not have undertaken blood tests; the court accepted this opinion. One GP, however, had been told of the night sweats and flushes that the patient was undergoing. The Court found that

investigation and referral should have followed on the basis of this information and this GP was liable. Causation was established on the basis of information from the cardiologist. The patient was awarded a significant sum representing the discomfort and loss of amenity due to the requirement for further cardiac surgery, together with a smaller sum for loss of earnings.

**Heart Failure.** Failure occurs when the heart and circulation cannot maintain the requirements of the body chemistry. If the heart is unable to pump enough blood through the lungs, then carbon dioxide builds up and the patient becomes short of breath on minimal exercise or even at rest. Back pressure from the left side of the heart causes fluid to seep into the air spaces of the lung, causing coughing. Failure affecting the right side of the heart causes a gradual accumulation of fluid within the tissues, and in an ambulant patient this will naturally be the lowest point, usually the ankles and particularly towards the end of the day. In severe cases of failure this ankle oedema (swelling) can be as high as the knees. Heart failure is really pump failure and can be due to a number of causes. These may be a direct effect of the cardiac muscle (as in cardiomyopathy) or to loss of tissue due to cardiac infarction. Another important cause of failure is leakage or blockage of the valves, where the heart is contracting adequately but the flow is not maintained either because of obstruction or back flow. A certain degree of heart failure may simply be due to degenerative change, particularly in elderly patients, and is relatively common. If diagnosed it can be treated with medication. Diuretics stimulate urine flow and decrease the load on the circulation and may be used in urgent treatment of failure. **A**ngiotensin-**c**onverting **e**nzyme inhibitors (ace inhibitor medications have names ending in –opril such as captopril) have revolutionised the treatment of heart failure. They work by reducing the salt content and hence the volume of the blood in the same way as a diuretic. They also reduce the tension in the muscles of the medium-diameter arteries, allowing improved flow.

In order to treat the patient with heart failure, however, the condition must first be diagnosed. Ankle swelling towards the end of the day is so common that many doctors would consider it physiological. A patient presenting with a cough may (negligently) be diagnosed with a chest infection. In patients who are non-smokers and who do not have other clinical evidence of chest disease an infection should be regarded as a rarity. Careful auscultation (listening with a stethoscope) will reveal abnormal breath sounds (crackles, 'crepitations') particularly at the lung bases. This is a sign of failure and not infection. Treatment is with cardiac medication and not antibiotics.

An abnormality of the heart which may be associated with failure is *atrial fibrillation* (AF). Ventricular fibrillation has been discussed already. The causes of atrial fibrillation may be poor coronary artery circulation, damage to the mitral valve, or abnormalities of the thyroid gland. Excess alcohol intake is another cause. In all these cases it is not, however, primarily the loss of pumping action which is the source of disability. AF is not fatal and if properly managed the patient may lead a normal life. The fibrillating atrium has relatively little effect on the total cardiac output, but because there may be parts of the atria where the blood flow is static there is a tendency to form clots. If these clots then break away and are pumped into the circulation they may cause stroke or pulmonary embolus. For this reason patients with atrial fibrillation should be put on medication to slow the heart in an attempt to control the arrhythmia. It is also important to reduce the tendency to form clots by giving warfarin or some other medication to reduce the tendency to form clots. Patients on warfarin are subject to the complications of the drug – it is also used as rat poison – and have to have regular tests. Warfarin dosage must be adjusted very carefully to maintain the international normalised ratio (INR) between 2.5 and 3.5. This means that the blood will take between two-and-a-half and three-and-a-half times longer to clot than normal blood. If the INR falls below 2.5 the patient is at risk from clots forming in the fibrillating atrium. If the ratio rises much above 3.5 there is a risk of bleeds, particularly haemorrhagic stroke. For this reason doctors should be very clear as to who has the responsibility for supervising the warfarin dose, and should take urgent action particularly if the target INR is exceeded.

**Case report**
A 56-year-old man required a prosthetic aortic valve. The surgery was performed without incident, but it was recommended that because artificial valves can promote blood clots the patient should be provided with anticoagulants with an INR between 2.0 and 2.5. Regular testing was performed at the GP's surgery with variation in warfarin dose. The patient was also, intermittently, tested at the local hospital and because he found this more convenient he requested the GPs to pass the control of his warfarin dose to the local haematology department. This was declined. The GPs had difficulty in keeping the patient at the right level, and for about 12 months the average INR was around 1.6. He then suffered a blood clot, resulting in partial loss of vision. It was found that, particularly in view of the difficulty of controlling the INR the GPs should have requested further input from the local haematology department.

More recently the pharmaceutical industry has developed anticoagulant drugs which require less monitoring. It is likely that problems with warfarin will become a thing of the past.

DIAGNOSIS IN PATIENTS WITH CARDIAC DISEASE – THE DOCTOR'S JOB

**History.** Patient complaints suggesting heart disease classically include swelling of the ankles, shortness of breath, and palpitations. Heart disease is not always obvious, and indeed the doctor must be aware that other, apparently unrelated, complaints may be due to problems with the heart. As mentioned above, a patient with a cough may not have a chest infection – he may have heart failure. Conversely, a patient with oedema of the lower limbs may not have heart failure – he may have a surgical problem such as a mass within the pelvis causing back pressure on the veins. History taking should always be done with a broad differential diagnosis in mind. Once the patient has recounted the complaint from his own point of view, the doctor must elaborate on this by asking direct questions. For example, a patient complaining of chest pain may need prompting before he says that this occurs principally when he is climbing stairs. This is an indicator of exercise-induced angina, whereas chest pain on coughing may be due to a pleurisy infection. Another patient may volunteer that he only gets the chest pain when eating curry, and that he can cure it easily with a proprietary indigestion preparation – an indicator of gastritis rather than significant cardiac disease. Even so, the history alone cannot be relied on for eliminating serious or life-threatening conditions from the differential diagnosis.

**Case Report**
A 56 year old lady, known to be a smoker, presented to her GP with chest pain for the second time in a week. He recorded: – "Chest pain but better with analgesia. Chest clear, Abdo soft, no masses generally tender. On examination heart sounds normal. No cardiac murmur. Respiratory system examined no apparent disorder". At a further consultation two days later he recorded: "has worked out that pain is brought on by food and aspirin so prescribe and advise Lansoprazole capsules, Gaviscon Advance."

This was the last record of the general practitioner consultations. The next entry in the notes was dated two days later stating that the patient had died. Post mortem examination had shown a blood clot in the coronary arteries. In this case, although the history pointed to indigestion, the doctor had not taken reasonable steps to discard coronary artery disease from his working diagnosis. A simple blood test for the products of blood clotting (troponin) and an ECG would probably have allowed intervention early enough to save her life.

**Examination.** The first basic examination to be done is measurement of the pulse rate and blood pressure. Blood pressure (BP) varies with age. The systolic and diastolic figures represent the peaks and troughs of what is actually a wave form, representing the higher level just after the heart has contracted and the lower level when it has finished filling and just before it is ready for the next stroke. The technique of blood pressure measurement is discussed in the chapter on circulation. There is no 'ideal' BP. In terms of preventing damage to the arteries, the lower the better, provided the patient has enough blood circulating in the brain to prevent fainting. As a rule of thumb 150mm systolic should not be exceeded but some elderly patients need a systolic blood pressure higher than this to keep them conscious or stop them having a stroke. The lower, diastolic, figure should usually be 90mm or less. The British National Formulary(1) has a recommended schedule for management of blood pressure. Any doctor who persistently allowed his patient to maintain blood pressures significantly higher than those recommended in the Formulary would be open to criticism if he did not attempt to intervene and an expert could well advise the Court that he had fallen below an acceptable standard, amounting to negligence.

One problem with measuring the blood pressure is that the measurement itself may cause it to rise – a phenomenon that is sometimes described as white coat hypertension. The effect of this can largely be eliminated by use of 24-hour monitoring, where the patient wears an automatic blood pressure cuff attached to a recording device. The intermittent blood pressure is recorded over a period of time and assessment of possible hypertension can be made with a fair degree of accuracy.

The pulse rate is normally around 60 beats per minute (bpm). Most doctors will feel the pulse and if it is around this figure then it may just be described as normal. If it is obviously very slow (below 40) or very fast (100 or more) then the rate should be checked with a watch and recorded. Cardiologists may also describe the character of the pulse, variously described as a 'slow rising' or 'water hammer' but this cannot reasonably be expected of the average general practitioner. While checking the pulse (usually by feeling the radial artery at the wrist) the doctor should check for finger clubbing. This is a sign indicating chronic (long-term) oxygen deprivation to the tissues and causes swelling of the ends of the fingers, which lose the angle between the nail and the nail bed. Clubbing occurs in lung disease as well as heart disease.

Where heart disease is suspected it is of course important to listen to the heart — although it has to be said that the first use of the stethoscope is in measuring the blood pressure. The bases of the lungs may collect fluid in left-sided heart failure. This should be detectable as crackles — described as crepitations, and usually abbreviated to 'creps' in the notes. This should be checked by listening at the lower part of the chest. Valve disease will usually cause turbulence and this should be detected by a reasonably competent general practitioner as a murmur. Students are taught the various fine points of describing a murmur in order to reach a diagnosis, but in general practice anyone with a murmur should be sent to a cardiologist. Precise diagnosis at primary care level, while perhaps intellectually satisfying, is not critically important. What is important is that a patient with a murmur who is generally feeling ill or complaining of night sweats should be suspected of having endocarditis, in which case urgent referral is mandatory.

**Investigations.** A patient suspected of having had a heart attack should be sent to hospital straightaway, but a GP may save some time by taking a blood sample. Myocardial infarction may cause an area of damaged heart muscle which releases a protein called troponin which can be detected in the blood. Urgent situations apart, what tests may be helpful in the early detection of coronary artery disease? One relatively simple investigation is measurement of the electrical effects of the rhythmical contraction of the heart muscle – an *electrocardiogram* or ECG. Most GP surgeries now have the facility to do ECGs. The tiny current produced by the heart muscle may be picked up by placing electrodes on the skin and putting the signal they detect through an amplifier to produce a trace of the wave. A resting ECG is helpful in established cases of myocardial infarction or ischaemic heart disease. A resting ECG is not, however, reliable in patients who are complaining of intermittent cardiac symptoms, notably chest pain. This is because if the heart is not under stress then the electrical changes associated with ischaemia will not be apparent. A doctor who relies on a resting ECG taken in his surgery to eliminate the possibility of ischaemic heart disease is negligent. The appropriate ECG test in patients suspected of suffering from cardiac ischaemia is the so-called treadmill or exercise test, where the patient is put through a graduated series of exercises while connected to the ECG machine. The test is done in hospital under supervision and with ready access to resuscitation facilities should these be required. Characteristic changes in the electrical tracing give a clue to strain on the heart.

Other hospital investigations will include an echocardiogram. This is an ultrasound investigation, does not involve any x-rays and so is non-invasive. It is useful for checking the function of the valves. Many patients are familiar with ultrasound, having seen scans done during pregnancy. Cardiac patients should also have a chest x-ray which will show the size of the heart and the possible presence of fluid in the lung.

## Cardiovascular System – The Heart

More invasively, other hospital investigations may include an x-ray of the coronary vessels themselves. This is usually referred to as *catheter investigation* or *angiogram* when a thin plastic tube (the catheter) is put into the arterial system at one of the lower limb arteries (femoral artery puncture) and run up against the flow of blood into the aorta and then into the opening of the coronary arteries. A shot of dye, which can be picked up an x-rays, is then injected into the blood supply and a picture obtained of the coronary arteries. When a patient is complaining of angina it is usually found that there is blockage of one or more of the coronary arteries.

**Case report**
A 54 year old lady, known to be a smoker, attended her general practitioner who recorded: "History: patient had episode of chest pain started 2 days ago. ?After drinking hot drink, slept well last night but awoke this a.m. and whilst brushing teeth started with burning pain across whole chest and over both shoulders, similar to indigestion and flu. Examination looks well. Chest clear. Abdo – NAD. BP 142/78. Medication Omeprazole 20mg template entry current smoker health education smoking comment does not sound cardiac but for ECG to rule out acute changes." A resting ECG was taken. The machine was equipped with automated reporting software which recorded:– "Interpretation (unconfirmed) sinus rhythm with first degree AV block anterior infarction, probably old. Abnormal repolarisation, possibly non-specific." A handwritten annotation on the tracing reads: Poor R wave progression no acute changes. File."
The patient remained ill for about 10 days but then recovered. She changed doctors and some time later had a further episode of chest pain. She was immediately referred to a cardiologist who found that she was suffering from single vessel coronary artery disease and cardiomyopathy. She required a stent, and now has significant reduced exercise tolerance.

*Comment*: It is likely that this lady had suffered at least two myocardial infarctions prior to diagnosis. The first doctor was found to have been negligent, firstly in relying on a resting ECG to make a diagnosis in acute chest pain, and secondly because he recognised that the patient may have had coronary artery disease but failed to seek a cardiology opinion which could have led to earlier treatment.

**Screening for Coronary Artery Disease.** Nowadays, many perfectly fit people have 'well person' medicals purely to see if their coronary arteries are being damaged. This is because the process is both insidious and hidden. Up until recently, the case of sudden unexpected death, as described in the first case report above, was all too common and clearly tragic for the patient's family. Successive governments have paid attention (although sometimes more with lip-service rather than action) to preventative care. These initiatives may include public health measures such as advice on diet, smoking and exercise – all factors intended to reduce the development of the underlying pathology of atheroma. As well as these general public health preventive measures, however, the individual patient may be investigated by standard screening processes. A blood test may reveal high lipids (loosely referred to as cholesterol). This test is useful in otherwise healthy people who may have a strong family history of heart disease. While many health screening programs offer an ECG, this is usually useless because the resting ECG may be perfectly normal, the muscle requiring only the minimum blood supply. This can still be adequate even in the presence of significant coronary artery disease so the electrical signal will not show the effects of ischaemia. The best non-invasive test for assessing coronary artery disease is an exercise ECG. This of course needs sophisticated resources and requires medical supervision so is not realistically available for the whole population. At present the man in the street must take his chance, but the availability of efficient screening methods for non-symptomatic people does mean that if there is any doubt at all (that is, possible signs or symptoms indicating coronary artery disease) then the GP has a duty of care. In these circumstances, in the presence of possible coronary artery disease, a GP should make a referral for further cardiac investigations and failure to do so would be seen as a breach of duty.

**Treatment of Coronary Artery Disease.** A patient with symptoms of coronary artery disease will usually have an exercise test and then a catheter X-ray – angiogram. The extent of the atheroma will then be known. At this stage the cardiologist will decide on the best treatment. Using a technique similar to the catheter approach, it is possible to insert a balloon appliance into a coronary artery to expand the arteries against the atheroma. A dilator (stent) can be left inside an artery to produce an increase in blood flow. The long-term effect of these techniques is still under research, but since the whole procedure can be done through a small incision in the groin they have considerable benefit, particularly in the elderly. Stenting and dilating procedures are known collectively as angioplasty.

More advanced treatment is by surgery for **c**oronary **a**rtery **b**ypass **g**rafting. This is abbreviated CABG in the notes. (Rather confusingly to the layman, doctors will sometimes discuss among themselves the benefits of a "cabbage"). Here, the chest wall must be opened to give the surgeon access to the heart. It is usually necessary to stop the heart and put the patient on a bypass pump, although this is not always necessary with a quick surgeon. Coronary artery bypass grafting is generally successful but is a complicated and expensive procedure. Under the National Health Service rigorous criteria are applied as to who may receive the benefit. The decision as to who may receive the treatment is emphatically not, however, a matter for the general practitioner. All patients likely to be suffering from coronary artery disease should at least be accorded the benefit of a cardiology opinion and failure to make a referral, irrespective of the likelihood of angioplasty or surgery, represents substandard care.

**Case report**
A 58-year-old man attended his general practitioner with chest pain. A resting ECG was undertaken which the GP decided was normal. The pain continued, but the patient was able to control this to a large extent by reducing his exercise activity. The patient reached retirement age and moved house, registering with another doctor. He mentioned the chest pain and was sent for detailed cardiac investigation which revealed significant coronary artery disease. The patient was subjected to coronary artery bypass grafting and the pain resolved completely. The man sought legal advice on the basis of the significant delay in diagnosis of his coronary artery disease. Expert cardiology opinion confirmed that the first general practitioner should indeed have made a referral for advanced cardiac investigation. However, the experts also advised that since the patient had not had any irreversible damage the late provision of coronary artery bypass grafting had made no significant difference to his long-term survival. If anything, it had increased it because a graft has a limited lifespan. Any damages would therefore have been limited to discomfort. The patient was advised not to proceed with the case, not least because of the expense and associated stress. He accepted this advice and litigation was discontinued.

This case is quoted to show that, even when a doctor has made a mistake, it is not always necessary, or appropriate, to pursue a claim for compensation. This applies particularly to patients with cardiac problems. The difficulties of litigation could well make the patient worse – a salutary thought for those contemplating legal action.

REFERENCE

1. British National Formulary. BMA & Pharmaceutical Society of Great Britain

Chapter 11

# CARDIOVASCULAR SYSTEM – CIRCULATION

Having considered the heart, the pump of the cardiovascular system, it is time to look at the plumbing – the arteries and veins which carry the blood round the body. Here too there is unfortunately plenty of scope for medical accidents to occur.

SUMMARY OF VASCULAR CASES
There were nine cases of deep vein thrombosis (clots). It was found that doctors were in error in all these cases. Problems occurring less frequently were temporal arteritis (inflammation of the arteries) involving three cases. There were two cases of overdosing with anticoagulant medication, both involving errors. The remaining cases involved isolated episodes of more unusual conditions. Nonetheless, even unusual conditions are diagnosable if proper consideration is given to the presenting symptoms. A common thread running through the errors was failure to consider a differential diagnosis to include possible urgent and dangerous conditions, rather than simply those which were most likely.

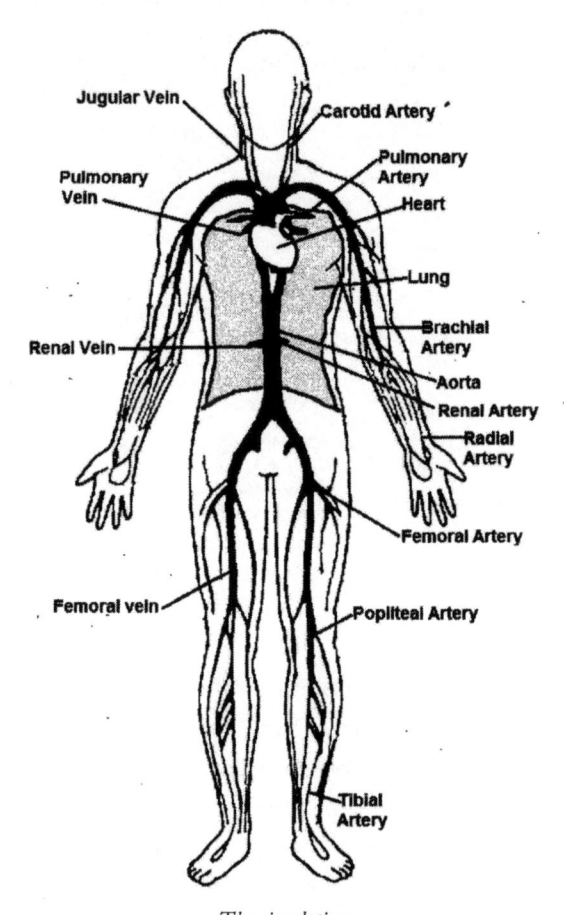

*The circulation*

To get an understanding of the background of these cases, look at the basic science of the blood vessels, and the blood within them.

**Anatomy.** *Arteries* carry blood away from the heart. *Veins* carry it back. Large vessels throughout the body have names. The names refer to the area of the body the vessels supply, and are often rather obscure but they appear from time to time in medico-legal reports so the more important ones are worth noting. These are the aorta itself, the carotid arteries up to the head and brain, the renal arteries to the kidneys and the femoral arteries to the legs. From the arteries, the oxygenated blood passes into smaller vessels, the arterioles. It then passes into the very small vessels that actually supply the tissues – the capillaries.

As may be expected, the arteries (which are high pressure vessels) are thick walled and elastic. Between the named arteries and the capillaries lie the arterioles. These vessels are not simply passive hollow tubes. They have muscles in their walls. These muscles can contract and relax, changing the diameter of the vessels and therefore their resistance. The veins are large vessels but have quite thin walls because they are not normally required to carry blood at high pressure.

The *blood* itself consists of the formed elements (cells) and the plasma (fluid part). The formed elements arise in the bone marrow. The most plentiful are the red cells which carry oxygen. White cells also circulate throughout the system. The white cells provide body defences as part of our immunity (ability to attack bacteria, viruses and other foreign substances). The blood also contains small fragments of cells called platelets which assist in clot formation.

*Plasma* is a slightly sticky yellowish fluid. It contains many different proteins. Of these proteins, albumin is found in the greatest concentration. Other proteins take part in the clotting process, resulting in the final clotting protein, thrombin. Antibodies constitute a further important group of proteins in the plasma. The fluid also contains dissolved salts, principally sodium and potassium, and all the products derived from the diet: glucose, products from digested protein (amino acids) for rebuilding the body, and fat. In addition to food products the blood carries low concentrations of control agents for different body functions. These are referred to collectively as hormones and are an important way of ensuring that the body reacts as a single unit under varying circumstances. The blood also carries dissolved waste products, principally urea, which pass through the kidneys to be removed in the urine.

**Physiology.** To understand the circulation it is useful to consider the two sides of the heart as separate pumps. As explained the last chapter the blood is pumped by the right side of the heart to the lungs. In the lungs it collects oxygen and gives up carbon dioxide. The blood then passes from the lungs to the left side of the heart from which it is pumped into the aorta and so through the rest of the body. The heart and lungs are connected one after the other or 'in series' as electricians would say, with the two sides of the heart pumping the blood round as a continuous circulation. This continuous flow is really just a transport system. Although different parts of the body (organs) perform different tasks the same basic life processes have to take place in all of them. Nearly every cell in the body needs energy-rich fuel in the form of glucose. This combines with oxygen to produce energy, with carbon dioxide as a by-product. The glucose may come direct from the intestines where it has been absorbed, or the liver where it is stored. This means that there has to be a transport mechanism between the liver in the abdomen and, say, the muscles which moves the big toe which are obviously nowhere near the abdomen. After passing through the capillaries where the exchanges take place, the blood goes into the veins and then back to the heart to be pumped round again.

**Blood Pressure.** Most people have a vague idea of what blood pressure is and are aware that having high blood pressure is considered a bad thing. Many people also know that low blood pressure can cause a faint. So what does it actually mean in scientific terms, and how is it measured? The first attempts to measure blood pressure were done by poking a glass rod into the carotid artery of an unfortunate horse and holding the end up to a height (about 9 feet) to assess the pressure in this large vessel. This method does not, however, recommend itself to blood pressure measurement in humans — not least because the measurement could only be done once! Fortunately, it is possible to measure the blood pressure indirectly. The large arteries have elastic walls which may be compressed from the outside. This is done with an inflatable rubber cuff connected to a column of mercury. Mercury is chosen because it is a fluid about 14 times heavier than water, and so we do not need such a long tube to provide the necessary pressure. A 300 mm column of mercury can be accommodated in an instrument contained in a portable box. This column of mercury can provide the same pressure as a column of blood over 4 metres high. By connecting the column of mercury by a rubber tube to a cuff round the arm the pressure inside the cuff can be measured in millimetres of mercury. The pressure is gradually increased by pumping more air in from a rubber bulb acting as a simple pressure pump. By raising the pressure to the point where the cuff compresses the artery we effectively have the pressure inside the artery, but measured indirectly from the cuff round the arm. The point at which the artery is compressed is found by applying a stethoscope and listening beyond the cuff, and waiting for the disappearance of the sound made by the flowing blood.

The highest blood pressure reading occurs when the heart has just contracted and the aorta is full of high pressure blood. This is systole and the high point of the blood pressure is called the *systolic*. The aortic valve then closes and pressure in the aorta is gradually released as the blood flows round the body. Some pressure is still maintained, however, because of the elastic walls of the aorta and other large vessels, and the blood pressure will only fall to a certain point during diastole, maintaining the *diastolic* blood pressure before the heart contracts again. Both systolic and diastolic blood pressures are important, and the difference between them (called the pulse pressure) is also significant.

What should 'normal' blood pressure be? The systolic pressure must be enough to keep the blood flowing, but not so high as to damage the vessels – usually up to 150mm. The diastolic blood pressure should be less than 90, and preferably around 80mm. The blood pressure is usually recorded in the notes by putting 2 digits separated by a slash, e.g. 150/90. This convention is universal. The digits may be preceded by the abbreviation "BP" but are often not labelled as the entry of the digits is self-explanatory. Blood pressure is so important that anybody examining medical notes for legal purposes should immediately be able to recognise not only a blood pressure entry but also to assess whether it is too high or low.

**Clotting** is a complex and important physiological process. In addition to obvious damage because of trauma it is important to realise that the vascular system consists of fragile vessels which requires constant attention to repair potential leaks. The process allows clot to form in any damaged area. A clot consists of platelets surrounded by a mesh of thrombin. It will prevent further leakage from the system until the vessel repairs itself with the appropriate protein, initially collagen, and the final lining of the vessel in the form of the endothelium. In other tissues such as bone or skin the clot is, in due course, removed and replaced by similar tissue. The clotting process is often overlooked when considering the physiology of the blood, but is in fact a highly dynamic system, consisting of constant clot formation and clot removal.

**Pathology.** Although vascular disease is hugely important in terms of morbidity in the population, the pathology (*i.e.* the things that can physically go wrong) of the blood vessels is relatively straightforward. They are like any other piece of plumbing:

they can either get worn, burst, or get furred up. In the arterial system the pathological equivalents of these plumbing disasters are inflammation (*vasculitis*), *aneurism* (bursting), or *atherosclerosis* (furring up). It is also important for doctors to remember that a clot in the wrong place – a *thrombosis* arising in the vessels – can do as much damage as no clot at all.

**Vasculitis** simply means inflammation of the blood vessels. The cause is often unknown but the underlying pathology may be infection or an abnormal immune response. It may be generalised and if it occurs it commonly affects the temporal arteries. Temporal arteritis is relatively unusual in general practice, but nearly all doctors who have undertaken a junior post in surgery will have been involved in temporal artery biopsies and so the diagnosis is not so obscure as to be a rarity. If it is missed, it is because Dr Botchup has simply made a 'best guess' diagnosis in a patient with a headache on the basis that common things are common, rather than considering the signs and symptoms and casting a wider diagnostic net.

### Case report
A 59-year-old man started to develop pain in his head together with a sore throat and pain up the side of his face and up around his ears. He consulted his GP who recorded : "upper respiratory tract infection not otherwise specified. Sore throat symptoms. Congested throat, otherwise OK. General advice". The pain continued and at a second consultation the GP wrote: "sinusitis. Pain moved from throat to sinuses and ears. On examination ears waxy, temporal arteries pulsatile, throat no apparent disorder. Prescribed amoxycillin". There were then three further consultations, after which a chest x-ray was ordered. This was normal. Further antibiotics were prescribed. The patient telephoned for further advice, because the pain had now been going on for four weeks. The GP recorded: "facial pain persist, especially cheeks – no nasal

congestion – abdo upset with antibiotics. Advised take 250 4 times a day rather than 500mg bd. Continue Paracetamol, if not better ?for investigations or refer". The patient again telephoned the surgery and the GP recorded: "still pain in face, temp on and off for past few weeks". The consultation record with the GP noted: "as above. bilateral maxillary sinus pain improved at present". The remaining three lines of the record were then devoted to the government requirement for clinical data collection under the doctor's contract. The GP then requested blood tests including inflammatory markers. The ESR was 109mm/hour (normal up to 12mm!). The plasma C reactive protein was 61mg/l (normal up to 5mg!). The next record says: "Discussed results. Still temp, intermittent. Doesn't feel any worse, still appetite less than normal. Check immunoglobulin and photo electrophoresis... raised ESR... plasma C reactive protein high". No referral was made and no treatment provided. The blood tests were repeated. Three days later the patient awoke with blindness in his right eye. He immediately contacted the surgery and was advised to contact the eye unit at his local hospital. The consultant ophthalmologist wrote back to the GP saying "the history of his temporal arteritis and monocular blindness is striking. It seems that he didn't have the classical scalp tenderness but had jaw claudication and then lost vision". The case was indefensible and was settled for a large sum.

*Comment*: the ophthalmologist was being charitable here. It is unlikely that the GP had even checked for scalp tenderness. The underlying problem was that he simply did not think of temporal arteritis. While unusual, it is sufficiently serious to be on the radar. As soon as the results of the inflammatory markers was known, instant action could have saved this man's eye.

**Aneurism** occurs when the artery starts splitting between its layers and then bursts. An aneurysm in the arteries of the brain may be responsible for the sudden and often devastating subarachnoid haemorrhage. An aneurysm may occur in any artery, but the aorta, being the largest vessel and subject to high blood pressure is particularly at risk. In days gone by, before the advent of antibiotics, the sexually transmitted disease syphilis particularly attacked the arch of the aorta. Soldiers who had survived the First World War but been unwise in their choice of companion while in France were particularly unfortunate in this respect. The abdominal aorta, however, remains vulnerable. The final event in an abdominal aortic aneurysm is a torrential bleed into the abdominal space with inevitable death. This does not, however, happen immediately and a progressive aneurysm will take several hours to develop – a process described as dissection – prior to this catastrophic event. Unfortunately, many abdominal conditions including relatively benign and self-limiting infections will also present as central abdominal pain. The diagnosis of an aneurysm is made by physical abdominal examination including palpation. If this is not performed then the doctor is negligent.

**Atheroma** is an abnormal waxy substance which forms on the inside of arteries. It has already been mentioned because of the problems it causes in coronary arteries, but it can occur anywhere. Atheroma is so important clinically, and has such significant medical and medico-legal consequences, that the pathology needs to be considered in some detail. Although it was known for a long time that the coronary arteries of elderly people had a certain amount of blockage in them due to atheroma, the extent of this pathology was not recognised until the Vietnam War. This was the first conflict in which large numbers of dead soldiers were subjected to post mortem examination. Many of them were in their late teens or early 20s. They were Americans, plentifully supplied with cigarettes and raised on a diet rich in fatty hamburgers. Atheroma was found to be almost universal, although at this age still in its early stages and otherwise undetected – except at post mortem. As the patient gets older the atheroma becomes more

| | |
|---|---|
| • Family history | • Diabetes |
| • Smoking | • Obesity |
| • Hypertension | • Animal fat diet |
| • Hyperlipidaemia | • Lack of exercise |

*Risk Factors for Atheroma*

severe and elderly patients may have extensive atheroma which becomes calcified, causing a narrow stiffened vessel which allows very little blood to flow.

What are the reasons for development of this dangerous substance? The table gives a list and it is worthwhile considering some of the important features. Firstly, consider genetic predisposition. If a doctor is concerned about the possibility of heart disease – as he should be in any patient with, for example, chest pain – he should ask about *family history*.

A doctor should also give his patient lifestyle advice if it is known that he has a poor family history of cardiac disease, stroke or peripheral vascular disease. The contract for general practitioners in the United Kingdom provides that lifestyle advice should be given to patients at risk of coronary artery disease. The lifestyle advice is based on reducing the risk for the development of atheroma – which in turn reduces the risk of clogging up the coronary arteries and therefore acute coronary syndrome.

*Smoking* is one of the most dangerous (and avoidable) activities indulged in by the inhabitants of the so-called developed nations. The tobacco companies are now concentrating their sales efforts on the Third World nations. Smoking tobacco causes a number of illnesses. The first to be recognised of these, and the best known, is lung cancer. Most patients who smoke will not, however, die of lung cancer because they will die of heart disease first. Consider the development of atheroma. The arteries are at high pressure with droplets of fat floating in them. One function of the cells lining the artery is to stop the fat getting pumped in between the cells of the lining. If the cells do not function properly because they have been poisoned by carbon monoxide in cigarette smoke there is an increased tendency for the atheroma to develop. From a clinical negligence point of view a doctor who allows his patient to remain in ignorance of the dangers of smoking is falling below an acceptable standard. The doctor cannot of course directly intervene to stop the patient smoking but he should inform the patient of the risk, and ensure that a record of the advice appears on the notes.

*Hypertension* and blood pressure measurement is discussed above. If a patient has too high a blood pressure then the tendency for the globules of fat to be forced in between the cells of the vessel lining is increased. For this reason it is important for the blood pressure to be controlled. If a patient is at risk of coronary artery disease, either because of suspicious clinical signs and symptoms or because of known family risk factors, a general practitioner should check and monitor the blood pressure. Where necessary, the blood pressure should be controlled with medication. Evidence suggests that if the blood pressure is controlled then the risk for arterial disease decreases accordingly. A doctor who simply records a high blood pressure and then does nothing about it is almost certainly failing in its duty of care to the patient in allowing a risk factor for the development of atheroma to persist.

*NICE guidelines on hypertension*: Because of the significance of high blood pressure and other cardiovascular risks it is not surprising that NICE have published comprehensive guidelines to practitioners. The trigger for further examination and/or investigation is a single measurement of 180/90. There is then an elaborate regime for monitoring the blood pressure, with advice on prescribing antihypertensive medication. At the same time GPs are recommended to address other cardiovascular risk factors – in effect the risks for the development of atheroma – particularly in the realm of public health in a state where healthcare must be met from the public purse. The Guidelines state: *"For all people with hypertension: test for the presence of protein in the urine by sending a urine sample for estimation of the albumin:creatinine ratio and test for haematuria using a reagent strip. [Offer to] take a blood sample to measure plasma glucose, electrolytes, creatinine, estimated glomerular filtration rate, serum total cholesterol and HDL cholesterol, [offer to] examine the fundi for the presence of hypertensive retinopathy, [offer to] arrange for a 12–lead electrocardiograph to be performed."*

In the UK, the 2004 GP contract introducing the quality of outcomes framework (QOF) made similar provisions. GPs wishing to claim additional fees under the scheme are obliged to keep a hypertension register. Target blood pressures are set, and GPs should provide the screening recommended in the above NICE guidelines.

*Hyperlipidaemia* is a three-part Greek word which simply means too much fat in the blood. This can either be because of a family trait or because the patient eats too much fat in the first place. Often it is a combination of both. The fat is found as cholesterol or as lipoproteins – molecules formed of fat and protein. The low density lipoprotein presents the highest risk. Lipids can easily be measured by taking a sample of blood from a vein and sending it to the laboratory. Most information is available if the blood is taken when the patient is fasting – therefore best done first thing in the morning. It was previously said that a cholesterol level below about seven units was normal, because it was about average. It is now recognised that even this level is dangerous – the average is too high! In patients who exhibit symptoms suggestive of arterial disease, or in patients who are at risk either because of the family history or other risk factors, a doctor should measure the lipids. If it is found that the lipids are high, there is a wide range of medication available, and indeed lipid lowering medications are now the basis of a multi-million dollar pharmaceutical industry. Failure to treat an abnormally high lipid level would almost certainly represent substandard care. This is particularly important in patients with familial hyperlipidaemia, where such treatment may be life-saving.

*Diabetes* is an important contributing factor to atheroma. Like tobacco smoke, diabetes is another cause of malfunction of the cells lining the blood vessels. In diabetics the cells do not work properly because they do not have access to the energy for their normal function – the lack of insulin prevents proper metabolism of glucose. Even though the blood outside the cells may be rich in sugar it cannot pass into the endothelial cells which function below their optimum and may allow fat build-up to occur. Diabetics who smoke hit the arterial lining twice over and rarely live to collect much of their pension. (The Chancellor wins twice over – first all that tobacco tax, and then no pension to pay out!) In addition to causing atheroma diabetes also affects the small vessels. This is particularly significant in the feet. Diabetics are (or should be) given detailed advice on foot care including regular chiropody. A further complication of diabetes, in addition to circulation problems, is that it affects the nerves. This peripheral neuropathy means that the in addition to having a poor blood supply the feet may be numb or at best lacking in sensitivity.

*Obesity, poor diet and lack of exercise* as a cause of atheroma may be considered together. Obesity is a risk factor of its own (irrespective of the cholesterol measurement) probably because having your own fat readily available means there is a ready source of lipid to get into the circulation and block up the arteries. The diet is obviously important and the type of fat (animal fat or vegetable fat) is probably one of the reasons why coronary artery disease is much rarer in southern parts of Europe where olive oil is used in cooking, compared with northern parts of Europe where the diet is rich in animal fat. Lack of exercise also contributes to atheroma, probably because it contributes to obesity and also because regular stimulation of the arteries is an aid to reduction in the build-up of the disease process.

**Thrombosis.** So far the emphasis on pathology of the vessels has concentrated on the arteries. However, it is the veins which cause the most trouble in terms of medical accidents involving misdiagnosis. The principles of abnormal clot formation were first described by the German pathologist Virchov, who in his day was sufficiently important to have a statue erected in his honour in Berlin. The statue is still there. 'Virchov's triad' describes the three factors necessary for abnormal clot formation: stasis, abnormal constituents of the blood, and abnormalities of the vessel wall. Blood flow is slowest within the venous system and it is therefore not surprising that this is a frequent site for abnormal clot formation, particularly in the large veins of the lower limb. Veins which have previously been inflamed (phlebitis) are more vulnerable. The combined contraceptive pill alters the constituents of the blood. Although the effect is relatively small it is significant because it can potentially affect millions of healthy young women. Stasis may occur in the veins due to lack of exercise. This is particularly important in bed-bound patients and it is estimated that up to 15% of all post-operative patients may sustain a deep vein thrombosis. Many of those will remain undiagnosed. In these patients the clot will be lysed (dissolved) with no untoward effects but if the clot enlarges then a part of it may break away and lodge in the lung. This pulmonary embolus can cause severe disruption to the blood flow within the lung and is potentially fatal.

CLINICAL ASSESSMENT OF CIRCULATION PROBLEMS –
THE DOCTOR'S JOB

One problem confronting a doctor faced by a patient with signs or symptoms in any given area of the body is to consider whether the pathology may be arising from the blood vessels – which are obviously present everywhere – or whether the problem is in other tissues in that particular limb or organ. The case quoted above where vasculitis caused a headache is an example. The history and examination must be influenced by this consideration.

**Peripheral vascular disease.** The arteries outside the heart – the 'peripheral' vessels – are subject to atheroma in the same way as the coronary arteries. The arteries of the lower limb are particularly vulnerable. Atheroma may affect the popliteal arteries and femoral arteries (see the diagram on p.202). The condition will progress insidiously and if severe may be accompanied by calcification of the vessel walls. This will produce reduced blood flow in the vessels and hence ischaemia. The muscles are starved of oxygen and lactic acid accumulates. This initially results in a clinical picture known as *claudication*. (This term was presumably first used by some clinical commentator with a classical bent who had in mind the Roman Emperor Claudius who walked with a limp). A patient complaining of pain in the legs should be closely questioned regarding the details. The characteristic picture of someone who claudicates is a smoke-stained middle-aged or elderly man who can walk only a few metres – certainly less than fifty – and then stops because of pain in his legs. After a rest he is able to continue. As the condition worsens the tissues can no longer recover even with rest. The patient may find that he is more comfortable if he sleeps with his leg hanging outside the bedclothes. The clinical picture now reveals a lower limb which is **p**ainful **p**ale **p**ulseless and **p**erishing with cold. This alliterative aide memoire should be within the knowledge of any competent clinician, and indicates advanced disease.

If the patient's history suggests peripheral vascular disease the doctor should examine the limb with particular attention to the pulses. The femoral (groin) pulse should be detectable in all but advanced cases. The popliteal pulse (behind the knee) and the posterior tibial and pedal pulses (ankle and foot) should also be palpated. Absence of these pulses is a strong indicator of vascular disease. Investigation of peripheral vascular disease can be done using Doppler ultrasound and district nurses are trained to use this technique. Any patient with signs or symptoms of peripheral vascular disease should be referred to a vascular surgeon for consideration of bypass grafting. Failure to make such a referral would be negligent in all but the most exceptional circumstances.

**Stroke.** This has been discussed in the section on nerves. The vessels within the brain are subject to the same pathology as any other vessels and may develop an aneurysm or atheroma, with the clinical consequences of either a bleed (haemorrhagic stroke) or a blockage (ischaemic stroke). Either will cause parts of the brain to die and this may leave the patient with permanent movement disabilities, loss of speech and possible mental impairment. An ischaemic stroke is usually so obvious (the acronym 'f.a.s.t.' applies) that even the least competent doctor should recognise it, and should then get the patient into hospital. A haemorrhagic stroke, however, may present without any immediate neurological signs – simply as a severe headache. It can happen without warning and the underlying cause may be an aneurysm which suddenly gives way, causing a subarachnoid haemorrhage. As described in the section on nerves, the important feature of the history here is the sudden onset.

In cases of stroke the risk factors for the underlying pathology may have legal significance because the stroke may have been preventable. In particular, persistent and untreated high blood pressure may be a causative factor and if it can be shown that the doctor responsible has ignored this then he may well be held liable for the development of the stroke.

### Case report
A 48-year-old senior executive was required to have a medical by a new company he was joining. His blood pressure was recorded at 190/100. The doctor told him he had high blood

pressure, advising him to see his general practitioner for a re-check, but at the same time reassured the executive that this was probably "white coat hypertension". The executive took the job, but three years later had a severe haemorrhagic stroke. It was discovered that his blood pressure had been high at the medical and his family brought a case against the company doctor. The doctor's defence organisation defended him on the basis that he had been employed by the company with whom he had a contract, and had no duty of care to the patient. This argument was dismissed by the Court, but it was held that the doctor's advice to the applicant to see his own doctor allowed him to fulfil his duty of care. The claimant lost the case.

*Comment*: This case illustrates the danger of reassuring patients when the opportunity has arisen for detecting an abnormality. In this case, dismissing the hypertension, or at best, providing reassurance as to its significance, was an error. Although a single high blood pressure reading should not be used to institute treatment it should certainly prompt a programme of regular surveillance. A further interesting aspect of this case was the judge's finding with relation to duty of care to the patient as well as the doctor's employer.

A less severe form of stroke occurs when the ischaemic episode is only temporary. Hence the term *transient ischaemic attack* (TIA). The underlying cause is the same as for full-blown ischaemic stroke, that is, a blood clot building up around atheroma in the arteries of the brain. The difference is that the blood clot dissolves within a few hours and the patient recovers. The preventative measures are therefore the same – stop smoking, do not drink too much alcohol, have a healthy diet, get your blood pressure checked and take exercise. A patient who has consulted the doctor and been advised they have a transient ischaemic attack should certainly be given the above advice. The doctor should also check for atrial fibrillation (a small clot may develop in the fibrillating atrium and go through to the brain). A blood test should check for cholesterol and as always the blood pressure should be checked, and controlled if necessary.

**Deep vein thrombosis (DVT).** The signs of lower limb deep vein thrombosis are pain in the leg, accompanied by swelling and reddening. The start may be insidious and the patient may attribute the problem to minor trauma. The doctor must, however, remain acutely aware of the possibility of a deep vein thrombosis and any patient with lower limb pain, particularly in the absence of significant trauma, should be assumed to have a deep vein thrombosis until proved otherwise. A DVT is diagnosed with Doppler ultrasound, but cuts in the health service have meant that although the diagnosis needs to be made urgently the means for investigation may only be provided intermittently. This is clearly regrettable; in practice the problem is overcome by assuming that a patient who *may* have a DVT *does* have a DVT! Subcutaneous heparin is started as an anticoagulant, to prevent an extension of the clot. The rationale is that if the treatment is necessary then it has been started immediately. When the ultrasound is done, if it turns out that there has been no DVT, then a couple of days anticoagulation will (probably) have done no harm. In practice, a doctor suspecting a patient of having a DVT is therefore obliged to administer subcutaneous heparin. In most circumstances failure to do so will be negligent.

### Case report
A 54-year-old lady was found to have osteoarthritis in her left knee and was admitted as a surgical day case for arthroscopy and washout. She was discharged the same day. Two days later she developed pain, swelling and blistering over her left leg. She contacted her general practitioner's surgery and spoke to one of the reception staff and was given a routine appointment. In the early hours of the next morning the

patient had an episode of reduced consciousness resembling a faint. Her husband contacted the Surgery at 8.00am and requested a home visit but this was declined. The patient was advised to take a taxi and attend Surgery. Before she was able to attend the Surgery she had collapsed and was taken by ambulance to the hospital. Sadly, she could not be resuscitated. She had sustained a deep vein thrombosis causing a pulmonary embolism. The general practitioner was found to be in breach of his duty of care for failing to attend, but the Court accepted a report produced by an expert instructed by the doctor's defence organisation. It was impossible to demonstrate causation because it was found in that the timings were such that the lady would have had the embolism in any event, even had the doctor seen her reasonably promptly.

*Comment*: This case illustrates the risk, always present in doctors' surgeries, of making a preliminary assessment over the telephone. As a minimum, a patient with a specific complaint should be formally triaged by clinical staff – usually a trained nurse. The case also illustrates the difficulty of the litigation process in that it is not sufficient to find a doctor in breach of his duty of care; it is also necessary to demonstrate causation of injury.

**Abdominal aortic aneurysm** may be recorded in the notes simply as 'AAA'. A patient presenting with unexplained sudden severe abdominal pain should always be properly examined; that is, lying on the doctor's couch with the abdomen exposed while the doctor carefully palpates the area. Except in very obese patients an abdominal aortic aneurysm will be felt as a large pulsatile mass. Middle-aged or elderly men, particularly smokers, are vulnerable. This is a surgical emergency and the patient should immediately be sent to the nearest vascular surgery unit. The condition is sufficiently common to warrant screening, which is done by ultrasound. Mass population screening has demonstrated that, in fact, many patients have an early aneurysm which is completely asymptomatic. It may be appropriate to monitor these but if symptoms develop, or the mass enlarges, then surgery becomes essential.

**Case report**
While on call one evening I received a request to visit a middle-aged man with abdominal pain. I was detained with another case and it was nearly an hour before I was able to attend. On arrival the patient's wife said that the pain had suddenly got worse and she had called for an ambulance. At that point the telephone rang. The call was from the hospital. The lady explained to the caller (the accident and emergency sister) that her doctor was with her. The sister asked to speak to me, and stated that the patient had died. I thanked her, and had to break the news to the patient's wife as best I could. Because I had not seen the patient for some time, and in any event no diagnosis had been made, a post mortem examination was necessary. I attended this the next morning and assisted the pathologist. On opening the abdomen there was a profuse amount of blood and it was clear that the patient had succumbed to an abdominal aortic aneurysm, which had never been suspected.

*Comment*: Although there had been a delay in attending, it is unlikely that even immediate admission would have saved this unfortunate man's life. The patient's widow accepted this, and was (perhaps unjustifiably) grateful that I had been there.

In summary, the blood vessels are present throughout the body and like any other tissues are subject to different types of pathological change. In reaching a diagnosis of some of these problems can be difficult to diagnose and are sometimes overlooked.

Chapter 12

# GYNAECOLOGICAL PROBLEMS

This part of the book looks at women's problems treated by the gynaecologist – breast pathology is dealt with in its own chapter. The female reproductive organs – the bits below the belt – are subject to a variety of pathology, not only because of the usual 'shocks' but also because of problems with pregnancy.

SUMMARY OF GYNAECOLOGICAL CASES
In the time under consideration there were twelve cases of late diagnosis of pelvic infection of which seven were found to have been mis-managed. There were four cases of ectopic pregnancy having been missed; none of these was defensible. Uterine and cervical cancer represented four cases, all of which were negligently missed. On the other hand, there were two cases of ovarian tumours, neither of which represented substandard care on the part of the general practitioner. There were two cases of coil perforations, neither of which was attributable to the fault of the operator.

BASIC MEDICAL SCIENCE

**Anatomy.** The *uterus* is a bag of muscle called myometrium. It is lined with special tissue called endometrium which changes throughout the monthly cycle. The non-pregnant uterus is about the size of a fist. The pregnant uterus is about the size of a rugby ball. The *ovaries* lie within the pelvis, at the outer end of the fallopian tubes. These arise from the upper outer part of the uterus. The *vagina* is a muscular tube passing upwards and backwards from the *vulva* and ending in the *cervix* (neck of the uterus).

**Physiology.** The menstrual cycle occurs on average over 28 days – interestingly the same duration as the lunar cycle; speculation regarding any evolutionary connection here is outside the scope of this book! The cycle is arbitrarily considered to start at day 1 when the endometrium is shed, producing the menstrual bleed or 'period'. From about day 5 the endometrium starts to proliferate again, until about day 14 when the lining of the uterus is ready for implantation of the fertilised ovum. An ovum (or sometimes more than one) is released from the ovary and passes to the uterus via the fallopian tube. As well as producing the eggs the ovary is also an endocrine gland and produces the hormones oestrogen and progesterone which act on the lining of the uterus. The ovaries themselves are controlled by hormones released from the pituitary gland at the base of the brain, follicle stimulating hormone (FSH) and luteinising hormone (LH). If pregnancy occurs the fertilised ovum becomes implanted and a placenta is formed which nourishes the foetus until birth at 40 weeks. The birth process consists of contractions of the muscular uterine wall to expel the baby through the vagina. If pregnancy does not occur – as is usually the case – then the rich endometrial lining of the uterus is shed during the menstrual period, and the process starts again. Interestingly, menstruation is relatively unusual among mammals, causing as it does a significant loss of iron in the menses with the potential for anaemia.

**Pathology.** The huge growth capability of the body of the uterus is reflected in its tendency to form tumours. Fortunately, most of these tumours are benign. The formal pathological name for them is *leiomyoma*. They are very common and usually just described as *fibroids,* although they are not strictly fibrous. They are really just enlargements of the muscular wall of the uterus and are frequently the source of abnormal or increased menstrual bleeding (menorrhagia) particularly in the older woman. Cancer of the uterine muscle (*leiomyosarcoma*) is relatively rare. The endometrium (lining of the uterus) has a high cell turnover and so is more prone to cancer, although this is still uncommon. When endometrial cancers do occur they tend to present early as an abnormal bleed, usually after the menopause.

*Cancer of the cervix.* In contrast to cancer of the body of the uterus, this is the 12th most common cancer in women in the UK, with about three thousand new cases per year. About one in three of these women will, sadly, die from the disease, accounting for about 1% of cancer deaths. There is a wide variation of incidence of cervical cancer. As in many cancers, genetics may play a part but the family history is unlikely to be greatly significant. An important cause is infection with the human papilloma virus, HPV. This causes microscopic growths on the cervix which may subsequently become malignant. This virus is spread by sexual intercourse, the incidence rising with the number of partners. This was first recognised in the 19th century by Rigonni-Stern(1) of Verona, Italy, who noticed the low incidence in Catholic nuns, who are supposed to be sexually inactive. The virus is carried on the penis, although it does not appear to cause any problems in men. There is a low incidence of cervical cancer among Jewish women, and one theory is that the preponderance of male circumcision in their (also Jewish) partners inhibits the lodgment of the virus.

The link between HPV and cervical cancer has therefore been known for many years but a programme of vaccination against the virus has been instituted only recently. Vaccination is offered to 13-year-old girls in the UK in the optimistic hope that they will be prevented from acquiring the virus before they become sexually active. The other significant public health measure, instituted in 1988 in the UK, is cervical cancer screening. The figures show that there has been a 42% reduction from 1988 to 1997, and so the NHS-implemented screening programme has been highly successful, screening the highest-risk age group (25-49 years) every 3 years, and those ages 50-64 every 5 years. The test consists of obtaining cells from the cervix for microscopic examination (cytology). This is less invasive than a biopsy but not as accurate, and a false negative report is always a possibility. Most women readily accept the test, but involving as it does intimate examination some women are reluctant. In the event of a positive cytology test, a more definitive examination is necessary. This involves colposcopy, the visualisation of the cervix through a special microscope, accompanied where necessary by cone biopsy – the removal of a section of the cervix for detailed histological microscopic examination.

MANAGEMENT OF GYNAECOLOGICAL PROBLEMS – THE DOCTOR'S JOB

**History.** This may include complaints of pain, vaginal discharge, swellings and irregularity of the periods. If the patient complains of pain, the doctor should, as always, enquire about precipitating factors – here including pain on intercourse – and attempt to elucidate the frequency and site of the pain. Vaginal discharge may be bloody or purulent (pus) indicative of infection. The doctor must take a careful history in order to distinguish an abnormal vaginal bleed from the normal menstrual cycle. In particular, if the woman is undergoing (or thinks she is undergoing) the menopause then the history of menstrual periods is important. In a postmenopausal woman a bleed must always, and immediately, be regarded as sinister and investigated. In a woman who is still having her periods it is necessary to determine the pattern of the bleed. The woman's 'normal' period timings should be established and note made of any departure from this. A complaint of discharge other than bleeding should prompt (tactful) questions regarding intercourse and the possibility of sexually transmitted disease.

**Examination.** This will be influenced by the nature of the complaint but should always include standard abdominal examination as well as any pelvic examination which may be necessary. A speculum may be used to visualise the cervix. The uterus can (usually) the felt on bimanual palpation (one hand on the lower abdomen while palpitating the vagina). Women with malignancies of the uterus or cervix will almost invariably present with vaginal bleeding. In all cases vaginal examination and bimanual palpation of the uterus must be undertaken, although this may be deferred for a few days – either until the woman has ceased bleeding, or until a longer time has elapsed than could reasonably be considered for a normal period. An abnormal intermenstrual bleed (that is, a bleed occurring between periods) with an apparently normal cervix requires investigation by ultrasound of the uterus. Bleeding from the cervix, either spontaneously or on intercourse, is a significant sign and the patient should be referred for colposcopy.

One further point about gynaecological examinations, notably where the practitioner is male, is that these involve additional legal hazards which have nothing to do with litigation for clinical negligence. This is because of the risk of accusation of sexual assault. While most women recognise the necessity for intimate examination, it must be said that such examination may be both embarrassing and unpleasant. Against this background, accusations of misconduct against the doctor may readily spring to mind. To avoid this, the practitioner should first take a careful history, being careful to maintain a 'distanced' and professional manner – no flippancy! This is particularly the case when making enquiries as to the frequency of sexual intercourse, and the number of partners – both of which may represent essential information. When examination becomes necessary the doctor should allow the patient to undress in the privacy of a curtained area and provide a sheet for temporary cover. It is a wise precaution to provide a running commentary as to the technical procedure so as to avoid any semblance of sexual interest and ensure that all manoeuvres are seen as purely clinical. GMC advice is that a chaperone should be present. While this is difficult in a busy general practice, requiring a nurse or receptionist to drop other pressing tasks, it is clearly essential in the majority of cases, particularly involving a relatively young male doctor and a younger patient. If these precautions are observed accusations of sexual impropriety will be avoided. If not, the un-chaperoned practitioner undertakes pelvic examination at his peril.

**Investigation** will also be dependent on the unfolding differential diagnosis; if infection is suspected a swab of any discharge may be taken and sent to the laboratory for microscopy and culture. If it is thought that symptoms may be due to a urinary tract infection, rather than a specific gynaecological problem, then the urine should be tested and, again, a specimen sent for microbiology. Imaging for gynaecological problems is best carried out initially with ultrasound. Some doctors' surgeries are equipped with ultrasound machines but the usual plan would be to make a referral for specialist diagnosis of suspected abdominal masses. If pregnancy is suspected the urine may be tested for human chorionic gonadotrophin (HCG). This is not as complicated as it sounds and can be done simply by testing the urine with sticks – or requesting the woman to get these herself at the local pharmacy.

*NICE Guidelines.* If *endometrial cancer* is suspected, the guidelines recommend a referral for an appointment within 2 weeks if the woman is aged 55 and over with post–menopausal bleeding. Postmenopausal bleeding is defined as *"unexplained vaginal bleeding more than 12 months after menstruation has stopped because of the menopause"*. As always, the guideline is a balance between the best clinical outcome and the resources available. In a younger woman who has had an early menopause (and there are many of these aged below 55 years) any recurrence of the bleeding should be regarded as suspicious.

In the case of *cervical cancer* the guidelines are less helpful, simply stating: 'Consider a suspected cancer pathway referral (for an appointment within 2 weeks) for women if, on examination, the appearance of their cervix is consistent with cervical cancer.'

**Treatment of gynaecological cancers.** In a woman past childbearing age, or in one who considers her family complete, tumours of the uterus and cervix are best dealt with by hysterectomy, the uterus, cervix and (usually) the ovaries being removed. In a woman with cervical cancer who wishes to have children it is possible to provide radiotherapy, although this causes significant scarring to the cervix and childbirth will almost invariably involve Caesarean section. Most tumours are benign – fibroids – but the first step is to establish this. Specialist investigation usually involves ultrasound which can detect abnormalities of the muscular wall of the uterus, and hysteroscopy (endoscopy of the interior of the uterus) to assess the endometrium. Even with benign tumours, the main problem experienced by the woman may be excessive menstrual bleeding. The bleeding may to some extent be controlled medically either by hormones or by medicine to alter the bleeding pattern, although many women may wish to opt for hysterectomy in any event.

**Case history**
A 35-year-old woman presented to her general practitioner three months after delivery of her second child. She complained of inter-menstrual bleeding. The delivery had been difficult, and she had experienced a cervical tear which had required suturing. The GP reassured her, saying that bleeding three months after such a delivery was to be expected. The bleeding persisted, occurring after intercourse which had also become increasingly painful. The doctor did a vaginal examination and took a smear, the result of which was negative. The woman was again reassured. She experienced continued intermittent vaginal bleeding for two years until she was finally referred for a gynaecology opinion. It was found that she had cervical cancer which had become locally invasive. She required surgery and radiotherapy. The radiotherapy caused complications in the form of bowel adhesions. The treatment was considered curative, but she had experienced significant amount of pain and suffering due to the additional therapy, as well as the experience of two years bleeding. She received substantial damages.

*Comment*: Persistent bleeding three months after delivery could not reasonably be attributed to the cervical tear, which would have healed within a matter of weeks. Cervical cytology is a screening test. It cannot be relied upon once a woman is symptomatic – in this case with frank bleeding. This patient should have been referred for a gynaecology opinion with colposcopy and cone biopsy two years earlier.

**Ovarian tumours**. A woman's risk of having an ovarian tumour at some time in her life is 6-7%. Two third of ovarian tumours occur in women of reproductive age. For all age groups, benign tumours are fortunately about five times more common than malignancies. A tumour may grow to considerable size before it is detected either by the woman or by her doctor, because the ovaries are suspended within the pelvis and may simply push the guts to one side, growing to a considerable size before they produce symptoms. For this reason ovarian cancer is often diagnosed only by ultrasound, sometimes when screening for other conditions. It may not necessarily have prompted previous medical consultations and late diagnosis is not invariably culpable.

*NICE Guidelines.* The guidelines for ovarian tumour reflect this difficulty in diagnosis. Urgent referral should be made if physical examination identifies ascites (fluid within the abdomen) or a pelvic or abdominal mass which is not, obviously, due to fibroids. Routine referral should be made for abdominal distension, loss of appetite, pelvic or abdominal pain or increased urinary frequency. The problem is that these features are all somewhat vague, difficult to define on history or examination, and can all be due to a variety of other conditions. There is a specific blood test for some ovarian cancers and if one is suspected, the general practitioner should take blood and request the laboratory to test for CA125. This is however not always indicative of the cancer and it may be necessary to follow the woman for some time before making a decision to refer.

**Case history**
A 65-year-old lady attended her general practitioner with a history of several months' intermittent abdominal pain. English was not her first language but the general practitioner recorded a careful history, having arranged a further appointment with an interpreter present. On abdominal examination it was found that the patient had an umbilical hernia. She was referred to the surgeons, who undertook further investigations including abdominal ultrasound, which failed to demonstrate any abnormality other than the hernia. This was duly repaired surgically, and

the patient returned to the care of her general practitioner. According to the patient (and later, her family) she continued to suffer abdominal pain, had feelings of being bloated and lost weight. She regularly attended the general practitioner for a variety of other, unrelated, conditions, an the abdominal symptoms were not mentioned in the notes. Eventually, she attended another general practitioner who organised a further ultrasound. On this occasion and ovarian mass was detected. Biopsy revealed that this was malignant. Unfortunately, by this stage it was not possible to provide curative therapy.

*Comment*: This case illustrates the difficulty of diagnosis of ovarian tumours in general, and cancer In particular. On this occasion the GPs had conducted an appropriate abdominal examination and attributed the pain to a hernia. While pain is unusual with an umbilical hernia this was also the conclusion reached by the surgeons, who undertook repair. Although the lady had continuing non-specific abdominal symptoms, it was considered that the general practitioners could not be faulted, since the patient had already been extensively investigated under the care of the hospital. Although preliminary investigations were made on behalf of the family, any case for compensation could not be sustained and the allegations against the general practitioner were dropped.

**Pelvic infection.** The ready availability of the pill led to a decrease in barrier methods of contraception – traditionally condoms. Over the last two generations there has consequently been an increase in sexually transmitted disease, STD. Pelvic infection is often (but not exclusively) caused by STD. Different organisms may be involved – N. gonorrhoea being the most notorious – but the final result is inflammation. This may cause pain and vaginal discharge. Significantly, the inflammation may cause adhesions within the tubes and lead to sterility. Perhaps understandably, in some instances where there is a vague abdominal pain, there is sometimes reluctance on the part of doctors to take a history of sexual activity and to suggest pelvic examination. This applies particularly in the case of a male doctor with a young female patient. The possibility of infection should nonetheless be considered in any female with unexplained pain or abnormal vaginal discharge. Most general practitioners will recognise this, and tactfully refer the patient for specialist care. Unfortunately this involves attendance at the clinic for genitourinary medicine, politely described as the Sexual Health Department but often referred to as the 'clap clinic'. This may further explain the reluctance both on the part of the doctor and the patient.

**Case Report**
A 21-year-old single girl, a known diabetic, attended her general practitioner who recorded: "Cervical smear test, copious amount of discharge, milky/grey in appearance, high vaginal swab culture sensitivity and Trichomonas." The smear result was reported "all cell types seen. Negative smear, actinomyces-like organisms present." Prior to this it had been noted, within the last three years, that the lady in question had had sexual contact with a boyfriend suffering from gonorrhoea, and on a subsequent occasion had also acquired a chlamydial infection. She was relying for contraception on an intra-uterine contraceptive device (IUCD – coil). The general practitioners continued to treat her, over the course of two years, with a variety of antibiotics but the vaginal discharge persisted. Eventually she was referred to a gynaecologist who immediately recognised that an unusual organism, actinomyces, was present. This had been reported to the general practitioner after the previous smear result but had been ignored. Further investigation indicated that the woman had suffered extensive tubal damage due to the chronic infection and was probably unable to conceive unless she underwent IVF.

*Comment*: This was eminently a case for specialist referral. There were at least three significant risk factors. Diabetes will always predispose to infection. It was known that the lady's lifestyle predisposed her to infection. She had an IUCD, which can harbour infection. An early referral should have been made, preferably to a genitourinary medicine clinic if acceptable, or alternatively to the gynaecology department. This was not a case where the general practitioners should have been providing treatment without expert assistance.

**Contraception and Pregnancy.** With a few notable exceptions, *Contraception* is likely to be used by nearly all women at some time in their reproductive years and often for a long time. In general, contraceptives are either hormonal, barrier, or an IUCD. All have their risks. Insertion of an IUCD may be done by general practitioners with special training. The procedure is described as mildly uncomfortable but should not be particularly painful. The depth of the uterus from the cervical os (entrance of the cervix) is measured with a sound. The coil is then inserted to the measured length. Provided this procedure is followed the insertion should be uneventful. The device is provided with threads which exit from the cervix and are visible on vaginal speculum examination. The woman should be taught to feel these threads herself, and to report to the general practitioner or family planning clinic if the threads cannot be detected. Should this happen, an x-ray is necessary to check the position of the device, which is treated to show up on x-rays. Even with appropriate technique, there is a small but recognised percentage of instances where perforation of the uterus can occur. This is not necessarily associated with undue force. Given that the burden of proof lies with the claimant, it is usually difficult to bring a successful claim for damages in the event of uterine perforation with an IUCD.

## Gynaecological Problems

**Case history**
A 23-year-old lady gave birth to her second child, and 12 weeks later attended a clinic requesting contraceptive advice. Various methods were discussed and it was decided that she should be provided with an IUCD. This was inserted by a doctor who was undergoing training in contraceptive technique, under the guidance and supervision of a more experienced doctor. The trainee made a careful note of the procedure, including the measurements produced during the use of the sound and the technique used to deploy the device. He recorded that the procedure had been pain-free. The woman returned some weeks later complaining that she could not find the threads. X-ray examination revealed that the coil was present within the abdominal cavity, having perforated the uterus. This required laparoscopic removal under general anaesthetic. The woman brought a claim against the practitioner, but an expert advised that there would have to be a demonstrable breach of protocol to show that the treatment had been substandard. The detailed notes taken by the practitioner provided a defence to the claim; this was subsequently abandoned.

*Hormonal contraception*, 'the pill', has been in use, and universally popular, since the 1960s. The early pills had a high hormone content and were found to have a small but significant tendency to predispose to clots in the veins. As discussed in the section on vascular problems, these can have serious consequences and cause potentially fatal pulmonary embolism. Although the risk is very small it should be remembered by the prescriber that the pill is given to healthy women and not to treat an established medical condition. The only pathology in this situation can arise from the 'treatment' itself! The safety requirements are therefore stringent. The lowest dose compatible with contraceptive efficacy should be used. Manufacturers differ in their recommendations but it is usually advised that in women over 40, hormonal contraception should be replaced by a different method. Women with a history of DVT or other predisposition to clotting should avoid the pill.

**Pregnancy** is a normal natural condition and not an illness. It is however convenient (although by no means universal throughout the world) for a pregnant woman to be supervised by doctors and midwives and to deliver her baby in hospital. This arrangement is to guard against unrecognised complications of pregnancy, and to provide rapid treatment should such complications occur. In UK community practice antenatal care is generally shared between a general practitioner and a district midwife. The woman will be seen by one or other practitioner on a regular basis, the appointments being more frequent towards full term. The object of this supervision is to check for normal growth of the baby, and to check for complications which could affect the mother. For this reason antenatal appointments should include the woman's weight and blood pressure and check for the presence of sugar or protein in the urine.

**Eclampsia and pre-eclampsia.** These complications of pregnancy are associated with high blood pressure which may affect the mother's kidneys and also affect the function of the placenta. Clinically the condition consists of the triad of oedema, hypertension and proteinuria (protein found on testing the urine). Eclampsia is an obstetric emergency which may require immediate caesarean section.

**Ectopic pregnancy** occurs when the ovum (egg) passes down the fallopian tube but is fertilised prior to reaching the uterus. Once fertilisation has occurred the ovum starts to grow, even though it has implanted into the wall of the fallopian tube and not the uterus. The tube cannot accommodate the growth and within a matter of days or a very few weeks the woman starts to experience pain, often accompanied by abnormal bleeding. Clinically, any woman of childbearing age presenting with unexplained low abdominal pain should be questioned as to the possibility of pregnancy. This must be done tactfully but carefully, as some women are reluctant to admit the possibility of pregnancy. If in doubt a pregnancy test and ultrasound scan should be ordered to visualise the tubes and to discard this potentially serious condition from the differential diagnosis. This is because an ectopic pregnancy, if undiagnosed, will proceed to cause a tubal rupture with potentially catastrophic intra-abdominal bleeding.

**Case report**
A 40-year-old woman, who had had one child five years previously and who had been trying to conceive for the last two years presented to the general practitioner with bleeding outside her expected period time. The notes read: "Surgery attendance. intermenstrual bleeding 3 weeks. Cycle usually 5–7/28 days. Last Bleed (date given). No pain no dyspareunia. Trying to conceive 1 year. Bloods. TCI for smear 1 week. Examination lung function test not otherwise specified on examination blood pressure reading 110/85, height 149 cm weight 55 kg refer for ultrasound investigation. Urinalysis no abnormality MSU sent to lab high vaginal swab taken endocervical chlamydia swab". The blood tests ordered included routine liver function tests, kidney function tests, and full blood count to check for anaemia. In addition to this the doctor ordered measurement of follicle stimulating hormone (FSH) and luteinising hormone (LH), both of which rise significantly in a menopausal woman. No test for human chorionic gonadotropin (HCG) was ordered either on the blood or on the urine. Ultrasound examination was performed and was reported back to the surgery as negative. Notwithstanding this, the bleeding progressed and became more severe, eventually becoming torrential. The woman was "blue lighted" to hospital and required an extensive blood transfusion and emergency surgery for an ectopic pregnancy.

*Comment*: This was an unfortunate case, not only for the patient but also bad luck on the doctor who had apparently taken a good history, performed an examination and had ordered a battery of tests. Unfortunately the ultrasound, which has a recognised lack of sensitivity in early pregnancy, was negative. The Doctor relied on this whereas a hormone test for pregnancy should have been undertaken. It appears that he had considered that the abnormal bleeding may have been a manifestation of the menopause, hence the request for LH and FSH. In the event these were both low, indicating the strong possibility of pregnancy. A careful analysis of the situation suggested that although a differential diagnosis had been considered, he had not considered pregnancy. In hindsight this was clearly an error, because he had already noted that the woman was attempting to conceive. It was agreed that the woman would have lost her tube in any event. She was awarded relatively modest damages for psychological trauma (she had, after all, nearly died) and for the additional pain and discomfort.

This case demonstrates that, as may often happen with sensitive gynaecological issues, there is a wide variety of pathology and diagnosis and management can be difficult, even for the apparently conscientious clinician.

REFERENCE

1. Rigoni-Stern D. In: Rotkin Ricci JV, ed. *One Hundred Years of Gynaecology, 1800-1900*. Philadelphia: Blackstone Co. 1945.

Chapter 13

# THE SKIN

Although the skin is not obviously a 'system' like the skeleton or the gut, it is still an important structure – not least because in terms of its overall bulk it is the largest organ in the body. There is a tendency to dismiss the skin simply as a layer between the outside world and the rest of the body, a bit like the wrapping around the contents of a package. Unfortunately some doctors may share this tendency. During the ten years under consideration there were five cases of missed diagnosis of melanoma, five cases of inadequate management of skin ulceration, two cases of undiagnosed rash due to meningitis and one case of mismanagement of a localised skin infection. The reality is that the skin is highly complex, and to understand it we need to consider it in the same way as any other structure. That is, we need to look at the anatomy, physiology and pathology, and then consider clinical management.

BASIC MEDICAL SCIENCE

**Anatomy.** The skin on, say, the forearm, where it does not get much wear and tear, is about 1.5 mm thick. Areas subjected to wear, such as the hand and more particularly the foot, have skin which is considerably thicker. It is useful to describe the skin as two separate layers, the *dermis* and the *epidermis*. (Dermis is Latin for skin. Epi is Greek for 'close to'.)

The epidermis is the outermost part and described as consisting of five layers, starting with the *basal layer* and ending with the *stratum corneum* on the outside. Five layers are described in this way because that is what can be seen under the microscope, although in reality the cells start at a basement membrane and the same cells then grow through to the surface, changing gradually as they go. This type of tissue is known as stratified squamous epithelium, the squamous cells being the layer at the basement membrane with the other layers (strata) above them proceeding outwards. The basal layer consists of actively dividing *keratinocytes* which are formed from stem cells. The basal layer also has pigment-producing cells at this level, the *melanocytes*. The epidermis consists of epithelium only, that is, sheets of cells. It does not have its own blood vessels or other structures, although it is pierced by hairs and by the ducts of the sweat glands. The working parts of the glands are situated deeper, inside the dermis.

The *dermis* lies immediately deep to the epidermis, and is tightly connected to it. Within the dermis are small vessels, the capillaries. There is a superficial plexus (mesh) immediately beneath the epidermis, formed of very narrow blood vessels. This is supplied by a deeper plexus of vessels of a larger diameter. Other structures within the dermis are nerve fibres, sweat glands and hair follicles. The hair follicles have tiny muscles attached to them, the *arrectores pili*. In some areas, notably the face, the hair follicles also have sebaceous glands, secreting an oily substance onto the skin via the follicle.

The hypodermis lies beneath the dermis. It is not strictly part of the skin. It connects the skin, sometimes quite loosely, to the underlying structures. About half of the total body fat is found within the hypodermis.

**Physiology.** It is important to realise that the skin is a functioning organ, not just a barrier. The epidermis is constantly growing. The dermis is instrumental in maintaining body temperature irrespective of the outside climate.

The basal layer of the epidermis produces keratinocytes from its stem cells. These migrate out to the surface, changing as they do so. The stratum spinosum (spiny layer) develops projections between the cells, accounting for the tight impermeable structure of the skin. As the cells move outwards the stratum granulosum produces increasing amounts of a tough protein, keratin, while other structures within the cell gradually cease to function. At the stratum lucidum the cells have little or no activity. By the time the migration is complete, at the stratum corneum, the cells are dead and keratin is practically the only substance present. Although this is not particularly obvious, the epidermis is a highly active structure and skin has a remarkably fast turnover because of its constant growth. A significant portion of 'house dust' is in fact shed human skin; some estimates have put this as high as 70% of all dust. (This figure is unlikely to be accurate,[1] but even the anecdote makes the point!) As well as the keratinocytes at the basal layer, the stem cells also make melanocytes. These produce a brown pigment called melanin. The melanocytes vary in proportion and are responsible for the variation in pigmentation which is characteristic of racial differences in skin colour. Not surprisingly, since melanin provides protection against harmful ultraviolet radiation, the pigmentation characterising different races has evolved more or less according to the latitude of origin of that particular race. The nearer the equator, the more melanocytes – accounting for the obvious differences in skin colour between, say, Africans and Scandinavians.

The epidermis is responsible principally for isolation and protection and apart from its constant growth is largely passive. The dermis is highly active, helping to ensure that the internal environment (that is, the rest of the body) remains in a stable state whatever is going on outside. This is an essential requirement, because most of the chemical processes within cells can only take place within a narrow temperature range. The 19th-century physiologist Claude Bernard put it rather neatly, saying: *"he stability of the internal environment is the condition of a free life"*. (Actually he said this in French, which need not trouble us here.) In other words, we can survive and thrive in a wide range of external environments, from crossing a hot dry desert to swimming in cold salt water. It is the skin which helps to fix the inside of the body in a constant state. Temperature control is achieved by regulating the amount of heat dissipated through the skin. Heat loss may be promoted by sweating. When moisture evaporates the process requires energy. This latent heat of vaporisation is therefore lost from the body, producing a cooling effect. In contrast to this, heat is conserved by mobility of the hair, produced by arrectores pili muscles. This effect is, of course, minimal in humans although of significant importance in many animals, particularly in the colder regions of the earth. (The fur trade, when wearing furs was acceptable, was concentrated in the Arctic regions.) The action these hairs is now largely confined to a fight and flight stress reaction, when a response to stress produces a tendency to heat conservation – hence, the hairs standing up on the back of your neck.

The oxygen supply to the skin comes from the superficial and deep plexuses of blood vessels. The blood vessels can dilate, allowing an increased blood flow to the skin, which in turn provides an additional method of heat regulation. This dilatation may also occur as a stress reaction – blushing when an emotional stress occurs! The process of adaptation to the environment must also depend on picking up what is happening in that environment, and the dermis contains nerve endings, sensitive to pressure and temperature, providing an input to the sensory systems.

**Pathology.** Considering its situation as the barrier against the outside world, protecting the rest of the body, it is not surprising that the skin is subject to a range of pathological insults. The more obvious of these are infection and trauma. As well as this, because of the high cell turnover, aberrations in the growth process may allow development of tumours. Growth errors are particularly likely to happen where the skin is exposed to strong sunlight with its ultraviolet radiation that can damage the DNA.

**Infection.** It has been estimated that as many as a thousand different species of microorganism (i.e. germs) may inhabit the skin.[2] Many of these are harmless commensals and do not cause disease. Others are potential pathogens. In common with the inside of the gut, however, pathogenic bacteria (which may number literally billions) are held in check by the natural defences of the body. In the case of the skin this consists of the largely impermeable epidermis, together with the 'backup' of the blood supply of the dermis transporting white cells and antibodies. Even so, the surprising feature is not the occasional skin infection, but the fact that these occur relatively rarely. A swab taken from the skin and sent off for analysis at the microbiology laboratory will often be reported as "skin commensals only" – the bugs are a normal finding. Most organisms on the skin, provided they stay there, produce no harm. It is when the skin bacteria pass through a break in the natural defences of the impermeable epidermis that infections may occur. This is likely to happen if the bacteria are present in sufficient numbers to overcome the immune system, or if the immune system itself is in some way deficient. It is a matter of common experience that small superficial cuts and grazes may sometimes get infected, but usually do not. The most frequently encountered pathogenic bacteria (that is, those likely to produce disease) are staphylococci and streptococci. Staphylococci often live just inside the nostrils. In theory at least, they can be spread with every breath. Staphylococci rank among the more sophisticated bacteria in that they are able to acquire resistance to many antibiotics. The notorious Methicillin Resistant Staphylococcus Aureus (abbreviated to MRSA) is among these and of great concern to the hospital microbiologists (and hospital managers!). Streptococci, given the opportunity to be in the wrong place at the wrong time, will produce enzymes which break down tissues and allow rapid spread of the bacteria. These are the "Flesh Eating Superbugs" beloved of headline writers. Happily these are rare, but may be lethal in some circumstances, or at best cause the loss of a limb. Another coccus, the meningococcus, may cause septicaemia (blood poisoning). As well as causing meningitis it also produces a characteristic skin rash. Other skin infections arise due to the presence of viruses rather than bacteria. The devastating, but happily now entirely eradicated, condition of smallpox was caused by a highly virulent virus. Childhood immunisation against the measles virus is highly efficient but the uptake is declining. As a result the disease is on the increase due to a combination of ignorance and reluctance on the part of parents. Chickenpox is another, highly contagious, viral condition of childhood. All these systemic infections are characterised by recognisable skin lesions. Local viral infections may give rise to warts on any part of the skin. When they occur in the feet as verrucae they may be painful. More significantly, the human papilloma virus (HPV), spread by sexual intercourse, may cause cervical warts. This is of concern because warts are precursors of cancer of the cervix, as discussed in the chapter on gynaecology.

**Tumours.** Benign tumours of the skin are relatively common. Any of the different cell types may be involved, for example producing

## The Skin

*papillomas* (simple skin tags) or pigmented *moles*. A common lump on the skin is the sebaceous cyst. This is not strictly a tumour, but arises from blockage of the duct of a sebaceous gland. The gland continues to produce sebum and swells accordingly.

With malignant tumours, the main areas of concern are basal cell carcinoma, squamous cell carcinoma and melanoma. All these tumours are associated with over-exposure to sunlight. In the case of melanoma it is of course ironic in that the melanocytes produce a screen against ultraviolet but are themselves susceptible to its pathological effects. The cells of the basal layer contain an enzyme called DNA re-polymerase, which allows rapid repair of DNA which has been damaged by ultraviolet. If this enzyme is missing or deficient – this can be a family trait – the chance of developing skin cancers is significantly increased.

### CLINICAL ASSESSMENT – THE DOCTOR'S JOB

As always, clinical assessment by the doctor should consist of history taking and examination. This may sometimes be followed by investigation – in the case of a single skin lesion this is usually a biopsy.

**History.** This will be guided by the nature of the patient's complaint. In the case of skin problems may be a generalised rash, or a single lesion. The single lesion may be an ulcer, an area of localised infection, or a growth of some sort. The patient should be questioned how long the lesion has been there, whether it is recurrent, if it has grown and if so how quickly. Additional features such as itching and bleeding should be questioned. The patient should also be asked about overall well-being. An isolated infected lesion can cause a generalised infection with pyrexia (raised temperature), although this occurs more often with one of the characteristic virus infections together with the rash.

**Examination.** Some general practitioners may use special lighting to do this. A green light will show up any reddening – it looks black under the light. Ultraviolet light from a Wood's lamp may show changes in pigmentation and some microorganisms, particularly yeasts and fungi. These techniques are, however, really only within the realm of specialist dermatologists and a reasonably competent general practitioner should not be expected to be familiar with their use.

Once the history taking and examination have been done, a competent doctor should be able to record a generalised rash using specific terms. Although this may appear to be technical jargon, precision is important. Terms which may be found in the notes include macule (a small flat area of altered skin colour), papule (a small circumscribed elevation of the skin), vesicle (a circumscribed fluid-containing elevation) and pustule (a pus-filled vesicle).

Once the history and examination are complete, the doctor will consider the differential diagnosis. In the skin, as elsewhere, there is ample opportunity for Dr Botchup to jump to a rapid conclusion with unfortunate results for his patient. Depending on the presentation, and whether a systemic illness is involved, the provisional diagnosis (impression) may need immediate refinement or, as in the case of non-specific viral childhood rash, the illness may simply be allowed to take its course. Single skin lesions may require biopsy, or it may be appropriate simply to watch and wait.

**Case report**
A 6-month-old baby was visited by a general practitioner. The mother complained that the child had developed a temperature, was not feeding, and was generally unwell. The GP conducted a thorough examination, checking ears nose and throat, listening to the chest, stripping the child to allow full examination of the skin and testing the urine. The skin was

normal. The GP diagnosed a non-specific viral infection, gave the mother advice and prescribed paracetamol syrup. Six hours later the parents telephoned the doctor again, saying that the child had become drowsy. The doctor re-attended, and found that the child was indeed only partly responsive. The temperature remained elevated. ENT examination was normal. No further skin examination was undertaken by the GP. The child was admitted to hospital under the care of the paediatricians on the basis of the drowsiness, and reached hospital some two hours later, when the paediatric senior house officer described a petechial rash. (This is a rash caused by inflammatory change within the vessels of the dermis, sometimes described as a haemorrhagic rash. It does not blanche even under pressure e.g. when seen through a glass. It is characteristic of meningitis.) Antibiotics were administered immediately but by this stage the child had developed severe brain damage and subsequently died.

*Comment*: This tragic case illustrates the rapidity with which meningitis may progress. The doctor concerned immediately recognised that a further skin examination should have been undertaken on her second visit. It is by no means certain that, at this stage, a rash would have been apparent but if it had been then it would have been standard practice to administer antibiotics immediately, instead of which they were provided some hours later in hospital. This delay may have been fatal. The loss to the parents was of course incalculable but the doctor was also traumatised by this tragic event, and subsequently resigned from her position. The case was investigated by the Primary Care Trust but no other proceedings were taken.

A severe generalised infection due to septicaemia, as in the case above, is fortunately rare. Localised infections affecting the skin, as in the following case, may be responsible for milder flulike illness. The infection will still need treatment to prevent progression.

**Case report**
A yachtsman in his late 60s sustained a prolonged period of wet feet, resulting in athlete's foot. He had experienced this before and thought little of it until he noted some reddening of the rest of the foot starting to spread up his leg. He sought informal advice from a member of his crew, who happened to be a doctor. Although the yacht's medical box had antibiotics, the doctor suggested that they would not be necessary because the infection would be self-limiting. Twelve hours later the redness had spread past the knee. The patient started to feel generally ill and had a raised temperature. At this point the doctor revised his opinion, having recognised the cellulitis, and suggested taking the antibiotics – starting with a double dose. He also recommended rest and elevation, with the skipper staying in his bunk. The doctor remedied his earlier misdiagnosis by offering to take the skipper's watch! Fortunately, the infection responded to the antibiotic treatment.

*Comment*: This was a 'near miss' situation in which no permanent harm was done, but illustrates the rapidity with which cellulitis may spread. It is likely that a streptococcal infection had started due to entry through the broken skin of the athlete's foot. Happily, this responded to the oral penicillin. (This case also illustrates the risks associated with the casual informal consultation!)

Skin problems in diabetics pose a particular problem, and any doctor dealing with a skin infection in a known diabetic patient should be aware of this. This is because the complications of diabetes include not only a predisposition to infection, due to the effects of diabetes on the immune system, but also damage to the blood vessels and to the nerves – so called peripheral neuropathy. This means that the sensory nerves may be affected, causing reduced sensation or even complete numbness. The patient may therefore experience trauma without realising it, and so take no avoiding action. This "triple jeopardy" applies particularly to the lower limbs, which is the reason why diabetics are strongly advised to undergo regular foot care.

NICE Clinical Guideline 119, published in March 2011[3] deals with diabetic foot problems. The guideline addresses the problem of diagnosis, pointing out that infection may easily be confused with the effects of ischaemia (tissue damage due to poor blood supply). NICE advice is that a diabetic with a foot ulcer should be referred urgently (within 24 hours) to a multidisciplinary team consisting of a diabetologist, chiropodist, vascular surgeon, and other specialists as may be appropriate. This guidance recognises the importance of making an early referral because of the vulnerability of diabetics in this respect.

**Case report**
A 55-year-old man who was a poorly-controlled type I diabetic attended his general practitioner complaining of discomfort and itching in his left fifth toe. The GP wrote a brief note: "Tip of toe black? Infected. Rx (prescribed) Amoxil". No follow up was provided. The patient took the antibiotics for a week and then returned. At this stage the whole toe was completely black. The doctor made a referral to the local surgical department, with a request for an urgent appointment (he did not telephone the hospital or request an emergency admission).) By the time the patient was seen the small toe was completely black, smelly, and the patient had started to experience pain even with his partial neuropathy. In the event he required not only amputation of the toe, but a failed bypass operation meant that he ultimately required a below-knee amputation. At this point a hospital registrar questioned the GP's earlier prescription of antibiotics, suggesting to the patient that earlier admission may have provided a better outcome. Because of the registrar's comments, the patient sued the general practitioner. There was no doubt that the GP's management was indefensible – he was clearly in breach of his duty of care and should have

made an immediate referral, having diagnosed gangrene. In the event however the causation experts, ultimately for both sides, agreed that on the balance of probabilities the patient had been suffering from advanced ischaemia (hardening of the arteries) and the amputation would have been necessary in any event.

*Comment*: This sad case demonstrates the vulnerability of diabetics to skin infection. It is also an example of the difficulties of litigation in clinical negligence. Even though the doctor was clearly in error there was found to be no causation of injury (see the next chapter).

**Treatment.** Because the skin is readily accessible, and because many general practitioners have expertise (or at least an interest) in minor surgical procedures, the NHS authorities encourage general practitioners to perform relatively straightforward surgical procedures in general practice. From a management point of view this is highly efficient, saving hospital resources. It does however have its risks. Benign skin tags, moles, tumours due to virus (verrucae) and minor blemishes are often treated in the surgery by general practitioners by cryotherapy (freezing). The basis of this treatment is that the lesion is treated with liquid nitrogen. This is extremely cold and produces an ice ball in the treated tissue. Cells contain at least eighty per cent water. When the water within the cell is frozen the cell contents are disrupted – very much like a burst pipe in domestic plumbing. The cell membranes remain intact however and so although the function of the cell is destroyed the tissue remains. This has the effect of 'killing' the tissue within the ice ball but providing an intact and still impermeable temporary cover. The adjacent skin then grows in so that by the time the dead tissue is shed the lesion has healed over. This is the theory. Unfortunately, as with any technique likely to produce tissue destruction, considerable care must be used for cryotherapy.

**Case report**
A 27-year-old woman attended her general practitioner complaining of a wart on her knee. She stated that she was a model and concerned by the unsatisfactory appearance. The GP, a locum, offered to treat the lesion with cryotherapy. This was done, but the patient later complained that in order to operate the apparatus delivering the liquid nitrogen the locum was obliged to consult an instruction manual during the procedure. Although the wart had been only a matter of 3 mm diameter, a subsequent photograph taken by the claimant showed a 40 mm area of inflammation after the ice ball had resolved. Within a few days the area ulcerated and became infected. This required several courses of antibiotics and eventually healed leaving a scar which, the patient claimed, was considerably worse from a cosmetic point of view than the original lesion. She brought an action against the general practitioner. Although it was agreed that her claim was significantly exaggerated, it was eventually settled, albeit for a relatively modest sum.

*Comment*: This case illustrates the importance of being able to demonstrate proper training in any technique. Additionally, practitioners and patients should be aware that doctors' defence organisations do not guarantee to provide cover when a procedure is undertaken for purely cosmetic reasons.

One disadvantage of cryotherapy is that the tissue is destroyed, and there is therefore no sample available for biopsy. In the case of an obvious diagnosis such as a skin tag this does not matter. In the case of a pigmented lesion, however, there is significant risk in failing to diagnose a melanoma and then providing inadequate follow-up treatment on the assumption that this is simply an innocent mole. Melanomas (see below) require extensive excision. Cryotherapy can also allow infection, particularly if the area is over-treated.

**Case report**
A 35-year-old woman attended the GP surgery complaining of a pigmented lesion on her abdominal wall. This had been present for many years but she had read in a women's magazine that skin conditions such as this could be treated at the doctor's surgery by "freezing". The GP took a careful history, noting that there had been no itching or bleeding. There had been no increase in size. The lesion had evenly distributed dark pigmentation throughout. Notwithstanding the patient's request for cryotherapy the general practitioner advised, and undertook, excision under local anaesthetic. He sent the specimen off for histology. To his surprise (and to that of the patient) the laboratory reported a melanoma. The deep border of the excision specimen was close to the edge of the tumour. The GP immediately referred the lady for wider and deeper surgical excision. Subsequent follow-up revealed no recurrence and it is likely that total cure had been achieved.

*Comment*: This was a case where the doctor had got the wrong diagnosis, in spite of taking a careful history and examination. It is unlikely that, even if the patient had complained, there would have been any grounds to demonstrate liability. He had however done exactly the right thing in declining the patient's request for "freezing" and in performing excision biopsy. The practitioner concerned immediately took corrective action, having contacted the local surgical department to arrange for urgent further treatment. Happily, at five years after the event, the patient remained well.

TUMOURS

As anywhere else in the body, tumours of the skin fall into two main categories, benign and malignant. Benign tumours are relatively common, and are sometimes referred to casually as 'lumps and bumps'. Unfortunately, malignant tumours are also quite common. These are basal cell carcinoma, squamous cell carcinoma and melanoma.

**Basal cell carcinomas** are sometimes stated only to be locally invasive and therefore classified as non-malignant because they never metastasise (spread). In fact, they may be extremely destructive and can proceed relentlessly unless treated. Basal cell carcinomas, usually abbreviated as BCC in the notes, typically occur on areas exposed to the sun, such as the face or the back of the hand. They are also known as rodent ulcers, because although the tumour starts as a small raised nodule the centre then breaks down, gnawing away and leaving a gradually spreading ring of destructive tissue. Although usually slow growing, a BCC may cause significant local problems. This is particularly the case if they occur on the skin near the eye.

NICE Guidance is that there should be a routine referral for most cases of BCC, but the two-week pathway should be followed if there is concern because of possible complications due to the site or size of the lesion. Unless the general practitioner has had previous surgical experience, or undergone special training, he or she should not attempt to treat BCC as a minor surgical procedure in the practice. Specialist assessment is advisable, particularly as excision is not always the best treatment; radiotherapy is often the preferred option and is equally effective.

**Squamous cell carcinoma** is often abbreviated SCC and is, like any other cancer, simply uncontrolled growth – in this case in the squamous cells of the epidermis. It is less common than the basal cell carcinoma. In the early stages SCC is indistinguishable from the red and scaly areas of so-called keratosis due to sun damage, which is usually how it starts. If these areas become open sores or start to develop a raised growth then SCC should be suspected. A fully developed tumour consists of an ulcer with raised rolled everted edges. In practice, a squamous cell carcinoma is unlikely to be missed by even the most careless doctor, because these lesions tend to be situated in an area of florid sun-damaged skin and to be sore, disfiguring and probably weeping. The patient is therefore likely to demand treatment and this is usually provided. If neglected a squamous cell carcinoma may spread, usually to local lymph nodes. In these cases they can be deadly. At best they are likely to be disfiguring, because the necessary surgery and radiotherapy are likely to leave areas of local tissue destruction requiring complex plastic surgery or grafting. For this reason any suspected lesion should be biopsied. Although this can be done in the surgery by trained GPs, referral is strongly advised.

NICE Guidance is that a squamous cell carcinoma should be suspected in if there is any non-healing or crusted tumour greater than 1 cm with significant induration (hardness) or with a documented expansion over eight weeks. SCCs are commonly found on the face, scalp or back of the hand. The condition should also be suspected in people who have had an organ transplant as squamous cell carcinoma arises more readily if the patient is immunosuppressed.

**Case Report**
An 86-year-old forestry worker attended his general practitioner, accompanied by his daughter who had persuaded him to seek advice on the basis of a crusting area on his scalp. The GP made a diagnosis of actinic keratosis due to sun damage and prescribed Efudix cream. This is a cream containing an anti-metabolite – effectively a chemotherapy agent – intended to reduce cell division. The GP accompanied this treatment with a request to return in six weeks for further assessment. The patient did not return at the advised time, but nearly one year later re-attended, again accompanied by his daughter. On this occasion there was a distinct ulcer. The general practitioner arranged for the patient to return later that day and undertook an incisional biopsy of a small sample from the edge of the ulcer. The laboratory reported this as a squamous cell carcinoma. The patient was referred urgently. He required extensive removal of the skin of the scalp followed by grafting. The patient (probably prompted

by his daughter) complained that the original treatment had been inadequate. The case was defended on the basis that the patient had failed to return in six weeks. Expert opinion confirmed that the original treatment had been reasonable, and was an appropriate initial step notwithstanding the probability that many general practitioners would have undertaken biopsy on the first occasion. The case was dropped.

**Melanoma** is the third most common skin cancer in the UK, but it accounts for more cancer deaths than all other skin cancers combined. In 2011 there were 13,348 new cases of melanoma and 2209 deaths. If treated early the long-term survival rate (i.e. cure) is about 80% but unfortunately cases are still missed. Although melanoma is more often diagnosed in older people, it is increasingly affecting younger people. More than 900 adults aged under 35 are now diagnosed with melanoma annually in the UK, and it is the second most common cancer in adults aged between 25 and 49. Melanoma therefore leads to more years of 'life lost' than many more common cancers. Another obvious feature of this bare statistic is that death at a young age is generally accompanied with far more associated family tragedy. NICE Guidance[5] is that

---

**Major features (2 points)**
- Change in size of the lesion
- Irregular pigmentation
- Irregular border

**Minor features (1 point)**
- Inflammation
- Itch or altered sensation
- Larger than other lesions (diameter > 7mm)
- Oozing/crusting of lesion

---

*Weighted 7-point check list for melanoma*

suspicious lesions should be assessed using a weighted 7-point checklist as in the table. A score of three points or more requires urgent referral within two weeks.

**Case report**
A 48-year-old lady requested advice for a mole on her back. She said that, as far as she knew, it had been present for some months but her husband had suggested she attend the doctor. In response to questioning about any symptoms, she stated that she occasionally caught the mole on her clothing, causing bleeding. She was uncertain as to whether the lesion had increased in size. The GP recorded: "Mole on back. Same size. Sometimes catches bra. OE. Looks all right. See SOS." The patient was reassured by this and took no further action for some months. She then saw another practitioner who made an immediate referral to a dermatologist, who in turn arranged urgent surgical excision. The lesion was shown to be an advanced melanoma, and by this stage it had spread to local lymph nodes and possibly centrally. The lady's prognosis is described as "uncertain", and it is likely that metastatic spread of the melanoma will prove to be a terminal event. The first doctor's management was indefensible and gave rise to a large claim.

*Comment*: This case again illustrates an unfortunate tendency on the part of some doctors to opt for what is 'likely' rather than ensuring that significant conditions are not ruled out from the differential diagnosis without good reason. In this case the doctor was only too ready to attribute the abnormal bleeding to occasional trauma. There had almost certainly been an increase in size but this had not been witnessed by the patient and was apparently discounted. There was no attempt to assess this potentially dangerous lesion against recognised criteria, in this case the seven-point check list.

In summary, and regarding skin problems in general, it is unfortunate that dermatology, the branch of medicine dealing with skin problems, is often regarded as something of an adjunct to the main specialties such as medicine and surgery. This is far from being the case, and approaching dermatological problems without a proper scientific assessment may lead to significant problems, as the above cases demonstrate.

REFERENCES

1. https://www.livescience.com/32337-is-house-dust-mostly-dead-skin.html
2. Molecular analysis of human forearm superficial skin bacterial biota. *Proc. Natl. Acad. Sci. U S A*. 2007 Feb 20; 104(8): 2927–2932.
3. https://www.nice.org.uk/guidance/ng19
4. https://www.nice.org.uk/guidance/csg8/resources/improving-outcomes-for-people-with-skin-tumours-including-melanoma-2010-partial-update-pdf-773380189
5. Melanoma and pigmented lesions. https://www.nice.org.uk/guidance/csg8/resources/improving-outcomes-for-people-with-skin-tumours-including-melanoma-2010-partial-update-pdf-773380189

Chapter 14

# WHEN THINGS GO WRONG

There is an ancient principle dating back to Roman law stating "*non bis in idem*", literally, "not twice in the same", meaning that a person should not have to answer twice for the same offence. In modern criminal law this is the defence referred to as double jeopardy and can be applied to serious crimes – although there are exceptions if new evidence emerges. The dissatisfied patient may be pleased to know that this principle does not apply to doctors. While it is true that errant doctors should only have to face criminal charges once – or hopefully not at all – there are in fact three more routes by which they may be brought to book. In theory it is possible that they may come face-to-face with any (or all!) of the following tribunals:

- Criminal Court.
- Civil Court.
- Registration authority.
- NHS tribunal.

This book does not pretend to offer legal advice or even to be an authoritative source of legal information. The following broad outline is offered for people who are concerned that their medical treatment has gone wrong, and wish to obtain redress or even – let's be blunt – revenge.

**Criminal** activity by a doctor is like any other type of criminal activity in that the charge requires a culpable act together with guilty intention – what the lawyers describe as *actus reus* and *mens rea*. Both must be present. This accounts for the difference between sticking a knife into someone in a brawl and an incision in the operating theatre. Most criminal offences with which a doctor may be charged are likely to come into the broad category of Offence Against the Person, a crime that is committed by direct physical harm or force being applied to someone. Since abortion has been legalised these cases are likely to be limited to sexual offences and gross negligence.

**Sexual offences** where the doctor undertakes any blatant sexual activity are fortunately rare, and generally obvious. More controversially, the practice of medicine inevitably involves some intimate physical examinations on patients of either sex. From the point of view of an anxious patient there can seem to be a very thin dividing line between an examination in order to obtain essential clinical information and a manoeuvre for the sexual gratification of the doctor. To make sure that there is no question of any sexual motive, a doctor should first explain to the patient why the particular examination is necessary – the patient must understand the reason in order to provide informed consent. Doctors are strongly advised to have a chaperone present during any such physical examination. In general practice this advice is occasionally neglected. An elderly doctor with an elderly patient whom he has known for years may sometimes undertake intimate examination without a chaperone. Conversely, a young male doctor with a new, young, female patient would be courting disaster to undertake the same manoeuvre without requesting the presence of a nurse or receptionist. It is a matter of common sense, but if in doubt a chaperone should be arranged even if it is inconvenient to get staff from other duties in a busy general practice. A patient who feels they have been assaulted needs to contact the police at the first opportunity but could well have an uphill battle to prove their case.

**Criminal negligence** charges may be brought against a doctor if things go badly wrong, and particularly if a patient dies. It is defined as a *gross* deviation from a reasonable standard of care and is a higher standard than the 'ordinary' negligence under tort law, which is discussed below. It has to be said that this definition is unclear, and one learned judge said he "could see no difference between negligence and gross negligence; that it was the same thing, with the addition of a vituperative epithet."[1] Other commentators describe gross negligence as being "the want of even slight or scant care" and note it as having been described as "a lack of care that even a careless person would use." [2] A further legal issue is the lack of 'mens rea' – the problem with criminal negligence is that it is not a deliberate intent, but lack of any consideration at all.

### Case Report
Lack of precision in defining criminal negligence led to a wrongful conviction for a gastrointestinal surgeon. One evening, as he was finishing his consultations in the local private hospital, this surgeon was requested by an orthopaedic colleague to see a patient who had developed abdominal pain. He suspected a perforated bowel, and ordered a CT scan. A witness from the hospital subsequently said that CT scanning and reporting was available 24-hours, although the scan was not done until the next day. Having

decided that he needed to operate, the surgeon was further delayed by the absence of an anaesthetist and the availability of theatre time. The upshot was that the necessary surgical procedure was not undertaken until more than a day after he had first been requested to see his colleague's patient. The patient died. A coroner's inquest had to be halted because the question of neglect had been raised. The police, and hence the Crown Prosecution Service, were then informed. The CPS obtained six different opinions from surgical experts, all of whom said that, while unfortunate, the delay did not amount to criminal negligence. A seventh expert, however, gave a different opinion – the only one which was heard in Court. He stated that the surgeon should have operated earlier. Significantly, this surgical expert went on to describe the management of his colleague as "grossly negligent". In this context, it was later decided by the Appeal Court that the trial judge should never have allowed this expert to give what amounted to a legal opinion defining gross negligence – in other words, criminal neglect. This aspect of the case was criticised by the three Appeal Court judges, and the conviction was overturned.

*Comment*: The Appeal Court judgement was made only after this highly respected surgeon had been committed to prison. He served fifteen months, initially in a high security unit where he shared a cell with murderers and rapists. To his enormous credit, after the Appeal Court decision the surgeon's first comment was not on the injustice done to himself, but to the family of the deceased patient. The question of the expert involved, and the extent of his immunity, has yet to be assessed.

From the point of view of a patient or relative who is concerned that the doctor has got things wrong, the question of a bringing a criminal prosecution, though possible, rarely arises. Prosecutions are normally only brought by the police and the Crown Prosecution Service. In any event, although there is perhaps a natural wish for some sort of retribution, even a successful prosecution of a failing doctor will provide no direct benefit to the injured patient.

**Civil** cases are brought under the law of *tort*. This is the French word for wrong and the allegation is made against the tortfeasor – who will be known as the Defendant if the case proceeds. While most criminal cases are brought because of an offence defined in an Act of Parliament – here the 1861 Offences Against the Person Act as Amended – civil cases in tort and brought by living patients are decided by case law. This means that once a judgement is made in a particular case it sets a precedent for future similar cases. Another important difference between civil and criminal cases is that in criminal cases the evidence is tested to see if the offence has been committed "beyond reasonable doubt". In civil cases the test is lower, the "balance of probability", meaning that 51% against 49% may be pleaded as a certainty. Although this is apparently an advantage to the would-be claimant, clinical negligence presents a particular difficulty in that it is often by no means clear exactly what a doctor is supposed to do in any given circumstance. An engineer who designs a bridge with a 50 foot span using materials which would only be expected to support a 30 foot span is clearly negligent because there will be plenty of information documenting the necessary design specifications. A doctor, however, usually has a variety of methods of treatment, any of which may be acceptable. For instance, a patient with a sore throat may be prescribed painkillers, advised to gargle, prescribed an antibiotic or just given advice. Even in exactly similar circumstances there are likely to be different groups of doctors applying different treatments, any of which may turn out to be effective and sensible. This difficulty is now assessed by what is known as the Bolam test. Although often simply referred to as "Bolam," it has formed the basis of clinical negligence litigation for 60 years. Any patient, or relative, pursuing litigation will almost certainly hear this case mentioned in conference by the lawyers and by medical experts. The circumstances of the case are worth considering:

In 1957 John Bolam was a voluntary patient in Friern Hospital. This was at one time the largest hospital of its kind in Europe, with 2,500 patients, when it was known as Colney Hatch Lunatic Asylum. As an undergraduate medical student in the 1970s I had an attachment in psychiatry at this hospital. On Monday morning a group of us students presented ourselves to the Senior Psychiatric Consultant, who greeted us with the words: "Well, I expect you chaps would like to see round a loony bin."!

While lacking in political correctness this expression was not far from the truth. In the so-called back wards groups of long-term patients were huddled into a hugely depressing Victorian building. They clearly had no hope of any treatment – or of release except by death. Of course, the hospital also provided psychiatric treatment of the more usual kind. It was here that Mr Bolam was provided with electroconvulsive therapy. ECT was, and still is, used for patients with severe clinical depression. In Friern Hospital the ECT unit was in a small room about the size of a domestic garage. It had a barred window and the floor was covered in brown linoleum. In the middle of the floor stood the treatment couch. This was probably the room in which Mr Bolam was treated – there was nothing to suggest that things had changed over at least 15 years. ECT treatment consists of giving the patient a short anaesthetic and then passing an electric current through electrodes on each side of the head. This has the effect of triggering the nerve cells. They then re-energise with benefit to the patient. Although the exact mechanism is not known, it is thought that the treatment changes the concentration of neurotransmitter substances at the junction of the nerve cells. One of the disadvantages of the treatment is that the current does not discriminate between the different type of cells within the brain, and the neurones controlling the muscle groups are also stimulated. This causes convulsive muscle contractions. At the time when John Bolam was treated the muscle contractions were sometimes controlled by manual restraint or sometimes controlled by giving the patient a muscle relaxant to induce paralysis. None of these measures is without risk, and there were therefore responsible doctors who preferred just to allow the patient to have the convulsion – some doctors provided a muscle relaxant and some did not. When Mr Bolam had his treatment he had a particularly powerful muscle contraction in both the gluteal muscles and the quadriceps – the big muscles at the front and back of the thighs. This had the effect of forcing the thigh bones up into their sockets on the pelvis. This happened on both sides and he was left with pelvic fractures and wrecked hip joints. Since the unfortunate Mr Bolam had already been depressed before any of this happened, it is not surprising that he sued the hospital. He lost. In this landmark case, Bolam v Friern Hospital Management Committee, Mr Justice McNair said that a doctor: "*…is not guilty of negligence if he has acted in accordance with a practice accepted as proper by a responsible body of medical men skilled in that particular art….a man is not negligent, if he is acting in accordance with such a practice, merely because there is a body of opinion who would take a contrary view.*"[3]

Friern Hospital closed in 1993. It was converted into luxury flats, many of which are now said to be inhabited by footballers and minor pop stars.

Over the years, the Bolam defence was used – some would say abused – to the extent that "a responsible body of medical men" was often claimed to exist even if it represented a small minority. The situation was clarified in another case, Bolitho v City and Hackney HA. James Bolitho was a young boy who suffered respiratory difficulty while an inpatient. The ward sister called the duty doctor who did not attend. While accepting that this was negligent, the defence argued that it was not possible to say what the doctor would have done even if she had attended. Causation of injury could not be proved because James may still have fared badly, the duty doctor stating that she would not have intubated James even if she had attended. The decision not to undertake the (hypothetical) intubation was held to be logical, even though supported only by three experts out of eight. The upshot was that although negligence was admitted James's claim failed. Almost as a by-product, however, the judgement clarified any doubt about the "responsible body" referred to in the Bolam test, saying that: *"the Court has to be satisfied that the exponents of the body of opinion relied on can demonstrate that such opinion has a logical basis"*.[4]

A further limitation in the applicability of the Bolam test was applied in the case of a Mrs Montgomery who sued her hospital because she had not been warned about potential damage to her baby during birth. She was not told about the risk of shoulder dystocia – a rare complication of childbirth where the infant's shoulder becomes lodged in the birth canal. It was argued that there would be a responsible body of opinion who would not have told her, but the Court found: *"The application of the Bolam test to this question* (ie the duty to warn the patient) *is liable to result in the sanctioning of differences in practice which are attributable not to divergent schools of thought in medical science, but merely to divergent attitudes among doctors as to the degree of respect owed to their patients."* [5]

It was found that she should have been warned and that the failure to do so was negligent. On behalf of her damaged baby Mrs Montgomery was awarded very substantial damages.

So much for the negligent act or omission – the breach of duty of care which establishes liability. In order to bring a successful case in tort however a claimant must satisfy not only the *liability* (breach) criterion, but also establish that the *duty of care* existed in the first place. As if that were not all, *causation* then has to be proved. These terms need some explanation.

**Duty of care** is not likely to be an issue if the claimant is clearly in a doctor/patient relationship, whether this is in a hospital or the GP's surgery. Difficulties may arise, however, in the case of a casual consultation, such as the friendly reassurance in the bar at the rugby club provided to a player with a hand injury. If, some weeks later, the player turns out to have had a fractured scaphoid bone in his hand the 'helpful' doctor could well be liable. While it may seem unfair, the Good Samaritan is vulnerable. If you have received casual medical advice, taken this to heart and suffered as a result, you are still in a position to bring proceedings. If a doctor does help, he should ensure that any help and advice as he offers is both within his scope and appropriate. He should always make a note, in some form or other, at the earliest possible opportunity and if it is likely that further treatment may be required he should inform the patient of this, or if this is not practical ensure that a responsible doctor will provide continuity of care.

**Causation** is the third hurdle which a claimant must overcome in order to be awarded damages. The question is: "The doctor may have failed in his duty of care but what damage did this cause?" It is often the most problematical. The test for causation means that many a defendant doctor guilty of negligence may still escape with no civil case against him. To the casual observer this may seem unrealistic and unfair, but a moment's thought indicates that the patient already had a problem before the doctor became involved. It is often found to be the case that this problem would have proceeded relentlessly, causing the patient illness or injury irrespective of anything the doctor did or failed to do. This is frequently the situation in cancer patients, where a delayed diagnosis may have made no difference to the patient's chances of survival. The Claimant also has what is called 'the burden of proof'. Even if negligent, it is not up to the doctor to show that his negligence caused no damage. It is up to the claimant to show that but for the negligence a different and more favourable outcome would have occurred.

**Case report**
A 30-year-old lady gave birth to her third child. She got a vaginal tear which required stitches. The day after the delivery she had pain in her hip joint. Her doctors at the hospital had initially said that this was due to the uncomfortable position she was put into while the repair was being undertaken. She was discharged from hospital even though feeling unwell. Over the succeeding days the pain in her hip got worse and she developed a temperature. She consulted her GP who ignored all this and continued to advise her that the pain was due to the strain on her hip. It was only after further time had passed that she went back to the hospital. She was found to have a septic arthritis – infected hip joint. The joint had been destroyed and at the early age of 30 she needed a total hip replacement. This will need to be re-done in 10 or 15 years. The general practitioner in the case was found to be negligent. An orthopaedic surgeon retained by the GP's solicitors, however, gave evidence to the Court that even if the GP had diagnosed septic arthritis at the first opportunity the patient would still have needed a replacement hip. The Court accepted this and she lost her case.

Fortunately for the claimant this "but for" test is not the only basis for a Court to decide that injury has been caused. If a doctor is negligent and the patient has sustained damage, there may be factors other than the negligence relating to the condition. For example, a patient who has sustained a heart attack because the doctor failed to treat his high blood pressure may also have been a smoker and have high cholesterol. The other causes (the smoking and the cholesterol) also contributed to the likelihood of heart attack. Even though the exact proportions cannot be defined the high blood pressure may be found to have made a "material contribution" and the claimant in this situation may still be awarded damages. "Material" in this case, is defined as non–negligible. *De minimis non cognovit lex* – the law does not take account of small matters. Anything else counts.

REFERENCES

1. Lord Rolfe. Approved by Lord Chelmsford in Giblin v McMullen (1868) LR 2 PC
2. W. Page Keeton, ed. (1984). *Prosser and Keeton on the Law of Torts* (5th ed.).
3. Bolam v Friern Hospital Management Committee [1957] 1 WLR 582
4. Bolitho v City and Hackney Health Authority, 1997
5. Montgomery v Lanarkshire Health Board [2015] UKSC 11

Chapter 15

# PUTTING THINGS RIGHT

The last chapter looked at the ways in which a doctor may be brought to book through the civil or criminal courts if he or she has got things wrong. The next step is to consider the ways to make the aggrieved patient feel better about it all.

**Learning.** In the chapter on management I discussed the prevailing attitude in the NHS that if something has gone wrong then the thing to do is to find someone to blame. This has the advantage from the management point of view that it shifts responsibility. From the point of view of the people actually providing healthcare this simply makes things worse – not only is the patient injured but the doctor or nurse is made to suffer professionally. One mistake after years of training and even more years of useful service may lead to a management decision effectively ending a career. Even if the mistake is due to a moment of inattention at the end of a long shift, or due to a practitioner being placed in a situation for which they have no training, sanctions may still be applied. Of course, it may still be necessary to apply corrective measures and as discussed below both the professional registration bodies and the NHS tribunal are there for this purpose. All this, however, ignores the fact that every time a critical incident or mistake occurs there is an opportunity for learning – one authority actually described medical accidents as "little nuggets of gold". In this respect both the NHS and Department of Health have a lot to learn from the Civil Aviation Authority. The CAA principle is that if a critical incident occurs that it must be reported. No automatic blame is allocated. The incident is regarded as a learning point rather than an opportunity for sanctions to be applied. Of course, the parallel cannot be drawn too closely because in an aviation 'near miss' there is no injury; if things are worse than that there is usually no one to blame anyway! Nonetheless, the principal of 'no blame' is an attractive one. Unfortunately, the health service has only gone half way. In the face of a complaint, nearly all responses will include a mealy-mouthed assertion that whatever unfortunate incident has occurred this has been a valuable learning point for the authority. In practice, it is often the case that little has changed. While doctors and nurses are encouraged, and even obliged contractually, to report any untoward incident it is still likely that an assiduous manager will take matters further and institute disciplinary proceedings. I was told by one trade union representative, a senior member of Unison, that the 'official' union advice was to report everything. In practice, if consulted about an incident, the representative would quietly tell her member: "Keep quiet, and just try and get it right next time!"

It is of course possible that some patients, or their relatives, may find some comfort from being told that their unfortunate experience has provided a learning point for doctors and nurses and has led to an overall improvement in the health service. Realistically, most people will want to take matters further.

**Damages.** The would-be claimant should remember that the main function of the Civil Court is to award compensation – known as *damages*. The Civil Court has no direct power to sentence a doctor to imprisonment, impose fines, sack him or strike him off the Medical Register. The Court is separate from any contractual or regulatory authority, although its findings may be passed to the NHS or the General Medical Council. It is worth remembering that although the aggrieved patient may lodge a complaint with these bodies they will not provide any compensation. When damages are awarded the Civil Court calculates the amount – called quantum – on the basis of Special Damages and General Damages. The idea is to provide a sum of money which is intended to put the claimant in the position he would have been had the negligence not occurred. Of course, this is a highly artificial situation – for example, no amount of money will compensate for the loss of sight. General damages are calculated to represent compensation for pain, discomfort and loss of amenity. A notional tariff is applied for these. Special damages are intended to reflect loss of earnings and the requirement for future care. Damages in the United Kingdom are often relatively modest compared with other administrations such as the United States. Nonetheless, special damages for a brain damaged child with a normal life expectancy but requiring constant care may amount to millions of pounds.

A slightly different situation applies in cases where *death* has occurred through doctors' negligence. Prior to Victorian times, a patient's family could not claim any compensation. Damages may have been due to the victim, but any right to compensation died with him. This was clearly unfair to the widow and children. Perhaps more persuasively for the politicians, it was likely to be a burden on the state. Parliament responded by passing the Fatal Accidents Act. This legislation applies today in cases of death due to clinical negligence, although the same rules of tort law apply.

**Experts.** Civil cases and criminal cases have a common feature in that they rely on experts. This is a term used to describe an expert witness, who will provide an opinion on the case in question, as opposed to finding the facts – these are determined by the Court. Like many legal terms, 'expert' is a slightly misleading description. The expert witness does not necessarily need to be a leading figure in his field (although many are). What is required is an understanding of the duties of an expert. This involves being independent and impartial and having the ability to explain, for the benefit of a judge who is not a doctor, the technicalities behind the issues of the case. This does not require great academic distinction. It does require an appreciation of the requirement to assist the Court in reaching a decision. The expert witness may base his opinion on material he considers suitable to support his position but at the end of the day his opinion is just that – an opinion – and is open to question and cross-examination. While it is possible (many say desirable) to have a single expert, most trials in the United Kingdom take place under an adversarial system. That is, each side will have its own team of lawyers and expert witnesses. On the one side is the Claimant (or Crown Prosecution in criminal cases) and on the other side is the Defendant. Although retained by one side or the other, an expert signs a statement to the effect that he is independent and there solely to assist the Court. This places considerable responsibility on the expert to ensure that he does not enter the role of advocate. He is there purely to enlarge on (and under cross-examination to explain) the opinion that he has provided in his report. This opinion will form the basis of the case that the lawyers instructing the expert will propose to the Court. While expert witnesses are sometimes accused of bias, the reality is that by the time a case gets to Court the experts on each side will have formed definite opinions and be in a position to explain and defend them. While in the past experts often saw themselves as being obliged to provide an opinion to suit the position of their instructing lawyers, in practice the days of the 'hired gun' are over and an expert may expect to receive severe criticism if he is seen to overstep the mark by appearing to advocate the case which is proposed by his instructing lawyers. In Civil cases the ultimate difficulty is for the trial judge, who at the end of the day must decide whether he prefers the expert evidence of one side over that of the other. Because many clinical negligence claims are complicated, these are decided by the judge alone. Juries are, of course, present in criminal cases because they represent the society which the criminal action is intended to protect. Although a jury was present in the days of the Bolam case, this no longer applies for civil cases and it is now up to a single judge to reach the decision.

Like most professionals, doctors make the occasional mistake. Most of these mistakes, however, do not result in the doctor having to face a Court, whether civil or criminal. They may, however, find themselves having to explain their management – or mismanagement – to their employing authority (for NHS cases) or to the General Medical Council. They may even have to face both.

**NHS Tribunals.** In December 2003, the Department of Health issued a document entitled *"High Professional Standards in the Modern NHS; a framework for the initial handling of concerns about doctors and dentists in the NHS"*.(1) This runs to 59 pages, and provides detail of the procedures to be adopted in the event of concern about professional practitioners in the NHS. These concerns could relate either to their personal conduct or to their professional skills. The document pointed out that concerns about a doctor's conduct or capability can come to light in a wide variety of ways. These may include concerns expressed by other NHS staff, complaints about care by patients or relatives of patients, information from the regulatory bodies, litigation following allegations of negligence, information from the police, or coroner's and Court judgements. The document sets out a framework for dealing with such complaints depending on the severity of the (alleged) misconduct. The employing authority may (rarely) apply an immediate suspension. There is then a complex system of investigation, which is intended to be fair to all parties concerned. There are then several possible pathways, including referral to the regulatory body (the GMC in the case of doctors) or referral to a body called the National Clinical Assessment Service. This organisation is an offshoot of the NHS Litigation Authority and provides a stable and supposedly reliable way of ensuring that professional standards are maintained.

At first sight the complexity of these organisations may provide just another indication of the over-bureaucratic administration of the National Health Service. The system does however provide a clear and transparent pathway, enforceable by the regulations, to which patients may turn should they have concern about a doctors' management. Although not of concern to a patient, from the point of view of the practitioner who may be deprived of his or her living, the existence of a fair system is essential.

In the early days of the general practitioner service, complaints against GPs were dealt with by a tribunal of their local NHS authority described as the Medical Service Committee. This consisted of a lay Chairman, three lay members, and three doctors. The doctors were proposed by the Local Medical Committee, the statutory body representing NHS doctors. Attendance on this committee was unpaid, and represented a considerable commitment on the part of the medical members. This unfortunately led to the occasional secondment onto the committee not only of those doctors interested in providing fair assessment for their peers, but also for those who gained some satisfaction of sitting in judgement. In the words of the assistant secretary to the Committee: "There's some folks that find this a little bit tasty!" This occasionally had unfortunate consequences:

An aggrieved parent made a complaint against his GP who had prescribed an antibiotic for his child's ear infection. The child concerned had vomited with the antibiotic and the father telephoned the doctor, who immediately provided an alternative. The child did not get better and the doctor complained that the GP should have re-examined the child. Although the GP had done exactly what most doctors would have done (and certainly a "responsible body of opinion" according to the Bolam test) there were at the time two GPs who had (for their own reasons) volunteered to sit on the Medical Service Committee. One of these doctors was under the impression that the committee was there to impose the highest standard possible. The other doctor had ambitions to serve on the Health Authority in an administrative role and was keen to demonstrate his impartiality towards colleagues. These inexperienced committee members chose to criticise their colleague, who had acted in a perfectly acceptable professional manner. In spite of my objections (I was only other medical member of the committee) the respondent doctor was found in breach of his terms of service – a criticism that remains with him for the rest of his career. Ironically this finding did not reflect particularly badly on the respondent doctor who went on to occupy a senior consultative role, responsible for appraisals and the standard of care throughout the county.

**The General Medical Council**, GMC, is the doctors' regulatory authority. It was established as a statutory body under the 1858 Medical Act as the General Council of Medical Education and Registration. Interestingly, the main impetus for the start of the GMC was its duty to keep a register. This enabled the public to see who was in fact a qualified doctor and who was not. Although this may surprise many people, it was, and still is, possible for anybody to set himself up as a 'medical practitioner'. The only difference is that it is a criminal offence falsely to claim to be on the medical register. An unregistered practitioner cannot use prescription-only medicines or issue certificates, although treating a patient with other remedies – even undertaking surgery – is perfectly legal as long as proper consent is obtained. (In the UK it is however illegal to treat an *animal* which you do not own!). The role of the GMC has expanded considerably since 1858 and the Council now sets standards of conduct that doctors in the UK have to follow. The main guidance that the GMC provides for doctors is a document called *Good Medical Practice*.[2] This outlines the standard of professional conduct that the public expects from doctors. It also explains the principles that form the basis of the GMC's Fitness to Practice decisions. When considering doctors whose performance is in doubt, it is the role of the GMC in this Fitness to Practice activity that concerns us here. Depending on the circumstances and severity of the case, the Counsel has a wide choice of disciplinary strategies. These may range from permanent erasure from the register – 'striking off', effectively depriving a doctor of his living – to a simple warning. The more severe cases are dealt with in a quasi-judicial setting, with both the respondent doctor and the GMC represented by barristers. The Council is likely to receive several thousand complaints about doctors every year. Of these, many are ill-founded or trivial. Until recently, however, even trivial complaints were managed in much the same way as serious allegations, causing great distress to the doctors concerned and achieving nothing by way of patient safety. Recent reforms to the Council are under way, and continue to be implemented. Even so, many doctors would say that the GMC procedures are ponderous and protracted – itself a source of considerable unfairness – and may cause a great deal of unnecessary stress. The Council is no longer elected by members of the profession, but appointed by what is described as an independent government body. Inevitably, this still means that there is a degree of political influence, which does nothing to help the credibility of the Council – at least from the point of view of a busy practising doctor.

**Action.** Having considered the variety of ways in which a poorly performing doctor, or one who has simply made a mistake, may be brought to book, the aggrieved patient may well ask: "Where do I turn now?" The answer to this general question will obviously depend on the circumstances of the case, but it has to be said that the majority of cases in which the patient believes the doctor has let them down are due to misunderstanding and may well be resolved by an explanation and apology. In nearly all cases, the best policy for an aggrieved patient is to write a (polite) letter to the doctor involved, explaining the circumstances of their concern and asking for an explanation. Provided a patient has suffered no serious or long-term harm then even if the doctor has clearly made a glaring mistake this may be sufficient to allow the situation to resolve. Of course, if the matter is more serious other steps need to be taken. Repeated mistakes, even of a trivial nature, may be an indicator of poor general performance and in this situation the best recourse is to the commissioning group in the case of general practitioners, or the hospital authority in the case of hospital doctors. This is more likely to bring some satisfaction of the patient, although the possibility of a complaint to the GMC may be borne in mind. Of course, a complaint either to the GMC or to the NHS authority will get the patient no direct benefit. Even so, an apology is often satisfying – a slice of humble pie from the doctor may well go a long way!

Another alternative for the aggrieved patient is the possibility of instituting criminal proceedings. This is mentioned here only for the sake of completeness, and in practice it is very unusual for the patient to do this directly. If the Crown Prosecution Service gets involved this is almost invariably through the police or the coroner. While it is possible to bring private prosecutions these normally require the Court's permission, and the patient is likely to have to bear the expense. In practice, while theoretically providing some satisfaction for the patient, a criminal prosecution may be of benefit to society, but does little to help the individual.

The majority of the cases described in this book are those that have been brought through solicitors and the civil Courts. The object here is not to discipline the errant doctor (although the cases can lead to that) but to get compensation. As has been seen, the process is complex, requiring not only proof that the doctor has breached his duty of care but also that that breach damaged the patient. In order to demonstrate both these features expert evidence is required, and this is expensive. Add to this the cost of the lawyer's time, which is even more expensive, and Court costs should matters proceed that far. Although there are assiduous attempts by the Department of Justice to bring the matter under control, the question of funding the cost of clinical negligence cases remains a huge issue:

**Case Report**
A 27-year-old lady fell on an icy pavement and sustained small but painful fracture of a small bone in her leg. She went to see her GP who missed it. At the time, it was possible for patients in her situation to obtain funding from the Legal Aid Board to bring a civil claim. The case proceeded accordingly. After about two years in preparation, and then a lengthy trial in the High Court, she won. She was awarded £8,000. The "costs" for this Claimant's solicitors and experts amounted to over £25,000 and it is likely that the defence organisation supporting the defendant doctor faced a similar bill. The solicitor supporting the Claimant is now a Member of Parliament.

**Solicitors.** Historically, nearly anybody could obtain legal advice, and if necessary bring a case through the Legal Aid Board. Provided the patient's income and means fell below a certain level the whole case would be funded from the public purse. This frequently led to the bizarre situation where one organisation was spending taxpayers' money to fund lawyers in a case against another taxpayer-funded organisation – the NHS. Since then, things have changed. Of course, a balance must always be struck and a patient who has suffered serious injury at the hands of his doctor must have the opportunity to obtain some degree of compensation, but it has to be said that the pendulum was far too far from the centre. It often seemed that the only beneficiaries of a clinical accident were the lawyers and medical experts. Some years ago I was approached by a solicitor representing a client who wished to sue her general practitioner. It subsequently transpired that the client saw him as 'her' solicitor because he had managed her house purchase. He had never previously managed a clinical negligence claim. Terms were agreed and at the solicitor's request I prepared a lengthy report, costing several hundred pounds. The patient was unfortunate enough to have acquired multiple sclerosis which had manifested itself in a number of very unusual ways. I had to advise the solicitor that there would be a responsible body of general practitioners who would have managed his client in much the same way. To put it bluntly, I explained, she had no case against the GP. Although it was outside my remit, in order to save the client additional expense, I also explained to the solicitor that in a case of multiple sclerosis there was unlikely to be any treatment, so even if the GP had been particularly astute and referred his client to a neurologist, she would still be in the same position. In other words, the causation criterion was not satisfied either. Perhaps not surprisingly the client was reluctant to accept this. Unfortunately, the solicitor was either unable or unwilling to explain that she had no case in law. There was then a protracted series of conferences and correspondence. The client then declined to pay the solicitor's fees which had accrued for all this. The lesson here was that if a patient wishes to bring a claim in clinical negligence only an experienced firm of solicitors can manage this. Such firms will often provide an initial *'pro bono publico'* – for the public good (i.e. free) – consultation for patients who are concerned about clinical negligence. Although not medically qualified, experienced clinical negligence solicitors will usually be able to advise a client if they have a case or, as is more usual, explain that although things may have gone wrong they are unlikely to be able to bring a successful claim. In instances where the solicitor considers that there may be a possibility of a successful action they may obtain an initial screening report from an expert (often at a reduced agreed rate) and then if this is encouraging proceed to make funding arrangements. Until recently solicitors were able to charge a success fee, effectively doubling their charges if the case was successful or working for nothing if it was not. Since they invariably only took cases where the chances of success were in excess of fifty per cent, this was a profitable way of doing business. Success fees are now no longer applicable, but lawyers may still take a case on a conditional fee arrangement, CFA. The experts, however, are not allowed to engage into any arrangement in which their fees are dependent on the outcome of a case. This would influence (or at least be held to influence) their impartiality. Expert fees must therefore be paid win or lose, and since these are likely to amount to several thousand pounds in a complex case, it is customary for the client to obtain 'after the event' insurance. For a one-off premium the insurer will cover the expenses of the expert reports.

Finally, a word of warning. Although for a claimant who has suffered serious and permanent loss civil litigation may be the only recourse it should not be entered into lightly. The process is likely to take some years and cause a great deal of stress and frustration for the patient and family – people who have already suffered from the original injury.

REFERENCES

1. www.dh.gov.uk/assetRoot/04/06/64/16/04066416.pdf).
2. https://www.gmc-uk.org/-media/documents/Good_medical_practice English_1215.pdf_51527435.pdf

# Index

abbreviations 7
affective disorder 171
alcohol 125, 179
anaesthetists 14
anatomy 5
aneurysm 208, 219
angina 185
angiogram 197
anxiety 168
appendix 126
arrythmia 184
atheroma 209
athlete's foot 246
atrial fibrillation 191
autoimmune 23
back   see spine   81 - 111
bacteria 28
basal cell carcinoma 251
bladder   see genitourinary
   133 - 152
   cancer 145

blood 203
blood pressure 194, 204
Bolam 110, 261
Bolitho 262
bones 57 - 80
breast 99 - 111
   anatomy 99
   assessment 102
   cancer 101
   examination 102
   infections 109
   investigation 103
   pathology 100
   physiology 100
   treatment 104
   tumours 100
Bristol Hospital 43
CABG 199
cancer
   pathology 22
   bladder 145

# Index

bone 66
cervix 223
colon 128,130
ovary 228
prostate 150
heart failure 190
cardiomyopathy 184
Care Quality Commission 52
caries 117
cauda equina 93
causation 264
cervical cancer 223
chaperone 225
circulation 184, 201 - 220
    anatomy 202
    diagram 202
    pathology 206
    peripheral 215
    physiology 204
Civil Aviation Authority 268
civil cases 260
claudication 215
clotting 206
coil 232
colon 128
conditional fee arrangement 278
congenital 19
congenital hip 64
contraception 232
contraceptive pill 233
coronary artery disease 185
    screening 198
    treatment 199
criminal act 257
criminal negligence 258
Crohn's disease 129

Crown Prosecution Service 259,270
cryotherapy 248
damages 269
degeneration 21
dentistry 35
depression 171 - 173
diabetes autoimmune 24
    atheroma 213
    skin 246
diagnosis 6
differential diagnosis 11
diastole 183
disc herniation 86
dislocation 77
diverticulitis 129
double jeopardy 256
drug abuse 180
duty of care 264
DVT 218
ECG 198
eclampsia 234
ECT 261
endocarditis 187
endocardium 183
examination abbreviations 8
experts 270
family traits 20
Fatal Accidents Act 269
fibro adenoma 100
fibroid 223
follicle stimulating hormone (FSH) 222
fractures 73
    spine 87
Friern hospital 261

gall bladder   123
gastrointestinal   see gut   112 - 132
general damages   269
General Medical Council   273
genetic   20
genitourinary   133 - 152
   anatomy   134
   assessment   136
   examination   137
   history   136
   investigations   137
   pathology   135,141
   physiology   134
gout   71
Greek   10
gut   112 - 132
   anatomy   112
   diagnosis   114
   diagram   117
   examination   115
   inflammatory   129
   investigation   115
   pathology   113
   physiology   113
gynaecology   221 - 236
   anatomy   222
   assessment   224
   cancer treatment   227
   examination   225
   history   224
   investigations   226
   pathology   223
   physiology   222
headache   162
heart   182 - 200
   anatomy   183
   assessment   192
   attack   187
   examination   194
   investigations   196
   ischaemia   185
   pathology   184
   physiology   183
   screening   198
hepatitis   125
hypertension   211
iatrogenic   29
immunity   23
incident reporting   268
infections   27
   viruses   27
inflammation   31
investigation   13
ischaemic heart disease   185
IUCD   232
jargon   10
joints   65 - 80
kidney   see genitourinary   133 - 152
Latin   10
liability   263
lipids   212
liver   124
luteinising hormone (LH)   222
managers   34 - 56
mastitis   109
material contribution   265
Medical Service Committee   272
medicines blacklist   41
melanoma   253
memory   159

# Index

metabolism 24
metastasis 23
Montgomery 263
mouth 116
movement control 61
MRSA 242
muscles 58
myeloma 67
myocardial infarction 187
myxoedema 24
National Clinical Assessment Service 272
neoplastic 22
nerves 53 - 180
    anatomy 155
    assessment 160
    compression 87,95
    physiology 156
neurology 160
neurones 156
neuroses 166
NHS history 34
NICE 54
    bladder cancer 145
    breast cancer 105
    colon cancer 131
    diabetic foot 247
    hypertension 211
    melanoma 253
    ovarian cancer 229
    pancreas 124
    prostate cancer 150
    renal failure 141
    spine 97
    squamous cell carcinoma 252
    urinary infection 143
    notes 10
NSAIDS 69
obesity 213
oesophagus 120
ophthalmitis 24
organic disorder 177
osteoarthritis 68
ovary 222
pain disorder 167
pancreas 123
papilloma virus 224
pathological fracture 76
pathology 18 - 33
    definition 6
    acquired 19
    bacteria 28
    cause of disease 32
    degeneration 21
    genetic 20
    iatrogenic 29
    immunity 23
    infections 27
    joints 64
    metabolic 24
    neoplastic 22
    spine 86
    toxins 28
    trauma 30
pelvic infection 230
periodontal disease 118
peripheral vascular disease 215
personality disorder 177
physicians 15
physiology 6

pregnancy   234
   ectopic   234
prostate
   anatomy   148
   cancer   150, 151
   hypertrophy   149
psychiatry   see nerves   154
   classification   166
psychosis   174
PTSD   169
quantum   269
registration   3
renal failure   140
rheumatoid arthritis   24
rheumatoid arthritis   70
schizophrenia   175
science   5
septic arthritis   71
sexual offences   257
sexually transmitted disease   230
skeleton   57 - 80
skin   237 - 255
   anatomy   237
   assessment   243
   cancer   251
   cryotherapy   248
   diabetes   246
   examination   244
   infection   241
   pathology   241
   physiology   239
   treatment   248
   tumours   242, 250
   virus   242
smoking   210
solicitors   276

special damages   269
specialists   14
spinal reflex   85
spine   81 - 111
   diagnosis   88
   examination   88
   fractures   87, 92
   infections   96
   investigation   89
   pathology   86
   sprains   87
   surgery   95
   treatment   90
squamous cell carcinoma   251
Staffordshire Hospital   45
stomach   121
stroke   216
surgeons   14
synapse   156
synovium   61
systole   183
teeth   117
temperature   27
teratogenic   19
testes   147, 148
thrombosis   214, 218
TIA   217
tort   260
toxins   28
training   2, 4
trauma   73
tribunals (NHS)   271
tumour   22
urinary system   see
   genitourinary   133 - 152
uterus   222

# Index

vascular disease   see circulation 201 - 220
vasculitis   207
vertebra   83
waiting lists   40
wisdom teeth   118
x-ray   89